J

POLITICAL SCIENCE

Library of Congress Classification

1995 EDITION

Prepared by the
Cataloging Policy
and Support Office,
Collections Services

Library of Congress, Cataloging Distribution Service, Washington, D.C.

The additions and changes in Class J adopted while this work was in press will be cumulated and printed in List 262 of *LC Classification—Additions and Changes*

Library of Congress Cataloging-in-Publication Data

Library of Congress. Cataloging Policy and Support Office.
Library of Congress classification. J. Political science / prepared by the Cataloging Policy and Support Office, Collections Services. — 1995 ed.
p. cm.
Includes index.
—— ——— Copy 3 Z663.7345 .L52 1995
1. Classification—Books—Political science. 2. Classification, Library of Congress. I. Title.
Z696.U5J 1995
025.4′632—dc20 95–44336
CIP

ISBN 0–8444–0900–6

For sale by the Library of Congress,
Cataloging Distribution Service,
Washington, DC 20541

PREFACE

The first edition of Class J, Political Science, was published in 1910, and the second in 1924. The second edition was reissued with supplementary pages in 1966. A revision of the second edition was published in 1991 integrating all changes that had been made between 1924 and 1991 into the text of the schedule itself. This 1995 edition has been produced using a new automated system developed at the Library of Congress for this purpose. The system will allow for the production of new editions on a regular and frequent basis.

In 1992, Rebecca Guenther, Network Development and MARC Standards Office, began overseeing the conversion of Library of Congress Classification data to machine-readable form using the provisionally approved USMARC format for classification data. In 1993–1994, the Catalog Distribution Service developed programs for producing printed classification schedules from the MARC records in cooperation with Lawrence Buzard, editor of classification schedules, Paul Weiss, senior cataloging policy specialist, and Rebecca Guenther. The Catalog Distribution Service also coordinated the layout and design of the new schedules.

This new edition of Class J is a fully revised edition. Captions have been updated to current terminology and geographic breakdowns have been revised to reflect the geopolitical landscape of the late twentieth century. Many legal topics formerly classed in J have been referred to K, where they are currently classed. The Library of Congress is now in the final stages of developing two new subclasses, JZ and KZ, for the literature of international relations and public international law. In anticipation of the adoption of these new subclasses, all numbers in subclass JX have been parenthesized. JX is being retained in the present schedule, however, for the benefit of those libraries who wish to continue it. Gabriel Horchler and James McGovern of the Social Sciences Cataloging Division were primarily responsible for this revision of Class J. They received valuable assistance and advice from Frederick Augustyn and Jurij Dobczansky, also of the Social Sciences Cataloging Division, as well as from Jolande Goldberg of the Cataloging Policy and Support Office.

New or revised numbers and captions are added to the L.C. Classification schedules as a result of development proposals made by the cataloging staff of the Library of Congress and cooperating institutions. Upon approval of these proposals by the weekly editorial meeting of the Cataloging Policy and Support Office, new classification records are created or existing records are revised in the master classification database. The classification Editorial Team, consisting of Lawrence Buzard, editor, and Barry Bellinger, Kent Griffiths, Nancy Jones, and Dorothy Thomas, assistant editors, is responsible for creating new classification records, maintaining the master database, and creating index terms for the captions.

The Library of Congress is grateful to the Edward Lowe Foundation for its financial assistance in producing this edition of Class J.

Barbara B. Tillett, Chief
Cataloging Policy and Support Office

September 1995

OUTLINE

Class	Numbers	Subject
J	(1)-981	General legislative and executive papers
	(1)-(9)	Gazettes
	10-(98)	United States
	80-82	Presidents' messages and other executive papers
	100-981	Other regions and countries
JA	1-92	Political science (General)
	1-26	Periodicals
	27-34	Societies
	35.5	Congresses
	60-64	Dictionaries and encyclopedias
	71-(80.2)	Theory. Relations to other subjects
	81-84	History
	86-88	Study and teaching. Research
	92	Collective biography of political scientists
JC	11-(607)	Political theory
	11-(607)	State. Theories of the state
	47	Oriental state
	49	Islamic state
	51-93	Ancient state
	109-121	Medieval state
	131-273	Modern state
	177-(178)	Thomas Paine
	311-314	Nationalism. Nation state
	319-323	Political geography
	327	Sovereignty
	328.2	Consent of the governed
	328.6	Violence. Political violence
	329	Patriotism
	345-347	Symbolism
	348-497	Forms of the state
	(501)-(607)	Purpose, functions, and relations of the state
JF	20-2112	Political institutions and public administration
	20-1177	General. Comparative government
	51-56	General works. History
	(201)-619	Organs and functions of government
	251-289	Executive. Heads of state
	331-341	Parliamentary government
	(441)-619	Legislation. Legislative process. Law-making

OUTLINE

JF		Political institutions and public administration
		General. Comparative govenment - Continued
	800-1177	Political rights. Political participation
	1338-2112	Public administration
	(1411)-1521	Civil service
	2011-2112	Political parties
JK	1-9993	Political institutions and public administration
	1-9593	United States
	(401)-1685	Government. Public administration
	501-(901)	Executive branch
	631-(873)	Civil Service. Departments and agencies
	(1001)-(1443)	Congress. Legislative branch
	1154-1276	Senate
	1308-(1443)	House of Representatives
	1606-1685	Government property, etc.
	1717-(2248)	Political rights. Practical politics
	(1756)-1761	Citizenship
	1846-(1936)	Suffrage
	(1961)-(2248)	Electoral system
	2255-2391	Political parties
	2403-9593	State government
	9663-9993	Confederate States of America
JL	1-3899	Political institutions and public administration
	1-500	Canada
	599.5-839	West Indies. Caribbean Area
	1200-1299	Mexico
	1400-1679	Central America
	1850-3899	South America
JN	1-9689	Political institutions and public administration
	1-97	Europe (General)
	101-1179	Great Britain
	1187-1371	Scotland
	(1400)-1571.5	Ireland
	1601-2191	Austria-Hungary. Austria. Hungary
	2210-2229	Czech Republic. Czechoslovakia
	2240	Slovakia
	2301-3007	France
	3201-(4980)	Germany
	5001-5191	Greece
	5201-5690	Italy

OUTLINE

OUTLINE

JS	(3)-8500	Local government. Municipal government
	55-67	History
	141-271	Municipal government and local government other than municipal
	300-1583	United States
	1701-1800	Canada
	1840-2058	West Indies. Caribbean Area
	2101-2148	Mexico
	2145-2219	Central America
	2300-2778	South America
	3000-6949.8	Europe
	6950-7509	Asia
	7510	Arab countries
	7520	Islamic countries
	7525-7819	Africa
	7820-7827	Atlantic Ocean islands
	7900-7906	Indian Ocean islands
	8001-8490	Australia. New Zealand. Pacific Ocean islands
JV	1-9480	Colonies and colonization. Emigration and immigration. International migration
	1-5399	Colonies and colonization
	1-9	Periodicals. Serials
	10-19	Societies
	61-151	History
	412-461	Administration and organization
	500-5399	Colonizing nations
	6001-9480	Emigration and immigration. International migration
	6001-6006	Periodicals. Serials
	6021-6032	History
	(6061)-(6149)	Emigration
	6201-(6348)	Immigration
	6403-7127	United States
	7200-7539	Canada, Latin America, etc.
	7590-(8349)	Europe
	8490-8758	Asia
	8760	Arab countries
	8762	Islamic countries
	8790-(9025)	Africa
	9029-9036	Atlantic Ocean islands
	9040-9047	Indian Ocean islands
	9100-9269	Australia. New Zealand
	9290-9470	Pacific Ocean islands

OUTLINE

JX	(1)-(6650)	International law
	(63)-(191)	Collections. Documents. Cases
	(221)-(1195)	Collections, cases, etc. By country
	(1261)-(1283)	Codification of international law
	(1305)-(1598)	Foreign relations
	(1621)-(1896)	Diplomacy
	(1901)-(1995)	International arbitration, organization, etc.
	(2001)-(6650)	International law

General Legislative and Executive papers
(1-9) Gazettes
see class K
9.5 General
Americas and West Indies
9.7 General works
United States
(10-75) Congressional documents
see KF16-KF43
Presidents' messages and other executive papers
Class here official messages and documents only
For the collected works of individual presidents, including nonofficial messages and papers, see the appropriate number in class E
For presidential messages on a specific subject, see the subject
For presidential papers, see CD3029.8+
For works about presidential messages, see JK587
80 Periodicals. Serials
Monographic collections covering more than two administrations
81 Collections issued before 1860
81.2 Collections issued 1860-1899
81.3 Collections issued 1900-1999
81.4 Collections issued 2000-
By president
George Washington
82.A1 Collections (both administrations)
Individual messages. By date of message
82.A11 1789
82.A12 1790
82.A13 1791
82.A14 1792
82.A15 1793
82.A16 1794
82.A17 1795
82.A18 1796
82.A19 1797
John Adams
82.A2 Collections
Individual messages. By date of message
82.A21 1797
82.A22 1798
82.A23 1799
82.A24 1800
82.A25 1801
Thomas Jefferson
82.A3 Collections
Individual messages. By date of message
82.A31 1801
82.A32 1802
82.A33 1803
82.A34 1804

Americas and West Indies
United States
Presidents' messages and other executive papers
By president
Thomas Jefferson
Individual messages.
By date of message -- Continued
82.A35 1805
82.A36 1806
82.A37 1807
82.A38 1808
James Madison
82.A4 Collections
Individual messages. By date of message
82.A41 1809
82.A42 1810
82.A43 1811
82.A44 1812
82.A45 1813
82.A46 1814
82.A47 1815
82.A48 1816
82.A49 1817
James Monroe
82.A5 Collections
Individual messages. By date of message
82.A51 1817
82.A52 1818
82.A53 1819
82.A54 1820
82.A55 1821
82.A56 1822
82.A57 1823
82.A58 1824
82.A59 1825
John Quincy Adams
82.A6 Collections
Individual messages. By date of message
82.A61 1825
82.A62 1826
82.A63 1827
82.A64 1828
82.A65 1829
Andrew Jackson
82.A7 Collections
Individual messages. By date of message
82.A71 1829
82.A72 1830
82.A73 1831
82.A74 1832
82.A75 1833
82.A76 1834
82.A77 1835

	Americas and West Indies
	United States
	Presidents' messages and other executive papers
	By president
	Andrew Jackson
	Individual messages.
	By date of message -- Continued
82.A78	1836
82.A79	1837
	Martin Van Buren
82.A8	Collections
	Individual messages. By date of message
82.A81	1837
82.A82	1838
82.A83	1839
82.A84	1840
82.A85	1841
	William Henry Harrison
82.B1	Collections
	Individual messages. By date of message
82.B11	1841
	John Tyler
82.B2	Collections
	Individual messages. By date of message
82.B21-B25	1841-1845
	James K. Polk
82.B3	Collections
	Individual messages. By date of message
82.B31	1845
82.B32	1846
82.B33	1847
82.B34	1848
82.B35	1849
	Zachery Taylor
82.B4	Collections
	Individual messages. By date of message
82.B41	1849
82.B42	1850
	Millard Fillmore
82.B5	Collections
	Individual messages. By date of message
82.B51	1850
82.B52	1851
82.B53	1852
82.B54	1853
	Franklin Pierce
82.B6	Collections
	Individual messages. By date of message
82.B61	1853
82.B62	1854
82.B63	1855
82.B64	1856
82.B65	1857

	Americas and West Indies
	United States
	Presidents' messages and other executive papers
	By president -- Continued
	James Buchanan
82.B7	Collections
	Individual messages. By date of message
82.B71	1857
82.B72	1858
82.B73	1859
82.B74	1860
82.B75	1861
(82.B8-B85)	Abraham Lincoln
	see E457.94
	Andrew Johnson
82.B9	Collections
	Individual messages. By date of message
82.B91	1865
82.B92	1866
82.B93	1867
82.B94	1868
82.B95	1869
	Ulysses S. Grant
82.C1	Collections
	Individual messages. By date of message
82.C11	1869
82.C12	1870
82.C13	1871
82.C14	1872
82.C15	1873
82.C16	1874
82.C17	1875
82.C18	1876
82.C19	1877
	Rutherford B. Hayes
82.C2	Collections
	Individual messages. By date of message
82.C21	1877
82.C22	1878
82.C23	1879
82.C24	1880
82.C25	1881
	James A. Garfield
82.C3	Collections
	Individual messages. By date of message
82.C31	1881
	Chester A. Arthur
82.C4	Collections
	Individual messages. By date of message
82.C41	1881
82.C42	1882
82.C43	1883
82.C44	1884

Americas and West Indies
United States
Presidents' messages and other executive papers
By president
Chester A. Arthur
Individual messatages.
By date of message -- Continued
82.C45 1885
Grover Cleveland I-II
82.C5 Collections
Individual messages. By date of message
82.C51 1885
82.C52 1886
82.C53 1887
82.C54 1888
82.C55 1889
Benjamin Harrison
82.C6 Collections
Individual messages. By date of message
82.C61 1889
82.C62 1890
82.C63 1891
82.C64 1892
82.C65 1893
Grover Cleveland II
82.C7 Collections
Individual messages. By date of message
82.C71 1893
82.C72 1894
82.C73 1895
82.C74 1896
82.C75 1897
William McKinley
82.C8 Collections
Individual messages. By date of message
82.C81 1897
82.C82 1898
82.C83 1899
82.C84 1900
82.C85 1901
Theodore Roosevelt
82.C9 Collections
Individual messages. By date of message
82.C91 1901
82.C92 1902
82.C93 1903
82.C94 1904
82.C95 1905
82.C96 1906
82.C97 1907
82.C98 1908
82.C99 1909
William H. Taft

Americas and West Indies
United States
Presidents' messages and other executive papers
By president
William H. Taft -- Continued
82.D1 Collections
Individual messages. By date of message
82.D11 1909
82.D12 1910
82.D13 1911
82.D14 1912
82.D15 1913
Woodrow Wilson
82.D2 Collections
Individual messages. By date of message
82.D21 1913
82.D22 1914
82.D23 1915
82.D24 1916
82.D25 1917
82.D26 1918
82.D27 1919
82.D28 1920
82.D29 1921
Warren G. Harding
82.D3 Collections
Individual messages. By date of message
82.D31 1921
82.D32 1922
82.D33 1923
Calvin Coolidge
82.D4 Collections
Individual messages. By date of message
82.D41 1923
82.D42 1924
82.D43 1925
82.D44 1926
82.D45 1927
82.D46 1928
82.D47 1929
Herbert Hoover
82.D5 Collections
Individual messages. By date of message
82.D51 1929
82.D52 1930
82.D53 1931
82.D54 1932
82.D55 1933
Franklin D. Roosevelt
82.D6 Collections
Individual messages. By date of message
82.D61 1933
82.D62 1934

Americas and West Indies
United States
Presidents' messages and other executive papers
By president
Franklin D. Roosevelt
Individual messages.
By date of message -- Continued

82.D63	1935
82.D64	1936
82.D65	1937
82.D66	1938
82.D67	1939
82.D68	1940
82.D69	1941
82.D691	1942
82.D692	1943
82.D693	1944
82.D694	1945
	Harry S. Truman
82.D7	Collections
	Individual messages. By date of message
82.D71	1945
82.D72	1946
82.D73	1947
82.D74	1948
82.D75	1949
82.D76	1950
82.D77	1951
82.D78	1952
	Dwight D. Eisenhower
82.D8	Collections
	Individual messages. By date of message
82.D81	1953
82.D82	1954
82.D83	1955
82.D84	1956
82.D85	1957
	John F. Kennedy
82.D9	Collections
	Individual messages. By date of message
82.D91	1961
82.D92	1962
82.D93	1963
	Lyndon B. Johnson
82.E1	Collections
	Individual messages. By date of message
82.E11	1963
82.E12	1964
82.E13	1965
82.E14	1966
82.E15	1967
82.E16	1968
	Richard M. Nixon

Americas and West Indies
United States
Presidents' messages and other executive papers
By president
Richard M. Nixon -- Continued
82.E2 Collections
Individual messages. By date of message
82.E21 1969
82.E22 1970
82.E23 1971
82.E24 1972
82.E25 1973
82.E26 1974
Gerald R. Ford
82.E3 Collections
Individual messages. By date of message
82.E31 1974
82.E32 1975
82.E33 1976
82.E34 1977
Jimmy Carter
82.E4 Collections
Individual messages. By date of message
82.E41 1977
82.E44 1980
Ronald Reagan
82.E5 Collections
Individual messages. By date of message
1981
82.E6 George Bush
82.E7 Bill Clinton
Administrative papers
83 Collections. Documents of several departments or agencies combined
Department of the Interior
84 Periodicals. Serials
General works, see JK868
(85) Other departments or agencies limited to a particular subject
see the subject
State executive papers
For state legislative documents, see KFA, KFW, KFZ
For legislative and administrative papers of the Confederacy, see KFZ8600+
For presidential messages of the Confederacy, see JK9718+
86 District of Columbia (Table J1)
87.A2 Alabama (Table J1)
87.A4 Alaska (Table J1)
87.A6 Arizona (Table J1)
87.A8 Arkansas (Table J1)
87.C2 California (Table J1)

Americas and West Indies
United States
Administrative papers
State executive papers -- Continued

87.C6 Colorado (Table J1)
87.C8 Connecticut (Table J1)
87.D3 Delaware (Table J1)
District of Columbia, see J86
87.F6 Florida (Table J1)
87.G4 Georgia (Table J1)
87.H3 Hawaii (Table J1)
87.I2 Idaho (Table J1)
87.I3 Illinois (Table J1)
87.I4 Indian Territory (Table J1)
87.I6 Indiana (Table J1)
87.I8 Iowa (Table J1)
87.K2 Kansas (Table J1)
87.K4 Kentucky (Table J1)
87.L8 Louisiana (Table J1)
87.M2 Maine (Table J1)
87.M3 Maryland (Table J1)
87.M4 Massachusetts (Table J1)
87.M5 Michigan (Table J1)
87.M6 Minnesota (Table J1)
87.M7 Mississippi (Table J1)
87.M8 Missouri (Table J1)
87.M9 Montana (Table J1)
87.N2 Nebraska (Table J1)
87.N3 Nevada (Table J1)
87.N4 New Hampshire (Table J1)
87.N5 New Jersey (Table J1)
87.N6 New Mexico (Table J1)
87.N7 New York (Table J1)
87.N8 North Carolina (Table J1)
87.N9 North Dakota (Table J1)
87.N95 Northwest Territory (Table J1)
87.O3 Ohio (Table J1)
87.O5 Oklahoma (Table J1)
87.O7 Oregon (Table J1)
87.P4 Pennsylvania (Table J1)
87.R4 Rhode Island (Table J1)
87.S6 South Carolina (Table J1)
87.S8 South Dakota (Table J1)
87.T2 Tennessee (Table J1)
87.T4 Texas (Table J1)
87.U8 Utah (Table J1)
87.V5 Vermont (Table J1)
Virginia
87.V6 To 1861 (Table J1)
87.V7 1861-1863/1864 (Richmond) (Table J1)
(87.V8) 1861-1863/1864 (Wheeling-Alexandria) see KFZ8600+
87.V9 1865- (Table J1)

Americas and West Indies
United States
Administrative papers
State executive papers -- Continued
87.W2 Washington (Table J1)
87.W4 West Virginia (Table J1)
87.W6 Wisconsin (Table J1)
87.W8 Wyoming (Table J1)
(95) Puerto Rico
see J164-J165
(97) Philippines
see J661-J663
(98) Virgin Islands of the United States
see J166
Canada
100 Lower Canada (Table J2)
101 Upper Canada (Table J2)
102 Province of Canada, 1841-1867 (Table J2)
103 Dominion of Canada, 1867- . Canadian confederation (Table J2)
104 Nova Scotia (Table J2)
105 New Brunswick (Table J2)
106 Prince Edward Island (Table J2)
107 Quebec (Table J2)
Including Quebec under French regime (New France), 1540-1759; and British regime, 1760-1867
108 Ontario (Table J2)
109 Manitoba (Table J2)
110 British Columbia (Table J2)
110.5 Vancouver Island (Crown Colony, 1849-1866) (Table J2)
(111) Northwest Territories
see J118
112 Alberta (Table J2)
118 Northwest Territories (Table J2)
119 Saskatchewan (Table J2)
121 Yukon Territory (Table J2)
125 Newfoundland (Table J2)
126 Greenland (Table J2)
131 Bermuda (Table J2)
132 Saint Pierre and Miquelon (Table J2)
West Indies. Caribbean Area
Including Federation of the West Indies, 1958-1962
133 General (Table J2)
135 Antigua and Barbuda (Table J2)
136 Bahamas (Table J2)
137 Barbados (Table J2)
137.5 Cayman Islands (Table J2)
138 Jamaica (Table J2)
Leeward Islands
Including Leeward Islands Federation, 1871-1956 and including the periods of British and Dutch rule

Americas and West Indies
West Indies. Caribbean Area
Leeward Islands -- Continued
139 General (Table J2)
139.13 Anguilla (Table J2)
Antigua and Barbuda, see J135
139.5 Montserrat (Table J2)
139.7 Saint Kitts and Nevis (Table J2)
140 Trinidad and Tobago (Table J2)
Windward Islands
Including the periods of British and Dutch rule
141 General (Table J2)
141.2 Dominica (Table J2)
141.4 Grenada (Table J2)
141.5 Saint Lucia (Table J2)
141.6 Saint Vincent and the Grenadines (Table J2)
(144) Belize
see J176
146 Guyana. British Guiana (Table J2)
(148) Falkland Islands
see J227
(150) Danish West Indies
see J166
Netherlands Antilles. Dutch West Indies
153 General (Table J2)
153.15 Aruba (Table J2)
153.2 Bonaire (Table J2)
154 Curaçao (Table J2)
154.2 Saba (Table J2)
154.3 Saint Eustatius (Table J2)
154.4 Saint Martin (Table J2)
(154.55) Surinam. Dutch Guiana
see J228
French West Indies
157 General (Table J2)
(158) French Guiana
see J230
159 Guadeloupe (Table J2)
160 Martinique (Table J2)
(161) Saint Pierre and Miquelon
see J132
Cuba
162 To 1898 (Table J2)
163 1898- (Table J2)
Puerto Rico
164 To 1898 (Table J2)
165 1898- (Table J2)
166 Virgin Islands of the United States (Table J2)
167 Haiti (Table J2)
168 Dominican Republic (Table J2)
Mexico
170 Spanish regime (Table J2)
171 Republic (Table J2)

	Americas and West Indies
	Mexico -- Continued
172.A-Z	States, A-Z (Table J2)
	Central America
175	General (Table J2)
176	Belize (Table J2)
177	Costa Rica (Table J2)
179	Guatemala (Table J2)
181	Honduras (Table J2)
183	Nicaragua (Table J2)
184	Panama (Table J2)
184.5	Panama Canal Zone (Table J2)
185	El Salvador (Table J2)
	South America
	For regional organizations, see KDZ, KG-KH, or JZ
200	General (Table J2)
	Argentina
201	General (Table J2)
202	States and territories, A-Z (Table J2)
204	Bolivia (Table J2)
	Brazil
207	General (Table J2)
208.A-Z	States, A-Z (Table J2)
211	Chile (Table J2)
	Colombia
214	Spanish régime (Table J2)
215	1819-1832 (Table J2)
216	1832-1885 (Table J2)
220	1885- (Table J2)
222.A-Z	Departments, A-Z (Table J2)
225	Ecuador (Table J2)
227	Falkland Islands (Table J2)
	Guiana
	Guyana. British Guiana, see J146
228	Surinam. Dutch Guiana (Table J2)
230	French Guiana (Table J2)
235	Paraguay (Table J2)
241	Peru (Table J2)
251	Uruguay (Table J2)
	Venezuela
257	General (Table J2)
259.A-Z	States, A-Z (Table J2)
	Europe
	For regional organizations, see KJC/KJE or JN
290	General (Table J2)
	Great Britain. England
301	General (Table J2)
305	Wales (Table J2)
305.5	Isle of Man (Table J2)
306	Scotland (Table J2)
307.3	Ireland. Irish Republic (Table J2)
307.5	Northern Ireland (Table J2)
307.8.A-Z	Channel Islands, A-Z (Table J2)

	Europe
	Channel Islands, A-Z -- Continued
307.8.J43	Jersey (Table J2)
308	Gibraltar (Table J2)
309	Malta (Table J2)
310	Austro-Hungarian Monarchy (Table J2)
	Austria
311	General (Table J2)
	States, provinces, etc.
	Including extinct jurisdictions
314	Austria, Lower (Table J2)
315	Austria, Upper (Table J2)
316	Bohemia (Table J2)
	Cf. J338+, Czechoslovakia
317	Bukowina (Table J2)
317.5	Burgenland (Table J2)
318	Carinthia (Table J2)
320	Dalmatia (Table J2)
321	Galicia (Table J2)
322	Görz and Gradiska (Table J2)
323	Istria (Table J2)
324	Moravia (Table J2)
	Cf. J338+, Czechoslovakia
325	Salzburg (Table J2)
326	Silesia (Table J2)
327	Styria (Table J2)
(328)	Trieste
	see J389
329	Tyrol (Table J2)
329.5	Vienna (State) (Table J2)
330	Voralberg (Table J2)
335	Hungary (Table J2)
(337)	Croatia
	see J460
(337.5)	Slovenia
	see J460.3
	Czechoslovakia. Czechoslovak Republic
	Cf. J316, Bohemia
338	General (Table J2)
338.2.A-Z	States, provinces, etc., A-Z
338.2.C97	Czech Socialist Republic (Table J2)
338.2.S577	Slovak Socialist Republic (Table J2)
338.2.S8	Sudetenland (Table J2)
338.3	Czech Republic (Table J2)
338.5	Slovakia (Table J2)
(339)	Bosnia and Herzegovina
	see J460.2
340	Liechtenstein (Table J2)
341	France (Table J2)
341.A2+	Documents before 1789 (Ancien régime) (Table J2)
341.B2+	Documents, 1789-1799 (Revolution) (Table J2)
343	Andorra (Table J2)
345	Monaco (Table J2)

Europe -- Continued
Germany. Germany (Federal Republic, 1949-)
Including German Confederation (1815-1866) and North German Confederation (1866-1870)
351 General (Table J2)
German states, provinces, etc.
Including extinct and mediatized states
352 Germany (Democratic Republic, 1949-1991) (Table J2)
353 Jülich-Berg (Table J2)
353.5 Nassau (Table J2)
354 Alsace-Lorraine (Table J2)
355 Anhalt (Table J2)
355.4 Anhalt-Bemberg (Table J2)
355.6 Anhalt-Dessau-Kothen (Table J2)
356 Baden (Table J2)
Baden-Württemberg, see J383.B3
357 Bavaria (Table J2)
357.5 Brandenburg (Table J2)
358 Bremen (Table J2)
359 Brunswick (Table J2)
359.5 Danzig (Table J2)
360 Hamburg (Table J2)
361 Hanover (Table J2)
362 Hesse (Table J2)
363 Lippe (Table J2)
Lower Saxony, see J383.S26
364 Lübeck (Table J2)
364.5 Mecklenburg (State, 1990-) (Table J2)
365 Mecklenburg-Schwerin (Table J2)
366 Mecklenburg-Strelitz (Table J2)
North Rhine-Westphalia, see J383.N6
367 Oldenburg (Table J2)
367.5 Palatinate (Table J2)
368 Prussia (Table J2)
370 Reuss, Elder Line (Table J2)
371 Reuss, Younger Line (Table J2)
Rhineland-Palatinate, see J383.R46
372 Saxe-Altenburg (Table J2)
373 Saxe-Coburg-Gotha (Table J2)
374 Saxe-Meiningen (Table J2)
375 Saxe-Weimar (Table J2)
376 Saxony (Table J2)
376.5 Saxony-Anhalt (State, 1990-) (Table J2)
377 Schaumburg-Lippe (Table J2)
378 Schwartzburg-Rudolstadt (Table J2)
379 Schwartzburg-Sondershausen (Table J2)
379.5 Thuringia (Table J2)
379.7 Thuringia (State, 1990-) (Table J2)
380 Waldeck (Table J2)
381 Württemberg (Table J2)
383.A-Z Other, A-Z
383.B3 Baden-Württemberg (Table J2)

Europe
Germany. Germany (Federal Republic, 1949-)
German states, provinces, etc.
Other, A-Z -- Continued
383.N6 North Rhine-Westphalia (Table J2)
383.R46 Rhineland-Palatinate (Table J2)
383.S2 Saarland (Table J2)
383.S26 Saxony, Lower (Table J2)
383.W884 Württemberg-Baden (Table J2)
383.W885 Württemberg-Hohenzollern (Table J2)
385 Greece (Table J2)
Italy
388 General (Table J2)
389.A-Z Provinces, A-Z (Table J2)
Malta, see J309
389.5 Trieste (Table J2)
Netherlands. Holland
391 General (Table J2)
392.A-Z Provinces, A-Z
392.B7 Brabant, North (Table J2)
392.D7 Drenthe (Table J2)
392.F5 Flanders, West (Table J2)
392.F7 Friesland (Table J2)
392.G4 Gelderland (Table J2)
392.G7 Groningen (Table J2)
392.H58 Holland (Table J2)
392.H6 Holland, North (Table J2)
392.H7 Holland, South (Table J2)
392.L5 Limburg (Table J2)
392.O8 Overijssel (Table J2)
392.U8 Utrecht (Table J2)
392.Z4 Zealand (Table J2)
393 Belgium (Table J2)
395 Luxembourg (Table J2)
397 Russia. Soviet Union (to 1991) (Table J2)
Including the Commonwealth of Independent States, and former Soviet republics (collectively)
397.2 Russia (Federation) (Table J2)
398 Finland (Table J2)
399 Poland (Table J2)
399.2 Ukraine (Table J2)
400 Belarus (Table J2)
400.2 Moldova (Table J2)
Baltic States
401 Estonia (Table J2)
401.2 Latvia (Table J2)
401.3 Lithuania (Table J2)
Scandinavia
402 General (Table J2)
403 Denmark (Table J2)
For Greenland, see J126
404 Iceland (Table J2)
405 Norway (Table J2)

Europe
Scandinavia -- Continued
406 Sweden (Table J2)
Spain and Portugal
409 Spain (Table J2)
Gibraltar, see J308
411 Portugal (Table J2)
Switzerland
415 General (Table J2)
Cantons
418 Aargau (Table J2)
419 Appenzell Ausserrhoden (Table J2)
420 Appenzell Innerrhoden (Table J2)
421 Baselland (Table J2)
422 Basel-Stadt (Table J2)
423 Bern (Table J2)
424 Fribourg (Table J2)
425 Geneva (Table J2)
426 Glarus (Table J2)
427 Grisons (Graubünden) (Table J2)
427.5 Jura (Table J2)
428 Lucerne (Table J2)
429 Neuchâtel (Table J2)
430 Saint Gall (Table J2)
431 Schaffhausen (Table J2)
432 Schwyz (Table J2)
433 Solothurn (Table J2)
434 Thurgau (Table J2)
435 Ticino (Table J2)
436 Nidwalden (Table J2)
437 Obwalden (Table J2)
438 Uri (Table J2)
439 Valais (Table J2)
440 Vaud (Table J2)
441 Zug (Table J2)
442 Zurich (Table J2)
Southeastern Europe
450 Albania (Table J2)
Bulgaria
451 General (Table J2)
452 Eastern Rumelia (Table J2)
1878-1885, Turkish vilayet with administrative autonomy. In 1885-1886, united with Bulgaria
453 Montenegro (Table J2)
455 Romania (Table J2)
457 Serbia (Table J2)
459 Yugoslavia (to 1992) (Table J2)
460 Croatia (Table J2)
460.2 Bosnia and Herzegovina (Table J2)
460.3 Slovenia (Table J2)
460.4 Macedonia (Republic) (Table J2)
(461) Turkey
see J691

Asia
South Asia. Southeast Asia
India
500 General (Table J2)
States and union territories
Including extinct jurisdictions
Agra, see J596+
507 Ajmere-Merwara (Table J2)
511 Andaman and Nicobar Islands (Table J2)
512 Andhra Pradesh (Table J2)
513 Arunachal Pradesh (Table J2)
Assam, see J527+
(519) Baluchistan
see J610
Bangalore, see J567
523 Baroda (Table J2)
Bengal and Assam
527 General (Table J2)
528 Assam (Table J2)
529 East Bengal (Table J2)
529.5 West Bengal (Table J2)
530 Bihar and Orissa (Table J2)
Cf. J575, Orissa
530.5 Bihar (Table J2)
531 Bombay Presidency (Table J2)
(535) Burma
see J648
541 Central India (Table J2)
543 Central Provinces and Bera (Table J2)
543.5 Chandigarh (Table J2)
547 Coorg (Table J2)
548 Dadra and Nagar Haveli (Table J2)
549 Delhi (Table J2)
550 Gao, Daman and Diu (Table J2)
551 Gujarat (Table J2)
552 Haryana (Table J2)
553 Himachal Pradesh (Table J2)
554 Kerala (Table J2)
555 Hyderabad (Table J2)
556 Lakshadweep (Table J2)
559 Jammu and Kashmir (Table J2)
563 Madras Presidency (Table J2)
564 Madhya Pradesh (Table J2)
565 Maharashtra (Table J2)
566 Manipur (Table J2)
567 Karnataka. Mysore (Table J2)
Including Bangalore
568 Meghalaya (Table J2)
569 Mizoram (Table J2)
570 Nagaland (Table J2)
571 Frontier Province (Table J2)
North West Provinces, see J596+

Asia
South Asia. Southeast Asia
India
States and union territories -- Continued
575 Orissa (Table J2)
Cf. J530, Bihar and Orissa
(577) Pakistan
see J610
(579) Bangladesh
see J603
580 Pondicherry (Table J2)
581 Punjab (Table J2)
581.5 Rajasthan (Table J2)
585 Rajputana (Table J2)
589 Sikkim (Table J2)
593 Sind (Table J2)
594 Tamil Nadu (Table J2)
595 Tripura (Table J2)
United Provinces of Agra and Oudh
596 General (Table J2)
597 Oudh (Table J2)
598 North West Provinces and Oudh (Table J2)
599 Uttar Pradesh (Table J2)
601.A-Z Other Indian states, A-Z
601.J26 Jaipur (Table J2)
601.M28 Malpur (Table J2)
603 Bangladesh (Table J2)
(605) Yemen (Peoples Democratic Republic). Aden
see J703
(608) British North Borneo. Sabah
see J618.S3
(609) Sarawak
see J618.S37
609.5 Brunei (Table J2)
610 Pakistan (Table J2)
611 Sri Lanka. Ceylon (Table J2)
(612) Cyprus
see J691.5
(613) Hong Kong
see J665
Malaysia. Malaya
Including Straits Settlements (to 1942), Federation of Malay States (1896-1942), and Malayan Union (1946-1947)
615 General (Table J2)
618.A-Z By state, A-Z
Brunei, see J609.5
618.J58 Johor (Table J2)
618.K45 Kedah (Table J2)
618.K5 Kelantan (Table J2)
618.P3 Pahang (Table J2)
618.P4 Perak (Table J2)
618.P5 Pinang (Table J2)

	Asia
	South Asia. Southeast Asia
	Malaysia. Malaya
	By state, A-Z -- Continued
618.S3	Sabah. North Borneo (Table J2)
618.S37	Sarawak (Table J2)
	Singapore, see J620
620	Singapore (Table J2)
625	Nepal (Table J2)
626	Bhutan (Table J2)
631	Indonesia (Table J2)
(638)	Pondicherry
	see J580
641	French Indochina. Indochina (Federation) (Table J2)
642	Cambodia. Kampuchea (Table J2)
643	Laos (Table J2)
644	Vietnam (Table J2)
	Thailand, see J681
648	Burma (Table J2)
651	Macao (Table J2)
(651.2)	Goa
	see J550
(651.3)	Timor
	see J631
	Central Asia
655	Kazakhstan (Table J2)
656	Kyrgyzstan (Table J2)
657	Tadjikistan (Table J2)
658	Turkmenistan (Table J2)
659	Uzbekistan (Table J2)
	Philippines
661	Spanish rule (Table J2)
662	United States rule, 1898-1946 (Table J2)
663	Republic, 1946- (Table J2)
	East Asia. Far East
665	Hong Kong (Table J2)
671	China (Table J2)
672	China (Republic, 1949-). Taiwan (Table J2)
674	Japan (Table J2)
677	Korea (Table J2)
	Including South Korea
677.5	North Korea (Table J2)
681	Thailand (Table J2)
682	Mongolia (Table J2)
	Southwest Asia. Middle East
685	Afghanistan (Table J2)
688	Iran (Table J2)
	Caucasus
690	Armenia (Table J2)
690.2	Azerbaijan (Table J2)
690.3	Georgia (Table J2)
691	Turkey (Table J2)

Asia
Southwest Asia. Middle East -- Continued
691.5 Cyprus (Table J2)
692 Arabia. Arabian Peninsula (General) Persian (Arabian) Gulf States (Table J2)
694 Bahrein (Table J2)
695 Iraq (Table J2)
Israel, see J698
696 Jordan. Trans-Jordan (Table J2)
697 Lebanon (Table J2)
698 Palestine. Israel (Table J2)
699 Qatar (Table J2)
700 Saudi Arabia (Table J2)
701 Syria (Table J2)
Trans-Jordan, see J696
702 United Arab Emirates (Table J2)
703 Yemen (Table J2)
Africa
704 General (Table J2)
English-speaking Africa
South Africa, Republic of
705 General (Table J2)
Provinces
706 Bobhuthatswana (Table J2)
707 Cape of Good Hope. Kaapland (Table J2)
708 Ciskei (Table J2)
711 Natal (Table J2)
715 Orange Free State. Oranje Wystaat (Table J2)
717 Transkei (Table J2)
719 Transvaal (Table J2)
719.5 Venda (Table J2)
Southern Africa. Central Africa
720 Swaziland (Table J2)
722 Lesotho. Basutoland, 1822-1964 (Table J2)
723 Botswana. Bechuanaland Protectorate, British, 1885-1964 (Table J2)
725 Rhodesia. Federation of Rhodesia and Nyasaland. British Central African Protectorate (Table J2)
725.3 Zambia. Northern Rhodesia (Table J2)
725.5 Zimbabwe. Southern Rhodesia (Table J2)
728 Malawi. Nyasaland (Table J2)
Southwest Africa, see J812
East Africa
Including East Africa Protectorate (British)
730 General (Table J2)
731 Kenya (Table J2)
Tanganyika, see J801
732 Uganda (Table J2)
733 Zanzibar (to 1964) (Table J2)
735 Somaliland, British (Table J2)
For Somalia, see J825
West Africa

Africa
English-speaking Africa
West Africa -- Continued
741 General (Table J2)
742 Gambia (Table J2)
743 Ghana. Gold Coast (Table J2)
Nigeria
745 General (Table J2)
745.2 Northern (Table J2)
745.4 Southern (Table J2)
745.6 Western Region (Table J2)
745.7 Eastern Region (Table J2)
Other states, A-Z
746.B464 Benue State (Table J2)
746.I474 Imo State (Table J2)
746.K364 Kano State (Table J2)
746.K384 Katsina State (Table J2)
746.L344 Lagos State (Table J2)
746.O956 Oyo State (Table J2)
746.P55 Plateau State (Table J2)
747 Sierra Leone (Table J2)
Anglo-Egyptian Sudan, see J868
753 Ascension (Table J2)
754 Saint Helena (Table J2)
755 Tristan da Cunha (Table J2)
758 Mauritius (Table J2)
759 Seychelles (Table J2)
Francophone Africa
Barbary States. The Maghrib
762 General (Table J2)
763 Algeria (Table J2)
Morocco, see J881
765 Tunisia (Table J2)
French West Africa
768 Benin. Dahomey (Table J2)
771 Guinea. French Guinea (Table J2)
773 Côte d'Ivoire. Ivory Coast (Table J2)
774 Mali. French Sudan (Table J2)
775 Mauritania (Table J2)
777 Niger (Table J2)
779 Senegal (Table J2)
780 Burkina Faso. Upper Volta (Table J2)
French Equatorial Africa
783 General (Table J2)
784 Central African Republic. Central African Empire (Ubangi-Shari) (Table J2)
785 Chad (Table J2)
786 Congo. Middle Congo (Brazzaville) (Table J2)
787 Gabon (Table J2)
788 Djibouti. French Somaliland (Table J2)
791 Madagascar. Malagasy Republic (Table J2)
792 Comoros (Table J2)
792.5 Mayotte (Table J2)

Africa
Francophone Africa -- Continued
793 Réunion (Table J2)
Other countries
800 German East Africa
801 Tanzania. Tanganyika (Table J2)
For Zanzibar, see J733
805 Cameroon (Table J2)
809 Togo. Togoland (Table J2)
812 Namibia. Southwest Africa (to 1967). German Southwest Africa (to 1967) (Table J2)
814 Ruanda-Urundi (Table J2)
815 Burundi (Table J2)
816 Rwanda (Table J2)
821 Italian East Africa (Table J2)
823 Eritrea (Table J2)
825 Somalia. Italian Somaliland (Table J2)
826 Libya (Table J2)
(827) Tripolitania. Cyrenaica
see J762
831 Zaïre. Congo Free State (Belgian Congo) (Table J2)
841 Angola. Portuguese West Africa (Table J2)
844 Cape Verde Islands (Table J2)
849 Mozambique. Portuguese East Africa (Table J2)
850 Guinea-Bissau. Portuguese Guinea (Table J2)
851 Sao Tome and Principe (Table J2)
855 Spanish West Africa (to 1958) (Table J2)
861 Ethiopia. Abyssinia (Table J2)
866 Egypt (Table J2)
868 Sudan. Egyptian Sudan (Table J2)
875 Liberia (Table J2)
881 Morocco (Table J2)
Pacific area
903 Australasia
Australia
905 General (Table J2)
907 Central Australia (Table J2)
911 New South Wales (Table J2)
912 Norfolk Island (Table J2)
913 Northern Territory. North Australia (Table J2)
916 Queensland (Table J2)
921 South Australia (Table J2)
926 Tasmania (Table J2)
931 Victoria (Table J2)
936 Western Australia (Table J2)
941 New Zealand (Table J2)
951 Guam (Table J2)
(953-956) Hawaii
see J87.H3
Philippines, see J661+
958 American Samoa (U.S. Territory) (Table J2)

	Pacific area -- Continued
960	Micronesia (Federated States). Trust Territory of the Pacific Islands (Table J2)
	For Gilbert and Ellice Islands Colony, see J968.G5
	For Guam, see J951
961	Fiji (Table J2)
964	New Guinea (Table J2)
967	Tonga (Friendly Islands) (Table J2)
968.A-Z	Jurisdictions, A-Z
968.C6	Cook Islands (Table J2)
968.G5	Gilbert and Ellice Islands Colony (Table J2)
968.N57	New Hebrides. Vanuatu (Table J2)
968.S6	Solomon Islands (Table J2)
	Formerly British Solomon Islands
981.A-Z	Other jurisdictions, A-Z
	Caroline Islands, see J960
	Marshall Islands, see J960
981.N3	Nauru (Table J2)
981.N4	New Guinea, British (Table J2)
981.N42	New Guinea, German (Table J2)
981.S6	Solomon Islands (Table J2)
	For British Solomon Islands, see J968.S6
981.W3	Western Samoa (Table J2)

Political science (General)
Periodicals. Serials
Class here general periodicals by place of imprint
1 United States
4 Canadian
5 Latin American
8 British
11 French
14 German
18 Italian
26 Other countries of imprint
Societies
27 International
28 American
29 British
30 French
31 German
32 Italian
34 Societies in other countries
35.5 Congresses
Collections, see JA66+
Yearbooks, see JA1+
Dictionaries. Encyclopedias
60 Polyglot
61 English
62 French
63 German
64.A-Z Other languages, A-Z
65 Terminology. Abbreviations. Notation
General works
66 English
67 French
68 German
68.5 Russian and other Slavic
69.A-Z Other languages, A-Z
70 Juvenile works
Theory. Method. Scope. Relations to other subjects
71 General works
Mathematical methods. Quantitative analysis
71.5 General works
71.7 Statistical methods
72 Mathematical models
72.5 Game theory
74.5 Relation to psychology. Political psychology
Relation to astrology, see BF1729.P6
75 Relation to law
(75.5) Relation to international law
see KZ
75.7 Relation to culture. Political culture
Relation to anthropology. Political anthropology, see GN492+

Theory. Method. Scope.
Relations to other subjects -- Continued
75.8 Relation to ecology. Political ecology
Including Green movement
Cf. GE1+, Environmental sciences
Cf. HC79.E5, Sustainable development
76 Relation to sociology. Political sociology
77 Relation to economics
78 Relation to history
79 Relation to ethics. Political ethics
Relation to religion, see BL65.P7
80 Relation to science
(80.2) Relation to literature
see PN51
Relation to poetry, see PN1081
Relation to drama, see PN1643
History of political science
For biography of political scientists, see JA92
81 General works
(82) Ancient and medieval (to 1500/1600)
see JC51-JC126
83 Modern
84.A-Z By region or country, A-Z
Study and teaching. Research
86 General works
88.A-Z By region or country, A-Z
School cities. School republics, see LB3093+
92 Collective biography of political scientists
For biography of statesmen and politicians, see classes D - F
For biographies of individual political scientists and political theorists, see JC under the appropriate time period

Political theory
State. Theories of the state
11 General works
Political anthropology
General works, see GN492+
Tribal government, see GN492.5
Village government, see JS271
47 Oriental state
(48) Buddhist state
see BQ4570.S7
49 Islamic state
By region or country, see JA84.A+
Ancient state. Political theory in antiquity
51 General works
55.A-Z Special topics, A-Z
55.L43 Legitimacy
55.P7 Plebiscite
61 Assyro-Babylonian Empire
For Code of Hammurabi, see KL2212.1
66 Egypt
67 Hebrews
Greece
Cf. KL4115, States and city states
71 Contemporary works. Biography
73 General works. History
75.A-Z Special topics, A-Z
75.A5 Amnesty
(75.A7) Archons
see DF83
Boule, see JC75.V6
75.C5 Citizenship
75.D36 Democracy
75.D4 Despotism
75.E9 Exiles
75.F3 Federal government. Federalism
75.J8 Justice
75.L63 Local government
75.R4 Resistance to government
75.S4 Secretaries (Grammateus)
75.S8 Suffrage
75.V6 Voule. Boule
(79) Local
see DF221-DF277
Rome
81 Contemporary works. Biography
83 General works. History
85 Special topics, A-Z
85.C5 Citizenship
85.C55 Civil rights. Human rights
Comitia
85.C7 General works
85.C73 Comitia Centuriata. Centuriate Assembly
85.D3 Democracy

State. Theories of the state
Ancient state. Political theory in antiquity
Rome
Special topics, A-Z -- Continued
85.E4 Elections
(85.J9) Judiciary
see KJA3040-KJA3050
85.L53 Liberty
(85.M2) Magistracy
see KJA2980-KJA3033
85.P9 Provincial administration
85.R4 Referendum
85.S4 Senate
85.S7 Sovereignty
85.T7 Tribunes
By period
88 The Republic
89 The Empire
(90) Local
see DG55-DG70
Byzantine Empire
91 Contemporary works. Biography
93 General works. History
Medieval state. Feudal institutions
For works on the political history of the Middle Ages, see D131
109 Dictionaries. Encyclopedias
111 General works. History
116.A-Z Special topics, A-Z
116.F8 Frank pledge
116.H7 Homage. Fealty. Allegiance
Land use, see HD141+
116.M4 Ministeriales
116.S4 Scutage
116.S5 Seigneur, Right of. Jus primae noctis
116.S7 Souffrance (Sufferentia)
116.V3 Vassals
(117) City State
see JC352
121 Contemporary works. Biography
By region or country
see JN - JQ
Modern state
131 General works
By period
16th century
134 General works. History
Contemporary works. Biography
137 English
139 French
141 German
143 Italian
145 Other

	State. Theories of the state
	Modern state
	By period -- Continued
	17th century
151	General works. History
	Contemporary works. Biography
153	English
155	French
156	German
158	Italian
160	Spanish
163	Other
	18th century
171	General works. History
	Contemporary works. Biography
	English
	Thomas Paine
	Collected works
177.A3	English. Editions by date
177.A32	French. Editions by date
177.A33	German. Editions by date
177.A34	Other. Editions by date
177.A4	General treatises on Paine's political theories
177.A5	Selections. By date
	Collected editions (Pts. I-II) By date of imprint
177.B3	English
177.B5	French
177.B8	Other
177.B9	Minor collections. "Maxima", etc.
	Rights of man, Part I
177.C11-C15	English editions of 1791
177.C16-C19	American editions of 1791
177.C21-C25	English editions of 1792
177.C26-C29	American editions of 1792
177.C31-C35	English editions of 1793
177.C36-C39	American editions of 1793
177.C41-C45	English editions of 1794
177.C46-C49	American editions of 1794
177.C51-C55	English editions of 1795
177.C56-C59	American editions of 1795
177.C61-C65	English ediitons of 1796
177.C66-C69	American editions of 1796
177.C71-C75	English editions of 1797
177.C76-C79	American editions of 1797
177.C81-C85	English editions of 1798
177.C86-C89	American editions of 1798
177.C91-C95	English editions of 1799
177.C96-C99	American editions of 1799
177.D2	Later editions. By date
	Rights of man, Part II
177.E21-E25	English editions of 1792

State. Theories of the state
Modern state
By period
18th century
Contemporary works. Biography
English
Thomas Paine
Rights of man
Rights of man, Part II -- Continued

177.E26-E29 American editions of 1792
177.E31-E35 English editions of 1793
177.E36-E39 American editions of 1793
177.E41-E45 English editions of 1794
177.E46-E49 American editions of 1794
177.E51-E55 English editions of 1795
177.E56-E59 American editions of 1795
177.E61-E65 English ediitons of 1796
177.E66-E69 American editions of 1796
177.E71-E75 English editions of 1797
177.E76-E79 American editions of 1797
177.E81-E85 English editions of 1798
177.E86-E89 American editions of 1798
177.E91-E95 English editions of 1799
177.E96-E99 American editions of 1799
177.F2 Later editions

French editions

177.G11-G15 Editions of 1791
177.G21-G25 Editions of 1792
177.G31-G35 Editions of 1793
177.G41-G45 Editions of 1794
177.G51-G55 Editions of 1795
177.G61-G65 Editions of 1796
177.G71-G75 Editions of 1797
177.G81-G85 Editions of 1798
177.G91-G95 Editions of 1799
177.H1 Later editions. By date
177.H3 Other languages (H3G, German, etc.)

Works about Rights of man, etc.

177.H5 English. By date
177.H7 French. By date
177.H9 Other
(178.A1-V4) Other works
see the topic
178.V5 Biography
(178.X2-X6) Trials
see KD
(178.Z2) Miscellaneous and controversial literature
see the topic
179 French
181 German
183 Italian
186 Spanish
189 Other

State. Theories of the state
Modern state
By period -- Continued
19th century
201 General works. History
Contemporary works. Biography
United States
211 Early works to 1815
212 1818-1860
213 1860-
217 Canada
219 Latin America
223 Great Britain
226 Netherlands
229 France
233 Germany
236 Italy
241 Scandinavia
244 Spain and Portugal
248 Other
20th century
General works. History. Biography
251 United States
253 Canada
255 Latin America
257 Great Britain
259 Netherlands
261 France
263 Germany
265 Italy
267 Russia. Soviet Union
269 Scandinavia
271 Spain and Portugal
273 Other
Nationalism. National state. Nation state
Cf. JC362, Internationalism
311 General works
312 Minorities
313 Particularism
314 Political messianism
Political geography. Geopolitics
319 General works
323 Boundaries. Frontiers
(325) Nature, entity, concept of the state
see JC11
327 Sovereignty
328 Allegiance. Loyalty
328.2 Consensus. Consent of the governed
328.3 Opposition. Resistance to government. Civil disobedience
Cf. JF518, Legislative bodies
328.5 Insurgency

State. Theories of the state -- Continued
328.6 Violence. Political violence
Cf. HM281+, Violence (Social psychology)
Patriotism
329 General works
By region or country
see JK - JQ
329.5 Political obligation
330 Power
Cf. HN49.P6, Sociology
(330.15) Public interest
see K3417
330.2 Stability
330.3 Political leadership
336 Social and evolutionary theories of the state
(341) The state as a moral organism
see JA79
Symbolism. National emblems. State emblems
Cf. CD5001+, Seals
Cf. CR191+, Official heraldry
345 General works
By region or country
346 United States
347.A-Z Other regions or countries, A-Z
Forms of the state
348 General works
352 City-state
355 Federal state. Federal government. Federalism
357 Confederation of states
359 Empire. Imperialism
362 World state. Internationalism. Cosmopolitanism
Cf. JC311+, Nationalism
Size of states
364 General works
365 Small states
366 Large states
(367) Ideal states. Utopias
see HX806-HX811
(370) Political anthropology
see GN492-GN494.5
(371) Village. Commune
see JS271
372 Theocracy
Cf. BV629+, Church and state
Ancient state, see JC51+
Feudal state, see JC109+
Monarchy
375 General works. History
381 Absolute monarchy. Despotism
389 Divine right of kings. Royal perogatives
391 Consecration. Coronation
392 Abdication. Deposition

	State. Theories of the state
	Forms of the state
	Monarchy -- Continued
393	Education of princes. Duties of kings and rulers. Mirrors for princes
405	Constitutional monarchy. Limited monarchy
(411-417)	Aristocracy. Nobility see HT647-HT653
419	Oligarchy
	Democracy
421	History
423	General works
	Peoples' democracies, see JC474
(471)	Democratic centralism see HX77
	Social democracy, see HX71+
	Federations, see JC355
474	Communist state. Peoples' democracies
478	Corporate state Cf. HD6479, Guild socialism
	Totalitarianism Cf. JC495, Dictatorships
480	General works. History
481	Fascism. National socialism Cf. D726.5, History Cf. DD253+, Germany Cf. DG571+, Italy
	Communism, see HX39.5.A2+, JC474
	Change of form of the state. Political change
489	General works
491	Revolutions Cf. HM281+, Sociology Cf. HX550.R48, Revolutions and socialism
492	Counterrevolutions
494	Coups d'etat
495	Dictatorships
497	Legitimacy of governments. Legitimation
	Purpose, functions, and relations of the state
(501)	General works see JC11
(510)	Church and state see BV629-BV631, Religion; JC372, Theocracy
	State and the individual. Human rights. Civil rights
571	General works. History
	Conservatism
573	General works
573.2.A-Z	By region or country, A-Z
	Liberalism
574	General works
574.2.A-Z	By region or country, A-Z
575	Equality
578	Justice. Equality before the law

State. Theories of the state
Purpose, functions, and relations of the state
State and the individual.
Human rights. Civil rights -- Continued
Rights of the individual
Liberty. Freedom. Libertarianism
Cf. HM271+, Sociology
585 General works
(589) Freedom of religion. Liberty of conscience
see BV741
(590) Academic freedom
see LC72-LC72.5
591 Freedom of speech
(593) Freedom of the press
see Z657-Z659
Right of privacy
596 General works
596.2.A-Z By region or country, A-Z
598 Freedom of information. Right to know
Cf. K3255, Law
Cf. Z711.4, Libraries
599.A-Z By region or country, A-Z
Under each country:
.x General works
.x2A-.x2Z Local, A-Z
Nationality. Citizenship, see JF801
Political rights, see JF799+
605 Property
Cf. HB711+, Economics
Cf. K721.5, Law
(607) Freedom of association
see K3256

Political institutions and public administration
General. Comparative government
Periodicals. Serials, see JA1+
Societies, see JA27+
Collections, see JF51+
Congresses, see JA35.5
Dictionaries. Encyclopedias, see JA60+
20 Directories
37 Handbooks, manuals, etc.
General works. History
51 English
52 French
53 German
54 Italian
55 Spanish and Portuguese
55.5 Russian and other Slavic
56.A-Z Other languages, A-Z
59 New states
60 Developing countries
127 Juvenile literature
128 Theory. Method. Scope. Relations to other subjects
130 Study and teaching. Research
195 Civil-military relations
Language policy, see P119.3+
197 Regionalism
Organs and functions of government
(201) General works
see JF51-JF56
(221) Sovereignty
see JC327
(223) Referendum
see JC491-JC497
225 Delegation of powers
229 Separation of powers. Checks and balances
Executive. Heads of state
Cf. JC375+, Monarchy
251 General works
Constitutional monarchy, see JC405
255 President
(256) War powers. Emergency powers
see K3344
(260) Legislative power
see K3350
(261) Veto power
see K3351
(269) Treaty-making powers
see K3342
274 Appointments and removals
285 Election. Succession
289 Installation. Inauguration
Parliamentary government. Cabinet system
331 General works
341 Ministerial responsibility

General. Comparative government
Organs and functions of government
Parliamentary government.
Cabinet system -- Continued
Parliamentary interpellation, see K3313
Civil service, see JF1601+
Legislation. Legislative process. Law-making
General works, see K3316+
(441) Legislative powers
see K3311
Referendum. Direct legislation
491 General works
By region or country
United States
494 General works
495.A-W By state, A-W
496.A-Z By city, A-Z
497.A-Z Other regions or countries, A-Z
Legislative bodies. Parliaments
501 History
General works
508 Early through 1800
511 1801-
Bicameralism. Unicameralism, see JF541+
513 Election. Dissolution. Term of office
514 Organization. Officers. Officials and employees
515 Parliamentary practice. Procedure
For individual legislative bodies, see class K
518 Opposition
Cf. JC328.3, Political theory
519 Obstruction. Filibusters
(525) Technique. Bill drafting
see class K
527 Legislative reference bureaus. Information services
529 Lobbying. Pressure groups
533 Parliamentary inquiries. Commissions. Committees
536 Salaries of members
538 Limitation of speeches
539 Reporting. Broadcasting of proceedings
540.5 Publishing of proceedings
Upper House
Including discussions of unicameral and bicameral systems
541 General works
549 Election. Dissolution. Term of office
Lower House
601 General works
619 Election. Dissolution. Term of office
Judiciary, see K3367

General. Comparative government -- Continued
(751) Federal and state relations. State rights
see JC355
Human rights, see JC571+
Political rights. Political participation
799 General works
801 Citizenship
(811) Naturalization
see K3224-K3230
Suffrage. Right to vote
831 General works
841 Voting age
Woman suffrage. Women's right to vote
847 Periodicals. Societies. Serials
851 General works. History
By region or country
see JK - JQ
Elections. Electoral systems. Voting
1001 General works
(1015) Universal suffrage
see JF831
1023 Plural voting
1031 Compulsory voting
1033 Absentee voting
1047 Abstention
1048 Election forecasting
Campaign management, see JF2112.C3
Campaign funds, see JF2112.C28
Representation. Representative government
1051 General works
Representation of economic and social groups
1057 General works
(1059) By region or country
see JK - JQ
Representation of minorities
1061 General works
(1063) By region or country
see JK - JQ
Proportional representation
1071 General works
1075.A-Z By region or country, A-Z
Political corruption
1081 General works
1083 Election fraud. Corrupt practices
(1085) Election contributions and expenditures
see JF2112.C3
Ballot
1091 General works
1104 Short ballot
Cf. JK2217, United States
1107 Secret ballot
1111 Australian ballot
Compulsory voting, see JF1031

General. Comparative government
Political rights. Political participation
Ballot -- Continued
1113 Voter registration
1128 Voting machines
1161 Vote count. Ballot counting
1177 Electoral college. Indirect election
By region or country
see JK - JQ
Public administration
Periodicals. Serials, see JA1+
Societies, see JA27+
Congresses, see JA35.5
Dictionaries. Encyclopedias, see JA60+
Mathematical methods, see JA71.5+
Statistical methods, see JA71.7
Study and teaching. Research
1338.A2 General works
1338.A3A-Z By region or country, A-Z
General works. History
1351 English
1352 French
1353 German
1354 Italian
1355 Spanish and Portuguese
1358.A-Z Other languages, A-Z
Civil service
Cf. HD8001+, State labor
For municipal and local civil service, see JS148+
(1411) General works
see JF1601-JF1678
1501 Bureaucracy
1521 Records management
1525.A-Z Special topics, A-Z
1525.A8 Automatic data processing. Electronic data processing
1525.C58 Commissions
1525.C59 Communications
Confidential information, see JF1525.S4
1525.C6 Consultants
1525.C65 Correspondence
1525.C66 Corruption
1525.C74 Crisis management
1525.D4 Decision making
Electronic data processing, see JF1525.A8
1525.E8 Ethics
Government information, see JF1525.S4
1525.I6 Intelligence service. Espionage
1525.L4 Leadership
1525.M37 Marketing
1525.O35 Office practice
1525.O45 Ombudsman
1525.O6 Operations research

Public administration
Special topics, A-Z -- Continued
1525.O73 Organizational change
1525.P67 Productivity. Government productivity
1525.P7 Property. Government property. Public buildings
1525.P8 Public relations. Propaganda. Government publicity
1525.P85 Purchasing. Government purchasing
Records management, see JF1521
1525.R46 Report writing. Government report writing
1525.S4 Secret and confidential information. Government information
1525.T67 Total quality management
Administrative law, see K3400+
Civil service
1601 General works
1651 Selection and appointment. Dismissal
1655 Job stress
1661 Salaries. Fringe benefits
Cf. HD4938+, State labor
Cf. JF536, Legislative bodies
1671 Pensions. Retirement
1674 Public relations
(1678) Trade-unions. Civil service societies
see HD8005-8013
(1800) Martial law
see K4754
1820 Military government
Cf. JF195, Civil-military relations
1900 Federal districts. Capitals
Colonial administration, see JV412+
Political parties
2011 History
(2049) Political participation
see JF799
2051 General works
2071 Party affiliation
Organization. Party machinery. Campaign methods
2085 Nominations for office. Primaries. Caucus
2091 Political conventions. Party platforms
2111 Political patronage. Party bosses
2112.A-Z Other topics, A-Z
2112.A4 Advertising. Political advertising
2112.C28 Campaign funds. Election finances. Election costs
2112.C3 Campaign management. Electioneering
2112.D43 Debating. Campaign debates
2112.P8 Public relations
Television in politics, see HE8700.75+

Political institutions and public administration
United States
1 Periodicals. Serials
3 Societies
4 Museums. Exhibitions
Directories. Registers
5 Official Register
6 Other directories
7.5.A-Z By region or state, A-Z
Class here directories of federal agencies and employees
For directories of state agencies and officials, see JK2701+
(8) Annuals
see JK1
9 Dictionaries. Encyclopedias
(11-19) Constitutional history. Constitutional law. Constitutions
see KF4501-KF4554
21 Addresses, essays, lectures
(27) Collected biography
see E176
31 General works
40 Juvenile works
Colonial period. The colonies
54 General works
66 Governor
Legislature
81 General works
83.A-Z Local, A-Z
(91) Judiciary
see KF361-KF364
Suffrage. Right to vote
96.A3 General works
96.A4-Z Local, A-Z
Elections
97.A3 General works
97.A4-Z Local, A-Z
99.A-Z Local, A-Z
Political parties
101 General works
103.A-Z Particular colonies, A-Z
1776-1820
116 General works
(128) Declaration of Independence
see KF4506
(130-136) Articles of Confederation, 1778
see KF4508
(141-148) Constitution of the United States, 1787-1788
see KF4520-KF4528.5

United States
1776-1820 -- Continued
155 Federalist
Class here works on the political theory of the Federalist
For the text of, and legal commentaries on, the Federalist, see KF4515
(161) State conventions
see KF4512
(168-170) Amendments
see KF4555-KF4558
1788-1789/1800
171 General works
(176) Virginia and Kentucky resolutions, 1798
see KF4621
181 1798/1800-1820
216 1821-1865
246 1866-1898
271 20th century
(291-295) American and other constitutions compared
see KF4554
Separation of powers
Cf. KF4565, Constitutional law
305 General works
(307) Treaty making power
see KF5055
Federal government. Federal-state relations. Federalism. State rights
311 General works
By period
316 To 1836
318 1836/40-1860
320 1861-1865
321 1866-1876/78
323 1876/78-1898
325 1899-
330 Civil-military relations
(339) War and emergency powers
see KF5060
(361) Church and state. Religion and the government
see BR516, Religion; KF4865, Law
Government. Public administration
(401) Directories. Registers
see JK5-JK7.5
404 Periodicals. Serials
411 History
(416) Administrative law
see KF5401-KF5402
421 General works
(448) Recall
see KF4884
467 Business and politics
468.A-Z Other special, A-Z

United States
Government. Public administration
Other special, A-Z -- Continued

468.A3 Advertising
468.A8 Automatic data processing. Electronic data processing
468.C7 Consultants. Executive advisory bodies
468.C75 Correspondence
468.E7 Ethics
Excutive advisory bodies, see JK468.C7
468.F5 Field service
468.I6 Intelligence service. CIA. Central Intelligence Agency. Espionage
468.L5 Lie detectors. Polygraphs
468.O4 Office practice
468.O6 Ombudsman
Cf. KF5423, Abuse of administrative power
468.P34 Paperwork
468.P64 Political planning. Public policy
Polygraphs, see JK468.L5
468.P75 Productivity
Public policy, see JK468.P64
468.P76 Public records management
Publicity, see JK849
468.S4 Secret and confidential information
468.T4 Telecommunication systems
468.T67 Total quality management
468.T7 Transportation
468.W54 Whistle blowing

Executive branch
For executive papers, see J80+
501 General works
President
511 History
516 General works
517 Juvenile works
Nomination
521 General works
522 Presidential primaries
Election
526 History
528 General works
529 Electoral college
536 Inauguration
550 Term of office
Salary. Compensation, see JK779
552 Staff. Executive Office of the President
554 Press conferences. Media relations
(558-562) War and emergency powers
see KF5060
(570-573) Treaty-making powers
see KF5055

United States
Government. Public administration
Executive branch
President -- Continued
Relations with Congress. Relations between Congress and Executive departments
585 General works
586 Veto power
587 Messages. State of the Union messages
Cf. CD3029.8+, Presidential papers
Cf. J80+, Texts of messages
606 Ex-Presidents
609 Succession. Disability
Cf. KF5082, Legal status
609.5 Vice President
Cf. JK1224, President of the Senate
Cabinet
610 Directories. Registers
611 General works
616 Relation to Congress
Civil Service
Cf. KF5338, Civil service law
Office of Personnel Managment. Civil Service Commission. Merit Systems Protection Board
631 Periodicals. Serials
639 General works
641 Presidents' messages
(643) Commissions or committees on departmental methods, economy, efficiency
see JK681-JK692
(645) Relation of the Civil service to Congress
see JK585
(646-656) Congressional documents
see KF16-KF49
661 Directories. Registers
666 Statistics
671 Periodicals. Serials
674 Societies
For trade-unions, see HD8005+
677 Congresses
681 General works
Including Civil Service reform
By period
686 Before 1883
691 1883-1977
692 1978-
692.5.A-Z By region or state, A-Z
Class here works on the federal civil service
For state civil service, see JK2465+
Biography
692.8 Collective
693.A-Z Individual, A-Z
698 Republican party and civil service reform

United States
Government. Public administration
Executive branch
Civil Service -- Continued
699 Democratic party and civil service reform
(711) Treatises
see JK681-JK692
Civil service examinations. Civil service schools
716 General works
717.A-Z Special subjects, A-Z
717.C54 Clerks. Clerical ability
(717.S7) Stenography
see Z53
717.S8 Supervisors
718 In-service training. Interns
Special classes of employees
Cf. JK766.4, Affirmative action programs
720 Veterans
721 Women in the civil service
723.A-Z Other special, A-Z
723.A34 Afro-Americans. Blacks
723.A4 Aliens
Blacks, see JK723.A34
723.B58 Blue collar workers
723.C6 Communists
723.D4 Deaf
723.E9 Executives
723.H3 Handicapped
723.H35 Mentally handicapped
723.H6 Homosexuals. Gays. Lesbians
723.M54 Minorities
723.O4 Older employees. Age and employment
723.S8 Students, College
723.V64 Volunteer workers
723.W5 Without-compensation personnel
Appointments and removals. Patronage. Spoils
731 General works
734 Loyalty and security investigations. Loyalty-security program
744 Dismissal. Reductions-in-force. Layoff systems
761 Political activity
Personnel management
765 General works
766.4 Affirmative action programs
766.5 Personnel records
766.6 Performance appraisal. Rating of employees
767 Promotions
768.3 Incentive awards. Meritorious service awards. Merit increases. Performance awards. Suggestion systems
768.4 Labor productivity

United States
Government. Public administration
Executive branch
Civil Service
Personnel management -- Continued
768.7 Discipline
768.8 Grievance procedures
769.5 Hours of labor
770 Annual leave. Sick leave
Salaries. Pensions. Fringe benefits
Class here works dealing with service under the state in all branches (not limited to civil service proper)
Cf. HD4938+, Wages of state labor
Cf. JK768.3, Salary increases as service awards
771 Salary lists
774 Periodicals. Serials
(775) Documents
see JK774, Periodicals; JK776, General works
776 General works
779 Salary of the President
781 Salaries of members of Congress
Including pensions
Salaries of the judiciary, see KF8777
791 Retirement. Pensions
794.A-Z Other, A-Z
794.H4 Health insurance
794.L5 Life insurance
(795) Travel regulations
see KF5387
849 Publicity. Media relations
850.A-Z Other topics, A-Z
850.A3 Accidents
850.A4 Alcoholism
850.B7 Bribery
850.C53 Charitable contributions
850.D4 Details and transfers
850.D77 Drug abuse. Drug testing
Drug testing, see JK850.D77
850.E48 Employee assistance programs. Problem employees
850.E5 Employers' liability. Workers' compensation
850.J62 Job satisfaction
Problem employees, see JK850.E48
850.R44 Relocation of employees
850.S9 Supplementary employment of civil service employees
850.T85 Turnover of employees
850.U5 Uniforms
Individual departments and agencies
(851-853) Department of State
see KF5112-KF5113

United States
Government. Public administration
Executive branch
Civil Service
Individual departments and agencies -- Continued
(854) Agency for International Development
see HC60
Department of the Interior
(864) Periodicals. Serials
see J84
868 General works
(873) Department of Justice
see KF5106-KF5107
Executive advisory bodies, see JK468.C7
Other departments or agencies limited to a particular subject
see the subject
(901) Independent regulatory commissions
see KF5406-KF5407
Congress. Legislative branch
(1001) Legislative process
see KF4945-KF4951
(1003) Legislative reference bureau
see JK1108
1012 Directories. Registers
1021 General works
1025 Juvenile works
Congressional committees
For rules of procedure, see KF4946
1029 General works
1029.2 Seniority system
1029.5.A-W Delegations. By state, A-W
1030 Collective biography
For biographies of individual legislators, see class E
History
By period
Colonial period, see JK81+
Continental Congress, 1774-1788
Journals
(1031) General
see KF4505
(1032) Secret journals, 1820-1821, 4 v.
see KF4505
1033 General works
Federal Congress, 1789-
(1036) Debates. Proceedings
see KF16-KF43
1041 General works
1051 Voting by members of congress

United States
Government. Public administration
Congress. Legislative branch
History
By period
Federal Congress, 1789- -- Continued
1059 By number of congress
e. g. 67th Congress, JK1059 67th.
Subarrange by main entry
(1061-1081) Constitution. Powers. Prerogatives
see KF4935-KF4944
Congressional employees. Staff members
1083 General works
1084 Capitol pages
Salaries of members, see JK781
(1091-1106) Procedure
see KF4937
1108 Legislative reference bureaus. Information services
1111 Conference committees
1118 Lobbying. Pressure groups
1121 Ethics
(1123) Investigations
see KF4942
1128 Reporting
1129 Broadcasting of proceedings
1130 Term of office. Term limits
Senate
1154 Directories. Registers
1161 General works. History
Juvenile works, see JK1276
(1166-1197) Constitution. Powers. Prerogatives
see KF4988-KF4989
Organization. Administration
1220 General works
Officers
1224 President
1226 President pro tem
1227 Majority leader
Committees
For rules of procedure, see KF4986+
1236 Directories. Registers
1239 General works
(1240) Individual committees
see KF4987
1251 Executive session
Employees. Staff members
1255 General works
1257 Secretary of the Senate
1259 Sergeant at arms
(1266-1274) Procedure
see KF4982-KF4984
1276 Juvenile works

United States
Government. Public administration
Congress. Legislative branch -- Continued
House of Representatives
1308 Directories. Registers
1319 General works
(1326-1333) Constitution. Powers. Prerogatives
see KF5053-KF5069
Congressional districts. Election districts.
Gerrymandering
1341 General works
1343.A-W By state, A-W
For election districts of state
legislatures, see JK2493
1379 Ethics
Organization. Administration
1410 General works
1411 Officers. Speaker
Committees
For rules of procedure, see KF4996+
1426 Directories. Registers
1429 General works
(1430) Special committees
see KF4997
1431 Employees. Staff members
1432 Clerk of the House
(1435-1443) Procedure
see KF4992
(1507-1603) Judiciary
see KF8700-KF8709
1606 Capital. Site of the capital
Cf. F191+, History of the District of
Columbia
Cf. KF5750+, Law
Public buildings
Cf. NA4195+, Architecture
1613 General works
Including works on federal buildings
For state buildings, see JK1651.A1+
Washington
1616 Capitol
Cf. F204.C2, History
1617 Senate offices
1618 House offices
1621 White House
Cf. F204.W5, History
Departments
1625 General works
1626 State department
1637.A-Z Other buildings, A-Z
1637.C6 Commerce Department building
1637.I6 Interior Department building
1641.A-Z Other cities, A-Z

United States
Government. Public administration
Public buildings -- Continued
State buildings
1651.A1 General works. States collectively
1651.A2-W By state, A-W
1661 Government property (other than public buildings)
For property of the individual states, see JK2701+
Supplies. Government purchasing
(1671) Federal
see JK1673
1672 General Services Administration
1673 General works
1677.A-Z Special kinds of supplies, apparatus, etc., A-Z
1677.A8 Automotive spare parts
1677.C6 Coal
1677.C65 Computers
1677.C67 Copying machines
1677.D3 Data tapes
1677.D4 Desks
1677.D7 Drugs
1677.E4 Electron tubes
1677.L37 Lasers
1677.M7 Motor vehicles
1677.O4 Office equipment and supplies
1677.P3 Paper
1677.P4 Petroleum
1677.R3 Radio equipment
1677.T4 Teletype
1679 Specifications, standards, product descriptions
Cf. TS155+, Production management
1683 States collectively
For individual states, see JK2701+
Public printing
1685.A1 General works
1685.A2-W By state, A-W
Political rights. Practical politics
For civil rights and human rights, see JC571+
For political participation, see JK1764
1717 History
1726 General works
(1731) Right of petition
see KF4780
(1736) Trial by jury
see KF8975
Citizenship
(1756) Legal treatises
see KF4700-KF4720
1758 Manuals for foreign-born citizens. Citizenship test. "Americanization"
1759 General works
(1760) Study and teaching
see JA86-JA88

United States
  Political rights. Practical politics
    Citizenship -- Continued
1761 National holidays
  For individual holidays, see the subject or event being commemorated
1764 Political participation
  Cf. JK2255+, Political parties
(1800-1836) Naturalization
  see KF4706-KF4710
Suffrage. Right to vote
  For Colonial period, see JK96.A3+
1846 General works
(1861-1863) Election laws
  see KF4891-KF4901
(1872) Voting by psychiatric hospital and mental retardation facilities patients
  see KF4896
(1873-1874) Absentee voting
  see KF4901
(1876-1878) Voting by soldiers
  see KF4894
Woman suffrage. Women's right to vote
1880 Periodicals. Serials
Societies
1881 National
1883 State
1885 Congresses
(1889) Election laws
  see KF4895
1896 General works
1898 Juvenile works
1899.A-Z Biography, A-Z
1911.A-Z By state, A-W
Afro-American suffrage. Afro-American voters
1924 General works
1929.A2 Southern states. South
1929.A3-W Other states, A-W
(1936) By state
  see JK2701-JK9593
Electoral system. Elections. Voting
  Cf. JK1846+, Suffrage
  For Colonial period, see JK97.A3+
  For election of the president, see JK526+
(1961-1963) Election laws
  see KF4885-KF4921
History
1965 General
(1966) By state
  see JK2701-JK9595
Statistics. Election returns. Voting behavior
1967 General works
1968 By date of election

United States
Political rights. Practical politics
Electoral system. Elections. Voting
Statistics. Election returns. Voting behavior -- Continued
By state, see JK2701+
1976 General works
1978 Juvenile works
(1982) Election districts. Voting districts
see JK1341-JK1343
(1984) Short ballot
see JK2217
1987 Abstention
Campaign funds. Election finances. Political action committees. Campaign contributions
1991 General works
1991.5.A-W By state, A-W
1994 Election fraud. Corrupt practices
(1997) Publicity of expenditures
see JK1991-JK1991.5
2007 Election forecasting
Election guides. Handbooks for election officials
(2021) General works
see JK1976
Law, see KF4885+
(2023) By state
see JK2701-JK9595
(2025) By city
see JS
Nominations for office
2063 General works
Primaries. Caucus
2071 General works
2075.A-W By state, A-W
Voter registration
2160 General works
2161.A-W By state, A-W
(2164) Laws
see KF4898
Ballot
2214 General works
2215 Australian ballot system
2217 Other systems
Including short ballot, coupon ballot, preferential ballot
(2241-2248) Electoral fraud
see JK1994
2249 Political corruption
Political parties
2255 Party platforms. Political conventions
History
For Colonial period, see JK101+
For comprehensive histories, see JK2261

United States
Political parties
History -- Continued
2260 1776-1860
2261 1860-
Including comprehensive histories
2265 General works
2271 Parties and the individual. Party affiliation
2281 Campaign management. Electioneering
2295.A-Z Local. By region or state, A-Z
For individual national parties functioning at the state level, see JK2301+
Particular parties
2301-2309 Federal Party (Table J3)
2311-2319 Democratic Party. Republican-Democratic Party (Table J3)
2320 National Republican Party (Table J5)
2326-2335 Whig Party (Table J3)
2336 Free Soil Party (Table J5)
2341 Know Nothing Party. American Party (Table J5)
2351-2359 Republican Party (Table J3)
Greenback Party, see HG604
2361-2365 Labor Party. United States Labor Party (Table J4)
2371-2375 Populists. People's Party of the United States (Table J4)
2381-2385 Prohibition Party (Table J4)
2386-2390 Progressive Party (Table J4)
2391.A-Z Other parties, A-Z (Table J6)
State government
Class here general works only
For individual states, see JK2701+
2403 Periodicals. Serials
2408 General works
(2410-2411) Admission of territories to statehood
see KF4545.S7
(2413-2428) State constitutions
see KF4529-KF4530
(2430-2491) Legislation
see KF4933
Public administration
2443 General works
2445.A-Z Special topics, A-Z
2445.A4 Advertising
2445.A8 Automatic data processing. Electronic data processing
2445.C58 Communication systems
2445.C7 Consultants
2445.E8 Ethics
2445.I57 Interstate relations, agencies, etc.
2445.P76 Productivity
2445.P82 Public records management

United States
State government
Public administration
Special topics, A-Z -- Continued
(2445.R4) Referendum
see JF494
2445.T67 Total quality management
(2446) "Short ballot" movement
see JK2217
Executive branch
2446.5 General works
Governor
2447 General works
2454 Veto power
2459 Lieutenant-governor
Civil service
2465 General works
2471 Appointments and removals
2474 Salaries. Pensions. Fringe benefits
Class here works dealing with service under the state in all branches (not limited to civil service proper)
Individual departments and agencies
2477 State department
Other departments or agencies limited to a particular subject
see the subject
2480.A-Z Special topics, A-Z
2480.E4 Employment tests. Civil service examinations
2480.H4 Health insurance
2480.I6 In-service training
2480.L24 Labor productivity
2480.M5 Minorities
2482.A-Z Special classes of officials and employees, A-Z
2482.E94 Executives
2482.W6 Women
Legislative branch
2484 History
2488 General works
2493 Representative districts. Election districts
For individual states, see JK2701+
2495 Organization. Administration
2498 Lobbying. Pressure groups
2506 Upper House
2508 Lower House
(2521-2525) Judiciary
see KF8700-KF8709
2556 Territorial government
Cf. JV500+, Colonial administration
Indians of North America. Indian nations. Tribal government, see E98.T77
Confederate states, see JK9803

United States
State government -- Continued
Directories. Registers
For directories of agencies and employees of individual state governments, see JK2701+
For directories of federal agencies and employees at the state level, see JK7.5.A+

2679	General
2681	New England
2683	Southern states
2685	Central states
2687	West. Pacific states
	Individual states and territories
2701-2793	District of Columbia (Table J7)
2801-2893	Maine (Table J7)
2901-2993	New Hampshire (Table J7)
3001-3093	Vermont (Table J7)
3101-3193	Massachusetts (Table J7)
3201-3293	Rhode Island (Table J7)
3301-3393	Connecticut (Table J7)
3401-3493	New York (Table J7)
3501-3593	New Jersey (Table J7)
3601-3693	Pennsylvania (Table J7)
3701-3793	Delaware (Table J7)
3801-3893	Maryland (Table J7)
3901-3993	Virginia (Table J7)
4001-4093	West Virginia (Table J7)
4101-4193	North Carolina (Table J7)
4201-4293	South Carolina (Table J7)
4301-4393	Georgia (Table J7)
4401-4493	Florida (Table J7)
4501-4593	Alabama (Table J7)
4601-4693	Mississippi (Table J7)
4701-4793	Louisiana (Table J7)
4801-4893	Texas (Table J7)
5101-5193	Arkansas (Table J7)
5201-5293	Tennessee (Table J7)
5301-5393	Kentucky (Table J7)
5401-5493	Missouri (Table J7)
5501-5593	Ohio (Table J7)
5601-5693	Indiana (Table J7)
5701-5793	Illinois (Table J7)
5801-5893	Michigan (Table J7)
6001-6093	Wisconsin (Table J7)
6101-6193	Minnesota (Table J7)
6301-6393	Iowa (Table J7)
6401-6493	North Dakota (Table J7)
6501-6593	South Dakota (Table J7)
6601-6693	Nebraska (Table J7)
6801-6893	Kansas (Table J7)
7001-7093	Indian Territory (Table J7)
7101-7193	Oklahoma (Table J7)
7301-7393	Montana (Table J7)

United States
State government
Individual states and territories -- Continued
7501-7593 Idaho (Table J7)
7601-7693 Wyoming (Table J7)
7801-7893 Colorado (Table J7)
8001-8093 New Mexico (Table J7)
8201-8293 Arizona (Table J7)
8401-8493 Utah (Table J7)
8501-8593 Nevada (Table J7)
8701-8793 California (Table J7)
9001-9093 Oregon (Table J7)
9201-9293 Washington (Table J7)
9301-9393 Hawaii (Table J7)
9501-9593 Alaska (Table J7)
Confederate States of America
Cf. E482+, History of the Confederate States of America
9663 Directories. Registers
(9671-9679) Constitution. Constitutional law
see KFZ9000-KFZ9027.8
(9695-9716) Legislative documents
see KFZ8606-KFZ8620
Executive documents
9717 General works
Messages of the President
9718 Collected
9719 Individual
(9778-9799) State documents
see KFZ8600-KFZ9199
9803 General works. History
9887 State relations. Equality and sovereignty
Executive branch
9909 General works. History
9919 Cabinet
9925 Civil service
Legislative branch
9933 General works. History
9939 Constitution, powers and prerogatives
9954 Senate
9961 House of Representatives
(9973-9975) Judiciary
see KFZ9108-KFZ9198.8
Political rights. Citizenship
9981 General works
9989 Suffrage. Right to vote
9993 Electoral system. Elections. Voting

Political institutions and public administration
Canada, Latin America, etc.
Canada
1 Periodicals. Serials
3 Societies
(5) Yearbooks
see JL1
15 General works. History
19 Separation of powers
27 Federal-Provincial relations
By period
Early, 1608-1792
41 General works
45 French rule, 1608-1763. New France
48 English rule, 1763-1792
53 Upper and Lower Canada, 1792-1840
55 Province of Canada, 1841-1867
65 Dominion of Canada, 1867- . Canadian Confederation
Government. Public administration
71 Directories. Registers
75 General works
86.A-Z Special topics, A-Z
86.A8 Automatic data processing. Electronic data processing
Confidential information, see JL86.S43
86.C67 Corruption
Electronic data processing, see JL86.A8
86.I58 Intelligence service. Espionage
86.O43 Ombudsman
86.P64 Political planning. Public policy
Public policy, see JL86.P64
86.P76 Public records
Public relations, see JL86.P8
86.P8 Publicity. Public relations. Propaganda
86.S43 Secret and confidential information. Government information
Executive
87 General works
88 Governor general
93 Privy council
(94) Commissions of inquiry
see K4765
Departments. Ministries
For departments limited to a particular subject, see the subject
95 General works
Cabinet
97 General works
99 Premier. Prime ministers
103 Department of the Secretary of State
Civil service

Canada, Latin America, etc.
Canada
Government. Public administration
Executive
Civil service -- Continued
(105) Directories. Registers. Civil service lists
see JL71
106 Periodicals. Societies. Serials
108 General works
111.A-Z Special topics, A-Z
111.A4 Alcoholism
111.D4 Details. Relocation
Employee suggestions, see JL111.I5
111.E84 Ethics
111.E93 Executives
111.I5 Incentive programs. Meritorious service increases. Employee suggestions
Meritorious service increases, see JL111.I5
Pensions, see JL111.S3
111.R38 Rating of employees
Relocation, see JL111.D4
111.S3 Salaries. Pensions. Fringe benefits
Including legislators' salaries and pensions
Transfers, see JL111.D4
111.W6 Women employees
Parliament. Legislative branch
131 Directories. Registers
136 General works
Procedure, see KE4535
148.5 Lobbying. Pressure groups
155 Upper House. Senate
161 Lower House. House of Commons
Representation
167 General works
168.A-Z By province, A-Z
179 Provincial legislative bodies
(181) Judiciary
see KE4775
186 Government property. Public buildings
186.5 Political rights. Political participation
187 Citizenship
(189) Naturalization
see K4351
Suffrage. Right to vote
191 General works
192 Women's right to vote
193 Elections. Electoral system. Voting
Political parties
195 General works
197.A-Z Special parties, A-Z
198 Provincial government
200-209 Newfoundland (Table J10)

	Canada, Latin America, etc.
	Canada -- Continued
210-219	Prince Edward Island (Table J10)
220-229	Nova Scotia (Table J10)
230-239	New Brunswick (Table J10)
240-259	Quebec (Table J9)
260-279	Ontario (Table J9)
280-299	Manitoba (Table J9)
300-319	Saskatchewan (Table J9)
320-339	Alberta (Table J9)
420-439	British Columbia (Table J9)
460-479	Northwest Territories (Table J9)
495	Yukon Territory (Table J11)
500	Prairie Provinces (Table J11)
590-599	Bermuda (Table J10)
599.2	Greenland (Table J11)
599.4	St. Pierre and Miquelon (Table J11)
599.5	West Indies. Caribbean Area (Table J11)
600-609	British West Indies. English-speaking Caribbean (Table J10)
609.2	Anguilla (Table J11)
610-619	Bahamas (Table J10)
620-629	Barbados (Table J10)
629.5	Cayman Islands (Table J11)
629.6	Grenada (Table J11)
630-639	Jamaica (Table J10)
	Leeward Islands
640-649	General (Table J10)
	Anguilla, see JL609.2
649.2	Antigua and Barbuda (Table J11)
649.5	Monserrat (Table J11)
649.7	Saint Kitts and Nevis (Table J11)
650-659	Trinidad and Tobago (Table J10)
	Windward Islands
660-669	General (Table J10)
669.2	Dominica (Table J11)
	Grenada, see JL629.6
669.4	Saint Lucia (Table J11)
669.5	Saint Vincent and the Grenadines (Table J11)
670-679	Belize (Table J10)
680-689	Guyana. British Guiana (Table J10)
690-699	Falkland Islands (Table J10)
(740-749)	Danish West Indies see JL1160-JL1169
	Netherlands Antilles. Dutch West Indies
760-769	General (Table J10)
769.3	Aruba (Table J11)
769.5	Bonaire (Table J11)
770-779	Curaçao (Table J10)
779.2	Saba (Table J11)
779.5-779	Saint Eustatius (Table J11)
779.7	Saint Martin (Table J11)
780-789	Surinam. Dutch Guiana (Table J10)

JL

Canada, Latin America, etc. -- Continued
French West Indies
790-799 General (Table J10)
810-819 French Guiana (Table J10)
820-829 Guadeloupe (Table J10)
830-839 Martinique (Table J10)
950-969 Latin America (Table J9)
1000-1019 Cuba (Table J9)
1040-1059 Puerto Rico (Table J9)
1080-1099 Haiti (Table J9)
1120-1139 Dominican Republic (Table J9)
1160-1169 Virgin Islands of the United States (Table J10)
1200-1299 Mexico (Table J8)
Central America
1400-1419 General (Table J9)
Belize, see JL670+
1440-1459 Costa Rica (Table J9)
1480-1499 Guatemala (Table J9)
1520-1539 Honduras (Table J9)
1560-1579 El Salvador (Table J9)
1600-1619 Nicaragua (Table J9)
1640-1659 Panama (Table J9)
1670-1679 Panama Canal Zone (Table J10)
South America
1850-1869 General (Table J9)
2000-2099 Argentina (Table J8)
2200-2299 Bolivia (Table J8)
2400-2499 Brazil (Table J8)
2600-2699 Chile (Table J8)
2800-2899 Colombia (Table J8)
3000-3099 Ecuador (Table J8)
Guianas
Guyana. British Guyana, see JL680+
Surinam. Dutch Guiana, see JL780+
French Guiana, see JL810+
3200-3299 Paraguay (Table J8)
3400-3499 Peru (Table J8)
3600-3699 Uruguay (Table J8)
3800-3899 Venezuela (Table J8)

Political institutions and public administration
Europe
1 Periodicals. Serials
2 Societies
(3) Collections
see JN5
General works. History
5 General
By period
7 Medieval
Modern
8 General works
9 16th-18th centuries
10 19th century
12 20th century
15 European federation and integration
16 Union of European Federalists
European Council, see JN33
16.5 European Movement
18 Council of Europe
For legal works and proceedings, see KJE100+
European Union. European Community. European communities
26 Periodicals. Societies. Serials
For official record and documentation, see KJE
27 Directories. Registers
30 General works
32 Executive branch
Including works on public administration
33 European Council
33.5 Commission of the European Communities
34 Council of the European Communities
35 Civil service
36 Legislative branch. European Parliament
40 Political rights. Political participation
45 Elections
50 Political parties
Regions
Northern Europe. Scandinavia, see JN7009.2+
94 Western Europe (Table J11)
96 Central Europe. Eastern Europe (Table J11)
97 Balkan Peninsula (Table J11)
Great Britain
101 Periodicals. Serials
102 Societies
106 Directories. Registers
(111) Constitutional law
see KD3931-KD3966
114 Dictionaries. Encyclopedias
General works. By date of imprint
117 Early to 1832
118 1832-
By period

Europe
Great Britain
By period -- Continued
131 To 1066
Medieval, 1066-1485
137 General works
141 Norman Conquest, 1066-1215
147 Magna Charta, 1215
Cf. KD3944+, Law
151 Magna Charta to end of 13th century
158 14th century. Plantagenet to 1399
Modern, 1485-
175 General works
181 16th century, Tudor, 1485-1603
17th century, Stuart. Revolution, 1603-1702
191 General works
193 Early Stuart
196 Commonwealth and Protectorate, 1649-1660
203 Restoration, 1660-1689
207 William and Mary, 1689-1702
18th century, 1702-1832
210 General works
214 Contemporary works
216 19th century, 1832-
231 20th century
248 Commonwealth of Nations. Imperial federation
(266) Church and state
see BX5157
(276) Imperialism. Imperial federation
see JN248
297.A-Z Special topics, A-Z
297.C58 Civil-military relations
297.F43 Federalism
297.I53 Insurgency
297.R44 Regionalism
Government. Public administration
Directories. Registers, see JN106
309 History
318 General works
329.A-Z Special topics, A-Z
329.C7 Consultants
329.C74 Correspondence
329.D43 Decentralization
329.E4 Electronic data processing
329.I6 Intelligence service. Espionage
Lobbying, see JN329.P7
329.O43 Ombudsman
329.P7 Pressure groups. Lobbying
329.P75 Public records management
329.P8 Publicity
329.S4 Secret and confidential information. Government information
Executive branch

Europe
Great Britain
Government. Public administration
Executive branch -- Continued
Crown
331 General works. History
By period
335 To 1066
336 Norman, 1066-1154
337 Plantagenet, 1154-1485
338 Tudor, 1485-1603
339 Stuart, 1603-1689
340 William and Mary, 1689-1714
341 Hanover, 1714-
(351) Royal prerogative. Divine right, succession, etc.
see KD4435-KD4456
359 Lord High Steward
365 Privy purse. Royal expenditures
371 Privy Chamber. Royal household
378 The Privy Council
389 Signet Office
Cabinet. Prime ministers
401 History
405 General works
407 Royal commissions
409 Executive advisory bodies. Other executive bodies
Civil service
425 General works
428 Civil service reform
431 Civil service examinations
441 Veterans and the civil service
442 Women in the civil service
443 Salaries. Fringe benefits
445 Pensions
447 Retirement. Superannuation
450.A-Z Other topics, A-Z
450.C6 Conflict of interest
450.I5 In-service training. Interns
450.M36 Manpower planning
450.P6 Political activity
450.R38 Rating of employees
450.S88 Suggestion systems. Incentive awards
450.T7 Travel
Departments. Ministries
For departments limited to a particular subject, see the subject
451 General
452 Cabinet Office
453 Home Office
Parliament. Legislative branch
500 Directories. Registers

Europe
  Great Britain
    Government. Public administration
      Parliament. Legislative branch -- Continued
        General works. By date of imprint
505 Early to 1800
508 1800-
        History. By period
513 To 1066
515 Medieval, 1066-1485
          Modern, 1485-
521 General works
525 16th century
534 17th century
539 18th century, to 1832
543 19th century, "Reform," 1832-1900
550 20th century
        Prerogatives of Parliament, see KD4246
558 Parliamentary representation
        Privileges, see KD4246
581 Salaries of members
        Parliamentary procedure
(591-608) General
            see KD4210-KD4242
611 Reporting. Broadcasting of proceedings
        House of Lords
617 Directories. Registers
621 General works
(627-653) Procedure. Prerogatives
            see KD4260-KD4290
        House of Commons
          Directories. Registers
671 Debrett
672 Other directories
673 History
677 General works
678 The Speaker
(679) Committees
            see KD4358-KD4361
(681-695) Procedure. Prerogatives
            see KD4354-KD4375
(750-841) Judiciary
          see KD4645
    Government property. Public buildings
851 General works
865 Government purchasing
    Political rights. Political participation.
      Practical politics
900 General works
906 Citizenship
(930-943) Naturalization
        see KD4056
      Elections. Voting. Suffrage. Right to vote

Europe
Great Britain
Political rights.
Political participation.
Practical politics
Elections. Voting.
Suffrage. Right to vote -- Continued
History
945 General
948 Early to 1640
951 1640 to The Reform Bill
955 1832-1945
956 1945-
961 General works
Woman suffrage. Women's right to vote
976 Periodicals. Societies. Serials
979 General works
(1001-1033) Election law
see KD4321-KD4349
1037 Election statistics. Election returns
1039 Campaign funds. Election finance
(1041-1071) Contested elections
see KD4380-KD4381
1088 Election fraud. Corrupt practices
Political parties
1111 Periodicals. Societies. Serials
1117 General works. History
By period
1118 Early to 18th century
1119 18th century
1120 19th century
1121 20th century
1125.A-Z Local, A-Z
1129.A-Z Special parties, A-Z
1150-1159 Wales (Table J10)
1170-1179 Isle of Man (Table J10)
Scotland
1187 Periodicals. Serials
(1201-1203) Constitutional law
see KDC750-KDC785
1213 General works. History
Government. Public administration
1228 General works. History
1231 Secretary for Scotland. Scottish Office
Executive branch. Crown
History
1233 General works
(1239) Right to the crown. Succession
see KDC779
1243 Civil service
Legislative branch. Parliament
1263 General works. History
1277 Representation

Europe
Great Britain
Scotland
Government. Public administration
Legislative branch. Parliament -- Continued
(1281) Procedure
see KDC766
(1282) Private bill legislation
see KDC768
(1283-1285) Judiciary
see KDC840-KDC920.6
Political rights. Political participation.
Practical politics
1290 General works
1291 Citizenship
1341 Elections. Voting. Suffrage. Right to vote
1361 Political corruption
Political parties
1370 General works
1371.A-Z Special parties, A-Z
Northern Ireland, see JN1572
Channel Islands, see JN1573
Ireland
(1400-1403) Constitutional law
see KDK1200-KDK1350
1405 General works. History
By period
1408 To 1500
1409 1501-1781
1411 1782-1921
1415 Irish Free State. Eire, 1922-
Government. Public administration
1425 General works. History
Executive branch
1435 General works. History
1441 Lord Lieutenant
1442 Governor-General
1443 Privy Council
1444 Cabinet
Civil service
1448 History
1457 General works
Legislative branch. Parliament
1468 General works
1477 Representation
(1481) Procedure
see KDK1308
(1483-1485) Judiciary
see KDK1580-KDK1713
Political rights. Political participation.
Practical politics
1490 General works
1491 Citizenship

Europe
Ireland
Political rights.
Political participation.
Practical politics -- Continued
(1505-1511) Naturalization
see KDK1250
1541 Elections. Voting. Suffrage. Right to vote
1561 Corrupt practices. Political corruption
Political parties
1571 General works
1571.5.A-Z Special parties, A-Z
1572 Northern Ireland (Table J11)
1573 Channel Islands (Table J11)
1576 Gibraltar (Table J11)
1580-1589 Malta (Table J10)
Austrian Empire. Austria-Hungary
1601 Periodicals. Serials
1604 Directories. Registers
(1605) Constitutional law
see KJJ2064-KJJ2660
1607 Dictionaries. Encyclopedias
1611 General works
History
1621 To 1273
1274-1804
1623 General works
1625 Pragmatic Sanction
1628 1805-1866
1629 Ausgleich, 1867. Austro-Hungarian compromise
1635 Dual Empire, 1867-1918
Austrian Republic, 1918, see JN2011+
1651 Separation of powers
(1653) Language question
see P119.32
Executive branch. Crown
1713 General works
Civil service
1715 General works
1721 Salaries. Pensions
Legislative branch
1751 Directories. Registers
1771 General works
1792 Austro-Hungarian Parliament
Austrian Parliament. Reichsrat
1815 General works
1845 Upper House. Herrenhaus
1865 Lower House. Abgeordnetenhaus
Hungarian Parliament, see JN2115+
(1901-1929) Judiciary
see KJJ1572-KJJ1979
1941 Government property. Public buildings. Government purchasing

Europe
Austrian Empire. Austria-Hungary -- Continued
Political rights. Citizenship. Political participation
1951 General works
(1965-1975) Naturalization
see KJJ2440
Elections. Voting. Suffrage. Right to vote
1993 General works
(1998) Law
see KJJ2506
Political parties
1998.8 General works
1999.A-Z Special parties, A-Z
Austrian Republic, 1918-
2011.A2 Periodicals. Serials
2011.A3 Directories. Registers
History
2012 General works
1918-1939, see JN2012
2012.2 1939-1945, Period of annexation by Germany
2012.3 1945-
(2014) Constitutional law
see KJJ2064.5-KJJ2660
2015 Federal-state relations. Regionalism. Federalism
Government. Public administration
(2017) Registers
see JN2011.A3
2018 General works. History
Executive branch
2021 General works
2021.2 President
2021.3 Chancellor
2021.4 Departments. Ministries
For departments dealing with a particular subject, see the subject
2021.5 Civil service
Legislative branch. National Assembly
2021.7 General works
2022 Federal Council. Bundesrat
2023 National Council. Nationalrat
(2025) Judiciary
see KJJ1572-KJJ1979
2025.5 Government property. Government purchasing
Political rights. Citizenship. Political participation
2026 General works
(2027) Naturalization
see KJJ2440
Elections. Voting. Suffrage. Right to vote
2029 General works
2029.5 Statistics. Election returns
Political parties

Europe
Austrian Republic, 1918-
Political parties -- Continued
2030 General works
2031.A-Z Special parties, A-Z
2041.A-Z Provinces, A-Z (Table J12)
Class here provinces of the Austrian Republic only
Hungary
2050 Periodicals. Societies. Serials
2052 Directories. Registers
(2053) Constitutional law
see KKF2064.5-KKF2660
2055 General works
History
By period
2057 To 1515
2061 1516-1847
2063 1847-1918
Including 19th century general
For Austro-Hungarian compromise, 1867, see JN1629
2066 1918-1989
Including 20th century general
2067 1989-
(2069) Treatises
see JN2055
2081 Civil-military regions
Government. Public administration
(2083) Directories. Registers
see JN2052
(2084) General works
see JN2055, JN2057-JN2067
Executive branch
2085 General works
2107 Civil service
Legislative branch. Parliament. Országgyülés
2115 Directories. Registers
2121 General works. History
2135 Representation
(2143) Procedure
see KKF2516
2151 Upper House. Főrendiház
2156 Lower House. Képviselőház
(2161) Judiciary
see KKF1572-KKF1979
2163 Government property. Public buildings. Government purchasing
Political rights. Citizenship. Political participation
2165 General works
(2171) Naturalization
see KKF2440
2183 Elections. Voting. Suffrage. Right to vote

	Europe
	Hungary -- Continued
2187	Political corruption
	Political parties
2191.A1	General works
2191.A2-Z	Special parties, A-Z
	Local, see JS4682.A+
	Local, see JS4685+
(2199.C4-C46)	Croatia see JN2202
(2199.R8-R86)	Ruthenia see JN6639
(2199.S44-S49)	Slovakia see JN2240
2201	Slovenia (Table J11)
2202	Croatia (Table J11)
2210-2229	Czech Republic. Czechoslovakia. Bohemia (Table J9)
2240	Slovakia (Table J11)
(2250-2269)	Bosnia and Herzegovina see JN9679.B6
2270-2289	Liechtenstein (Table J9)
	France
2301	Periodicals. Serials
2303	Directories. Registers
2306	Societies
	General works, see JN2597
	Ancien Régime (To 1789)
(2320)	Directories. Registers see JN2303
2325	General works
	History
	By period
2328	Early to 511
2331	Merovingian, 511-687
2334	Carolingian, 687-843
2337	Medieval, 843-1493
	House of Orléans, 1493-1789
2341	General works
2344	Contemporary works
	Executive. Crown
2358	General works
	History
	By period
2361	Early to 511
2363	Merovingian, 511-687
2365	Carolingian, 687-843
2367	Medieval, 843-1493
2369	House of Orléans, 1493-1789
2375	Succession to the Crown
2377	Crown properties and revenues
(2395)	Intendants see JS4843

Europe
France
Ancien R egime (To 1789) -- Continued
2409 Tiers Etat
Parliamentary Assemblies. Etats Généraux
For Assemblies of 1787-1789, see JN2471
For Parlements, see KJV3754
2413 General works
2417.A-Z By place, A-Z
(2423) Judiciary. Parlements
see KJV3745-KJV3758
(2433) Local. Provinces
see JS4845
Revolutionary and modern periods
2451 General works. History
By period
1789-1870
2461 General works
Revolution and First Republic, 1789-1804
2468 General works. History
2471 Assemblies of 1787-1789
2473.A-Z Local assemblies. By place, A-Z
(2475) Assemblée Constituante, 1790-1791
see KJV4074.5
2491 Napoleonic era, 1804-1815
2509 Restoration, 1815-1830
2521 Second Revolution, 1830
2529 Louis Philippe, 1830-1848
2552 Second Empire, 1852-1871
(2554) Gouvernement de la défense nationale, 1870-1871
see DC310
(2557) Commune, March 18-May 22, 1871
see DC310
Third Republic, 1871-1947
2562 General works
2592 Pétain regime
2592.5 Interim regime, 1943-1947
2593 Contemporary works
2594 Fourth Republic, 1947-1958
2594.2 Fifth Republic, 1958-
2597 General works
2606 Separation of powers. Delegation of powers
2610.A-Z Special topics, A-Z
2610.C58 Civil-military relations
2610.R4 Regionalism
Government. Public administration
(2615) Directories. Registers
see JN2303
General works, see JN2597
Executive
Cf. JN2358+, Ancien Régime
2625 General works
2665 President

Europe
France
Government. Public administration
Executive -- Continued
Executive power, see KJV4360
Council of Ministers. Ministries
For ministries dealing with a particular subject, see the subject
2681 General works
2685 Ministry of the Interior
2701 Council of State. Conseil d'Etat
Civil service. Fonction publique
Directories. Registers, see JN2303
2719 Dictionaries
2725 History
2728 General works
2738.A-Z Special topics, A-Z
Confidential information, see JN2738.S43
2738.C58 Consultants
2738.C6 Corruption
2738.C74 Crisis management
2738.E4 Electronic data processing
2738.E95 Executives
2738.H35 Handicapped
2738.I58 Intelligence service. Espionage
2738.O47 Ombudsman
2738.P36 Paperwork
2738.P8 Publicity and propaganda. Public relations
2738.S43 Secret and confidential information. Government information
2738.W67 Women employees
2741 Study and teaching. Examinations
2746 Selection and appointment. Dismissal
2748 Salaries. Pensions
(2749) Trade-unions. Civil service societies
see HD8005
Government property. Public buildings
2751 General works
2759 Records management
Legislative branch
2761 Directories. Registers
2771 History
For Ancien Régime, see JN2413+
2791 General works
2794 Lobbying. Pressure groups
(2809) Legislative powers
see KJV4321
(2815) Procedure
see KJV4326
Senate
2819 Directories. Registers
2826 General works. History
National Assembly. Chamber of Deputies

Europe
France
Government. Public administration
Legislative branch
National Assembly.
Chamber of Deputies -- Continued
2858 Directories. Registers
2863 General works. History
(2887) Judiciary
see KJV3721
(2913) Government property
see JN2751-JN2759
Political rights. Political participation
2916 General works
2919 Citizenship
(2931) Naturalization
see KJV377
Suffrage. Right to vote
2941 General works
2954 Woman suffrage. Women's right to vote
Elections. Electoral systems. Voting
2959 General works
2960.A-Z Local, A-Z
Class here works on local results of national elections
2988 Political corruption
Political parties
2997 General works
3007.A-Z Special parties, A-Z
Departmental government, see JS4903+
Regional government, see JS4902
3100-3119 Andorra (Table J9)
3130-3149 Monaco (Table J9)
Germany
3201 Periodicals. Serials
3202 Societies
3203 Directories. Registers
3211 Dictionaries. Encyclopedias
Constitutional history. Constitutional law.
Constitution, see KK4436+
3221 General works
History
By period
3241 Early to ca. 900
The Holy Roman Empire, ca. 919-1806
3249 General works
(3250) Constitutional history. Constitutional law
see KK290-KK378
(3251-3260) Early Feudal period
see JN3249
(3261-3270) Later Feudal period, 1273-1519
see JN3249

Europe
Germany
History
By period
The Holy Roman Empire, ca. 919-1806 -- Continued
3271 Charles V to the Peace of Westphalia, 1519-1648
3281 Peace of Westphalia to the dissolution of the Empire, 1648-1804
Period of confederation, 1806-1871
3295 General works
Confederation of the Rhine: Rhinebund, 1806-1815
3301 General works
(3303-3307) Constitution
see KK4444
3321-3331 Confederation of 1815. German confederation. Deutscher Bund, 1815-1866
3321 General works
(3323) Constitution. Bundesakte, 1815. Wiener Schlussakte, 1820
see KK4444.2-23
(3329) Movements and events of 1848
see DD207
3331 National Assembly. Frankfurt Parliament. Deutsche Nationalversammlung, 1848-1849
North German Confederation and the New Empire, 1867-1918
3357 General works
North German Confederation, 1867-1871
3368 General works
(3371-3379) Constitutional history
see KK4525-KK4544
Empire of 1871. Kaiserreich, 1871-1918
3388 General works
(3391-3444) Constitutional history
see KK4552-KK4705
Weimar Republic. Third Reich, see JN3951+
1945, see JN3971.A1+
1990, see JN3971.A1+
Government. Public administration
(3445) Directories. Registers
see JN3203
General works, see JN3221
Executive branch. Kaiser
Cf. KK4654+, Constitutional law
3463 General works
(3475-3489) Imperial Chancellor. Reichskanzler
see KK4667-KK4669
3501 Departments. Ministries
For departments limited to a particular subject, see the subject

Europe
Germany
Government. Public administration
Executive branch. Kaiser -- Continued
Civil Service
(3525) Directories. Registers
see JN3203
3548 General works
3565 Salaries. Pensions
Legislative branch
3571 Directories. Registers
3581 General works
(3593-3615) Parliamentary procedures. Legislative powers
see KK4629
Upper House. Bundesrat
3623 Directories. Registers
3633 General works
(3638-3643) Constitution, powers, and prerogatives
see KK4630-KK4636
Lower House. Reichstag
3669 Directories. Registers
(3671) Collections
see JN3674
3674 General works
(3678-3698) Constitution, powers, and prerogatives
see JN4636-JN4653
(3721-3753) Judiciary
see KK4696
3759 Government property. Public buildings
Political rights. Political participation
3770 General works
Citizenship
(3771) Legal treatises
see KK4590
3774 General works
(3785-3794) Naturalization
see KK4598
Suffrage. Right to vote
3809 General works
3825 Woman suffrage. Women's right to vote
3838 Elections. Voting
(3848-3887) Election law
see JN4626-JN4628.5
3901 Election fraud
Political parties
By period
3931 Early to 1871
3933 1871-1918
(3934) 1918-1945
see JN3970
1945, see JN3971.A979+
3946.A-Z Special parties, A-Z
Weimar Republic. Third Reich, 1918-1945

Europe
Germany
Weimar Republic.
Third Reich, 1918-1945 -- Continued
3951.A2 Periodicals. Serials
3951.A3 Directories. Registers
(3951.5) Constitutional history
see KK4710-KK4900
3952 General works. History
3955 Federal-state relations. Federalism
Government. Public administration
(3957) Directories. Registers
see JN3951.A3
(3958-3959) General works
see JN3952
Executive branch
3961 General works
3961.2 President
3961.3 Chancellor
3961.4 Departments. Ministries
For departments dealing with a particular subject, see the subject
3961.5 Civil service
National Council. Reichsrat
3962 General works
(3962.A3) Procedure
see KK4821
Reichstag
3963 General works
(3963.A3) Procedure
see KK4813
(3965) Judiciary
see KK4879
Political rights. Citizenship. Political participation
3966 General works
(3967) Naturalization
see KK4736
Elections. Voting. Suffrage. Right to vote
3969 General works
3969.5 Statistics. Election returns
3969.9 Political corruption
Political parties
For National Socialist Party, Nationalsozialistische Deutsche Arbeiterpartei, see DD253+
3970.A1 General works
3970.A2-Z Special parties, A-Z
1945-
Including West Germany to 1990, West and East Germany to 1990, and Reunified Germany after 1990
3971.A1 Periodicals. Societies. Serials

Europe
Germany
1945- -- Continued
3971.A12-A125 Directories. Registers
3971.A127 Dictionaries. Encyclopedias
(3971.A13-A32) Constitutional history. Constitutional law. Constitutions
see KK4436-KK5513
(3971.A34) Treatises
see JN3971.A58
3971.A38A-Z Special topics, A-Z
3971.A38C58 Civil-military relations
Federal and state relations, see JN3971.A38S8
Language policy, see P119.3+
Military-civil relations, see JN3971.A38C58
3971.A38M5 Minorities
3971.A38R343 Regionalism
3971.A38S8 State rights. Federal-state relations. Federal government
Government. Public administration
(3971.A4) Directories. Registers
see JN3971.A1-A125
3971.A5 History
General works, see JN3971.A58
3971.A56A-Z Special topics, A-Z
3971.A56A8 Automation. Electronic data processing
3971.A56C54 Communication systems
Confidential information, see JN3971.A56S4
3971.A56C55 Consultants
3971.A56C57 Correspondence
3971.A56C6 Corruption. Political corruption
3971.A56C75 Crisis management
3971.A56D42 Decentralization
3971.A56D45 Decision making
Electronic data processing, see JN3971.A56A8
3971.A56E8 Ethics. Political ethics
3971.A56I6 Intelligence service. Espionage
3971.A56I63 Investigations
3971.A56M37 Marketing
3971.A56O35 Office practice
3971.A56O4 Ombudsman
3971.A56P37 Paperwork
3971.A56R4 Records. Public records
3971.A56S4 Secret and confidential information. Government information
3971.A56W55 Whistle blowing
(3971.A57) Administrative law
see KK5569-KK5929
3971.A58 General works
Executive branch. President. Chancellor
3971.A61 General works

Europe
Germany
1945-
Government. Public administration
Executive branch.
President. Chancellor -- Continued
Departments. Ministries
For departments or ministries limited to a particular subject, see the subject
3971.A63 General works
Civil service
(3971.A66) History
see JN3971.A67
3971.A67 General works
3971.A69A-Z Special topics, A-Z
3971.A69A6 Appointments and removals
3971.A69C55 Classification
Dismissal, see JN3971.A69A6
3971.A69E87 Examinations
3971.A69E9 Executives
3971.A69I6 In-service training. Interns
3971.A69M54 Minorities
3971.A69P35 Part-time employment
3971.A69P44 Personnel management
3971.A69P64 Political activity
3971.A69P7 Promotions
Public relations, see JN3971.A69P85
3971.A69P85 Publicity. Propaganda. Public relations. Government publicity
3971.A69R3 Rating of employees
3971.A69R45 Relocation of employees. Transfers
Removals, see JN3971.A69A6
Selection and appointment, see JN3971.A69A6
3971.A69T7 Travel
3971.A69W6 Women in the civil service
3971.A69W68 Work sharing
3971.A691 Salaries. Pensions. Retirement
3971.A693 Ministry of the Interior
Legislative branch
For the Bundestag, see JN3971.A78
3971.A7 Directories. Registers
3971.A71 General works
(3971.A72-A75) Organization and procedures. Powers and duties
see KK5310-KK5378
3971.A76 Legislative reference bureaus
3971.A77 Federal Council. Bundesrat
Federal Assembly. Bundestag
Directories. Registers, see JN3971.A7
3971.A78 General works
3971.A78A-Z Special topics, A-Z
3971.A78B74 Broadcasting of proceedings. Reporting

Europe
Germany
1945-
Government. Public administration
Legislative branch
Special topics, A-Z -- Continued
3971.A78E45 Employees
3971.A78E85 Ethics
(3971.A78L39) Legislative power
see KK5329
(3971.A78L42) Legislative process
see KK5349
Lobbying, see JN3971.A78P7
3971.A78O6 Opposition
3971.A78P53 Political planning. Public policy
3971.A78P7 Pressure groups. Lobbying
(3971.A78P8) Publication of proceedings
see JN3971.A78B74
(3971.A78R4) Reporters and reporting
see JN3971.A78B74
3971.A78S65 Speaker. Presiding officer.
Bundestagsprasident
(3971.A8-A87) Judiciary
see KK5452
3971.A9 Government property. Public buildings
Political rights. Political participation.
Practical politics
3971.A91 General works
3971.A92 Citizenship. Civics
(3971.A93) Naturalization
see KK6044
Elections. Voting. Suffrage. Right to vote
3971.A95 General works
3971.A953A-Z Local results of national elections, A-Z
3971.A956 Election statistics. Election returns
(3971.A96) Election law
see KK5272
3971.A975 Election fraud
Political parties
3971.A979 General works
3971.A98A-Z Special parties, A-Z
3971.A988 State government (General and comparative)
For local government, see JS5301+
(3971.A99-Z8) By state
see JN4000-JN4980
3971.5 German Democratic Republic, 1949-1990 (Table J11)
(3971.5.A99-Z8) By state
see JN4000-JN4980
(3972) Reunified Germany, 1990
see JN3971
States
Including provinces and extinct states
For local government, see JS5301+

Europe
Germany
States -- Continued
4000-4019 Alsace-Lorraine (Table J9)
4020-4039 Anhalt (Table J9)
4040-4139 Baden (Table J8)
4139.5 Baden-Württemberg (Table J11)
4140-4239 Bavaria (Table J8)
4239.3 Brandenburg (Table J11)
4239.5 Brandenburg (State, 1990-) (Table J11)
4240-4259 Bremen (Table J9)
4260-4279 Brunswick (Table J9)
4279.5 Friesland (Table J11)
4280-4299 Hamburg (Table J9)
4299.5 Hanover (Table J11)
4300-4319 Hesse (Table J9)
4320-4339 Lippe-Detmold (Table J9)
4339.5 Lower Saxony (Table J11)
4340-4359 Lübeck (Table J9)
4359.5 Mainz (Table J11)
4359.7 Mecklenburg (State, 1990-) (Table J11)
4360-4379 Mecklenburg-Schwerin (Table J9)
4380-4399 Mecklenburg-Strelitz (Table J9)
4399.5 Nassau (Table J11)
4399.7 North Rhine-Westphalia (Table J11)
4400-4419 Oldenburg (Table J9)
4420 Pomerania (Table J11)
Prussia
4421 Periodicals. Serials
4424 Directories. Registers
4431 General works
History
Cf. KKB9171+, Constitutional history
By period
4445 To 1850
4451 1850-1918
4461 1918-1949
1949, see JN3971.5
Government. Public administration
(4484) Directories. Registers
see JN4424
General works, see JN4431
Executive branch. Crown
4487 General works
4508 Departments. Ministries
For departments dealing with a particular subject, see the subject
Civil service
(4527) Directories. Registers
see JN4424
4533 General works
4548 Salaries. Pensions
Legislative branch

Europe
Germany
States
Prussia
Government. Public administration
Legislative branch -- Continued
4551 Directories. Registers
4557 General works. History
(4563-4577) Procedure. Legislative powers
see KKB9194.7
4582 Upper house. House of Peers. Herrenhaus
4597 Lower house. House of Representatives. Abgeordnetenhaus
(4607-4613) Judiciary
see KK9149
Political rights. Citizenship. Political participation
4623 General works
(4633-4638) Naturalization
see KKB9188.5
Suffrage
4643 General works
4645 Qualifications
4648 Woman suffrage
Elections. Voting. Right to vote
4653 General works
(4656-4658) Election law
see KKB9194
4681-4683 Political parties
4681 General works
4683.A-Z Special parties, A-Z
States, see JN4000+
4700-4719 Reuss, Elder Branch (Table J9)
4720-4739 Reuss, Younger Branch (Table J9)
4739.3 Rhine Province (Table J11)
4739.5 Rhineland-Palatinate (Table J11)
4739.7 Ruhr Region (Table J11)
4739.8 Saarland (Table J11)
4740-4759 Saxe-Altenburg (Table J9)
4760-4779 Saxe-Meiningen (Table J9)
4820-4839 Saxony (Table J9)
4839.5 Saxony (State, 1990-) (Table J11)
4839.7 Saxony-Anhalt (State, 1990-) (Table J11)
Saxony, Lower, see JN4339.5
4840-4859 Schaumburg-Lippe (Table J9)
4859.5 Schleswig-Holstein (Table J11)
4860-4879 Schwarzburg-Rudolstadt (Table J9)
4880-4899 Schwarzburg-Sondershausen (Table J9)
4900-4909 Thuringia (Table J10)
4910 Thuringia (State, 1990-) (Table J11)
4915 Waldeck (Table J11)
4916 Westphalia (Table J11)
4920-4939 Württemberg (Table J9)

Europe
Germany
States -- Continued
4944 Würzburg (Table J11)
(4945) Other political divisions
see JN4000-JN4944
(4960-4980) States no longer existing in 1871
see JN4000-JN4944
Greece
For ancient Greece, see JC71+
5001 Periodicals. Societies. Serials
5004 Directories. Registers
Constitutional history. Constitutional law.
Constitutions, see KKE2050+
5016 General works
History
By period
5031 Early to 1822
5035 National Assembly at Piadi (1822) to establishment of monarch, 1833
Otto of Bavaria, King of Greece (1833-1862)
5041 General works
(5044) Constitution
see KKE2064.51843
George I (1863-1913)
5051 General works
(5053) Constitution of 1864
see KKE2064.51864
5056 Constantine I (1913-1922)
5057 George II (1922-1933)
Republic, 1924-
(5058) Constitution
see KKE2064.51925
5059 General works
(5060) Contemporary works
see JN5059
5061 Ionian Islands
(5062) General works
see JN5016
Government. Public administration
Directories. Registers, see JN5004
General works, see JN5016
Executive. Crown
5065 General works
5075 Departments. Ministries
For ministries limited to a particular subject, see the subject
Civil service
(5081) Directories. Registers
see JN5004
5093 General works
Legislative branch
5101 Directories. Registers

Europe
Greece
Government. Public administration
Legislative branch -- Continued
5107 General works
5116 Senate
5123 House of Representatives. Voulé
(5141-5143) Judiciary
see KKE283-KKE288
Political rights. Citizenship. Political participation
5147 General works
Elections. Voting. Suffrage. Right to vote
5165 General works
5166 Election statistics. Election returns
5181 Election fraud. Corrupt practices
Political parties
5185.A1 General works
5185.A2-Z Special parties, A-Z
Prefectures. Nomos
5190 General works
5191.A-Z By prefecture, A-Z (Table J12)
Italy
For ancient Rome, see JC81+
5201 Periodicals. Societies. Serials
5203 Directories. Registers
(5208) Constitutional history. Constitutional law. Constitutions
see KKH2050-KKH2677
5211 General works
History
By period
Early to French Revolution (ca. 1793)
5231 General works
Special states and regions
5251 Piedmont. Savoy
5256 Liguria. Genoa
5261 Lombardy. Milan
5266 Venice
5271 Emilia. Romagna
Including Modena and Parma
5276 Tuscany. Florence
5281 Rome. Marches. Umbria
5286 Naples. Sicily
5291 Sardinia. Corsica
5299.A-Z Other, A-Z
Nineteenth century (circa 1796-1900)
5345 General works
By period
5348 Napoleonic era, 1796-1814
1814-1870. Risorgimento
5381 General works
5383 1814-1848

Europe
Italy
History
By period
Nineteenth century (circa 1796-1900)
By period
1814-1870. Risorgimento -- Continued
5385 1848-1860/1870
Sardinia (Kingdom). House of Savoy
5391 General works
(5395-5401) Constitutional history
see KKH7191-KKH7200
5405 Executive branch
5411 Legislative branch
(5414) Judiciary
see KKH7184
Other states
5425 Lombardo-Venetian Kingdom
5429 Tuscany
5431 Papal States. Rome
5433 Kingdom of Naples and Sicily
5435.A-Z Other, A-Z
United Italy (1870-). Italian Republic
5441 Periodicals. Serials
5443 Societies
Constitutional history. Constitutional law.
Constitutions, see KKH2050+
5448 General works
History
By period
5449 1870-1922
5450 1922-1945
5451 1945-
(5471) Church and state
see BX1545
5477.A-Z Special topics, A-Z
5477.A8 Automation. Electronic data processing
(5477.D38) Data processing
see JN5477.A8
5477.D4 Decentralization
5477.I6 Intelligence service. Espionage
5477.P7 Pressure groups. Lobbying
5477.P83 Publicity
5477.R35 Regionalism
5477.S33 Secret and confidential information
Government. Public administration
(5478) Directories. Registers
see JN5204
(5479) General works
see JN5448, JN5449-JN5451
Special topics, see JN5477.A+
Executive branch
5483 General works

Europe
Italy
United Italy (1870-). Italian Republic
Government. Public administration
Executive branch -- Continued
(5489) Powers, prerogatives
see KKH2578
Departments. Ministries
For departments limited to a particular subject, see the subject
5493 General works
5494 Ministry of the Interior
5497 Council of state. Consiglio di Stato
Civil service. Bureaucracy
(5503) Directories. Registers
see JN5203
5511 General works. History
5519.A-Z Special topics, A-Z
5519.A6 Appointments and removals. Patronage
5519.E87 Examinations
5519.E9 Executives, Government
5519.I6 In-service training
5519.L5 Labor productivity
5519.W6 Women in the civil service
5526 Salaries. Pensions
Legislative branch. Parlamento
5531 Directories. Registers
5535 History
5537 General works
(5539-5540) Parliamentary practice
see KKH2516
Senate
5541 Directories. Registers
5544 General works
Chamber of Deputies
5564 Directories. Registers
5567 General works
(5581-5585) Judiciary
see KKH283-KKH288
5589 Government property. Public buildings
Political rights. Citizenship
5591 General works
5593 Political participation
(5596) Naturalization
see KKH2440
Elections. Voting. Suffrage. Right to vote
5607 History
Provinces
Class here works on national elections
For local elections, see JS5796.A+
For provincial elections, see JN5690.A+
5608.A2 General works
5608.A3-Z By province, A-Z

Europe
Italy
United Italy (1870-). Italian Republic
Political rights. Citizenship
Elections. Voting.
Suffrage. Right to vote -- Continued
5609 Election statistics. Election returns
5611 General works
(5619-5623) Election law
see KKH2506
5641 Corrupt practices. Political corruption
Political parties
5651 General works
5657.A-Z Special parties, A-Z
5690.A-Z By region or province, A-Z
Class here works on regional or provincial government
For local government, see JS5796.A+
5695 San Marino (Table J11)
5697 Vatican City (Table J11)
5700 Benelux countries (Table J11)
Netherlands
5701 Periodicals. Societies. Serials
5703 Directories. Registers
(5707) Constitutional history. Constitutional law. Constitutions
see KKM2050-KKM2677
History
5711 General works
By period
Early to 1789/1795
5718 General works
5731 1555 to 1648
5745 1648 to 1795
Nineteenth century
5755 General works
By period
5758 Batavian Republic (1795-1806)
5761 Kingdom of Holland (1806-1810)
5764 French annexation (1810-1815)
5770 Kingdom of Netherlands (1815-1830)
5773 Separation of Belgium
5789 Kingdom of the Netherlands (1830-)
5801 General works
(5803) Compends. Textbooks
see JN5801
Government. Public administration
(5809) General works
see JN5801
5810.A-Z Special topics, A-Z
5810.A8 Automatic data processing. Electronic data processing
5810.C67 Corruption. Political corruption

Europe
Netherlands
Government. Public administration
Special topics, A-Z -- Continued
5810.D43 Decentralization in government
Electronic data processing, see JN5810.A8
5810.P8 Publicity. Government publicity
5810.S4 Secret and confidential information
Executive branch
5813 General works
(5818) Powers, prerogatives
see KKM2578
Departments. Ministries
5828 General works
(5831) Powers and prerogatives
see KKM2602
Individual departments and ministries
5836 Ministry of the Interior
Other departments or ministries limited to a particular subject
see the subject
5837 Council of State. Raad van State
Civil service
(5841) Directories. Registers
see JN5703
5855 General works
5861 Salaries. Pensions
Legislative branch. Staten-General
5873 Directories. Registers
5881 General works
5883 Lobbying. Pressure groups
Upper House. Eerste Kamer
5887 General works
(5891-5897) Constitution, powers and prerogatives
see KKM2510-KKM2529
5901 Lower House. Tweede Kamer
(5921-5929) Judiciary
see KKM283-KKM288
5933 Government property. Public buildings
Political rights. Citizenship. Political participation
5935 General works
(5941-5945) Naturalization
see KKM2440
Elections. Voting. Suffrage. Right to vote
5951 General works
(5953-5955) Election law
see KKM2506
5971 Political corruption
Political parties
5981 General works
5985.A-Z Special parties, A-Z

Europe
Netherlands
Government. Public administration -- Continued
5999.A-Z By province, A-Z
For local government, see JS5950.A+
Belgium
6101 Periodicals. Societies. Serials
6105 Directories. Registers
Constitutional history. Constitutional law. Constitutions, see KJK2050+
History
6114 General works
By period
6135 1830-1893
6155 1893-
6165 General works
6175 Central-local government relations. Regionalism
Government. Public administration
(6183) General
see JN6165
6184.A-Z Special topics, A-Z
6184.E4 Electronic data processing
6184.P82 Publicity. Government publicity
Executive branch
6189 General works
(6199) Powers, prerogatives
see KJK2578
6205-6235 Departments. Ministries
For departments or ministries limited to a particular subject, see the subject
Civil service
(6215) Directories. Registers
see JN6105
6223 General works
6235 Salaries. Pensions
Legislative branch. Parlement
6243 Directories. Registers
6247 General works
(6248) Constitution, powers, and prerogatives
see KJK2510-KJK2529
6249 Lobbying. Pressure groups
6255 Senate
6271 Chamber of Representatives
(6283-6288) Judiciary
see KJK283-KJK288
6290 Government property. Public buildings
Political rights. Citizenship. Political participation
6301 General works
(6311-6315) Naturalization
see KJK2440
Elections. Voting. Suffrage. Right to vote
6331 General works

Europe
Belgium
Government. Public administration
Political rights.
Citizenship. Political participation
Elections. Voting.
Suffrage. Right to vote -- Continued
(6335-6339) Election law
see KJK2506
6355 Political corruption
Political parties
6365 General works
6371.A-Z Special parties, A-Z
Local
Provinces to 1830, see JN5999.A+
Provinces after 1830, see JS6020.A+
6380-6399 Luxembourg (Table J9)
6500-6598 Soviet Union. Russia. Former Soviet Republics (Table J8)
(6599) Individual republics
see JN6615-JN6745
6615 Estonia (Table J11)
6630-6639 Ukraine (Table J10)
6640-6649 Belarus (Table J10)
Caucasus
General, see JQ1759
(6650-6659) Armenia
see JQ1759.3
(6660-6669) Azerbaijan
see JQ1759.5
(6670-6679) Georgia
see JQ1759.7
6680-6689 Moldova (Table J10)
6690-6699 Russia (Federation) (Table J10)
For Siberia, see JQ1100+
(6700-6719) Finland
see JN7390-JN7399
Baltic States
6729 General (Table J11)
Estonia, see JN6615
6730-6739 Latvia (Table J10)
6745 Lithuania (Table J11)
6750-6769 Poland (Table J9)
Scandinavia. Northern Europe
Constitutional history. Constitutional law.
Constitutions, see KJC531+
7011 General works
History
By period
7021 To 1523
7036 Denmark and Norway (1523-1814)
7041 Norway and Sweden (1814-1905)

Europe
Scandinavia. Northern Europe
History
By period -- Continued
7042 1905-
Including the Nordic Council
7051 Executive branch
7056 Legislative branch
7066 Political parties
Denmark
7101 Periodicals. Societies. Serials
7104 Directories. Registers
(7105) Constitutional history. Constitutional law. Constitutions
see KJR2061-KJR2070
History
7111 General works
By period
7118 To 1814
7155 Kingdom of Denmark, 1814-
7161 General works
Government. Public administration
(7169) General works
see JN7161
7170.A-Z Special topics, A-Z
7170.D42 Decentralization in government
7170.E4 Electronic data processing
7170.P75 Productivity. Government productivity
7170.P8 Publicity. Government publicity
Executive branch
7178 General works
(7183) Powers and prerogatives
see KJR2578
7191 Departments. Ministries
For departments or ministries limited to a particular subject, see the subject
Civil service
(7207) Directories. Registers
see JN7104
7221 General works
7223 Salaries. Pensions
Legislative branch. Rigsdag
7228 Directories. Registers
7235 General works
(7238) Legislative powers and process
see KJR2510-KJR2529
7241 Lobbying. Pressure groups
7255 Upper House. Landstinget
7270 Lower House. Unicameral legislature. Folketinget
(7275-7289) Judiciary
see KJR283-KJR288
7279 Government property. Public buildings

Europe
Denmark -- Continued
Political rights. Citizenship
7295 General works
7296 Political participation
(7301-7305) Naturalization
see KJR2440
Elections. Voting. Suffrage. Right to vote
7321 General works
(7325-7328) Election law
see KJR2506
7355 Political corruption
Political parties
7365.A1 General works
7365.A2-Z Special parties, A-Z
7367 Faroe Islands
7370-7379 Greenland (Table J10)
7380-7389 Iceland (Table J10)
7390-7399 Finland (Table J10)
Norway
7401 Periodicals. Societies. Serials
7405 Directories. Registers
(7409) Constitutional history. Constitutional law. Constitutions
see KKN2061-KKN2070
History
7415 General works
By period
7421 To 1814
1814-1905
7431 General works
(7432) Rigsforsamlingen (1814). Eidsvold
see KKN2064.5
(7433) The Grundlow (1814)
see KKN2064.5
7451 1905-
7461 General works
(7471) Language question
see P119.32
Government. Public administration
(7479) General works
see JN7461
7480.A-Z Special topics, A-Z
7480.C67 Corruption. Political corruption
7480.E4 Electronic data processing
7480.P82 Publicity. Government publicity
7480.R43 Records. Public records
Executive branch
7483 General works
(7491) Powers and prerogatives
see KKN2578

Europe
Norway
Government. Public administration
Executive branch -- Continued
7501 Departments. Ministries
For departments or ministries limited to a particular subject, see the subject
Civil service
(7513) Directories. Registers
see JN7405
7525 General works
7528 Salaries. Pensions
Legislative branch. Stortinget
7541 Directories. Registers
7543 General works
(7544) Elections
see JN7651
7548 Ombudsman
7549 Pressure groups. Lobbying
7561 Upper House. Lagting
7581 Lower House. Odelsting
(7601-7605) Judiciary
see KKN283-KKN288
7606 Government property. Public buildings
Political rights. Citizenship. Political participation
7615 General works
(7631-7635) Naturalization
see KKN2440
Elections. Voting. Suffrage. Right to vote
7651 General works
7653 Election statistics. Election returns
(7655-7659) Election law
see KKN2506
(7681) Political corruption
see JN7480.C67
Political parties
7691.A1 General works
7691.A2-Z Special parties, A-Z
(7693) Counties
see JS6220
7695 Spitzbergen
Sweden
7721 Periodicals. Societies. Serials
7724 Directories. Registers
Constitutional history. Constitutional law.
Constitutions, see KKV2050+
History
7741 General works
By period
To 1905
7761 General works

Europe
Sweden
History
By period
To 1905 -- Continued
(7765) Constitution of 1809
see KKV2064.5
7799 1905-
7825 General works
7835 Central-local government relations
Government. Public administration
(7849) General works
see JN7825
7850.A-Z Special topics, A-Z
Confidential information, see JN7850.S4
7850.D43 Decentralization in government
7850.D45 Decision making
7850.E4 Electronic data processing
7850.P38 Paperwork. Government paperwork
7850.P75 Productivity. Government productivity
7850.P8 Publicity. Government publicity
7850.S4 Secret and confidential information
Executive branch
7853 General works
(7865) Powers and prerogatives
see KKV2578
7869 Royal household
7875 Departments. Ministries
For departments or ministries limited to a particular subject, see the subject
7877 Council of State. Statsradet
Civil service
(7888) Directories. Registers
see JN7724
7903 General works
7904 Salaries. Pensions
Legislative branch. Riksdag
7911 Directories. Registers
7913 History
7915 General works
7918 Ombudsman
7921 Upper House. Forsta Kammaren
7928 Lower House. Andra Kammaren
(7934-7936) Unicameral Legislature (1971)
see JN7911-JN7915
(7938-7941) Judiciary
see KKV283-KKV288
7943 Government property. Public buildings
Political rights. Citizenship. Political participation
7945 General works
(7951) Naturalization
see KKV2440

Europe
Sweden
Government. Public administration
Political rights.
Citizenship. Political
participation -- Continued
Elections. Voting. Suffrage. Right to vote
7958 General works
7958.2 Election statistics. Election returns
(7959-7963) Election law
see KKV2506
7985 Political corruption
Political parties
7995.A1 General works
7995.A2-Z Special parties, A-Z
(7997) Local
see JS6270-JS6285
Spain
8101 Periodicals. Societies. Serials
8103 Directories. Registers
(8107) Constitutional history. Constitutional law.
Constitutions
see KKT2050-KKT2677
8108 Dictionaries. Encyclopedias
History
8111 General
By period
To 1516
8118 General works
(8123) Cortes
see JN8298
The old kingdoms
8128 Majorca
8130 Asturias. Leon
8133 Navarre
8137 Aragon
8140 Castile and Leon
8142 Valencia
8145 Kingdom of Spain, 1516-1808
Nineteenth century
8155 General works
8157 Napoleonic era, 1808-1814
(8159) Constitution of 1809
see KKT2064.51809
(8161) Constitution of 1812
see KKT2064.51812
Period of constitutional struggle, 1814-1872
8173 General works
(8174) Constitution of 1837
see KKT2064.51837
(8174.5) Constitution of 1869
see KKT2064.51869

Europe
Spain
History
By period
Nineteenth century
Period of constitutional struggle, 1814-1872 -- Continued
(8179) Contemporary works
see JN8173
8183 Republic of Spain, 1873-1876
Kingdom of Spain, 1876-1931
8195 General works
(8197) Constitution of 1876
see KKT2064.51876
Republic and Franco era, 1931-1975
(8205) Constitution of 1931
see KKT2064.51931
8209 General works
8210 1975-
8221 General works
8230 Civil-military relations
8231 Regionalism. Autonomous communities
Government. Public administration
(8236) General works
see JN8221
8237.A-Z Special topics, A-Z
8237.A87 Automatic data processing. Electronic data processing
Corruption, see JN8386
Electronic data processing, see JN8237.A87
Executive branch. Crown
8246 General works
(8251) Powers and prerogatives
see KKT2550-KKT2564
Departments. Ministries
8258 General works
Individual departments or ministries
8261 Ministry of the Interior
Other departments or ministries limited to a particular subject, see the subject
8266 Council of state. Consejo de estado
Civil service
(8273) Directories. Registers
see JN8103
8281 General works
8289 Salaries. Pensions
Legislative branch. Cortes
8293 Directories. Registers
8298 General works
(8305) Powers and prerogatives
see KKT2510-KKT2529
8309-8311 Upper House. Senado
8309 Directories. Registers

Europe
Spain
Government. Public administration
Legislative branch. Cortes
Upper House. Senado -- Continued
8311 General works
Lower House. Congreso de los Diputados
8319 Directories. Registers
8321 General works
(8335-8338) Judiciary
see KKT283-KKT288
8340 Government property. Public buildings
Political rights. Political participation.
Practical politics
8341 General works
8343 Citizenship
(8351-8354) Naturalization
see KKT2440
Elections. Voting. Suffrage. Right to vote
8371 General works
(8374-8378) Election law
see KKT2506
8386 Political corruption
Political parties
8395.A2 General works
8395.A3-Z Special parties, A-Z
8398 State, provincial, prefecture government (General
and comparative)
8399.A-Z By region, province, or autonomous community, A-Z
Class here works on regional or provincial
government
For local government, see JS6320.A+
For the old kingdoms, see JN8128+
Portugal
8423 Directories. Registers
(8427) Constitutional history. Constitutional law.
Constitutions
see KKQ2050-KKQ2677
History
8436 General
By period
8444 To 1640
8461 Kingdom of Portugal, 1640-1807
8465 Napoleonic era, 1807-1826
8499 Kingdom of Portugal, 1826-1910
8502 Republic, 1910-
8509 General works
8514 Civil-military relations
8515 Regionalism
Government. Public administration
(8519) General works
see JN8509
8520.A-Z Special topics, A-Z

Europe
Portugal
Government. Public administration
Special topics, A-Z -- Continued
8520.E43 Electronic data processing
Executive branch. Crown
8525 General works
(8531) Powers and prerogatives
see KKQ2550-KKQ2564
8536 Departments. Ministries
For departments or ministries limited to a particular subject, see the subject
Civil service
(8547) Directories. Registers
see JN8423
8557 General works
8559 Salaries. Pensions
Legislative branch. Cortes
8565 Directories. Registers
8568 General works
8581 Upper House. Camara dos Pares. Senado
8585 Lower House. Camara dos Deputados. Assembly of the Republic
(8595-8599) Judiciary
see KKQ283-KKQ288
8600 Government property. Public buildings
Political rights. Citizenship. Political participation
8605 General works
(8611-8613) Naturalization
see KKQ2440
Elections. Voting. Suffrage. Right to vote
8623 General works
(8625-8629) Election law
see KKQ2506
8641 Political corruption
Political parties
8651.A2 General works
8651.A3-Z Special parties, A-Z
8660 State, provincial, district government (General and comparative)
8661 Azores
Switzerland
8701 Periodicals. Societies. Serials
8704 Directories. Registers
(8705-8709) Constitutional history. Constitutional law. Constitutions
see KKW2050-KKW2677
History
8711 General works
By period
8719 To 1648
1648-1874

Europe
Switzerland
History
By period
1648-1874 -- Continued
8758 General
(8759-8761) Constitution of 1848
see KKW2064.51848
(8762) Contemporary works
see JN8758
(8763-8765) Constitution of 1874
see KKW2064.51874
1874-
(8766) Contemporary works
see JN8767
8767 General works
8781 General works
8788 Federalism. Federal-Canton relations. Regionalism
(8791) Church and state
see BR1033
Language question, see P119.3+
8795 Minorities
Government. Public administration
Executive branch
8801 General works
(8809) Powers and prerogatives
see KKW2578
8812 Federal Council. Bundesrat
Civil service
(8825) Directories. Registers
see JN8704
8831 General works
8839 Salaries. Pensions
Legislative branch. Federal Assembly.
Bundesversammlung
8845 Directories. Registers
8850 General works
8852 Pressure groups. Lobbying
(8853) Powers and prerogatives
see KKW2510-KKW2529
8855 Upper House. Council of States
8862 Lower House. Nationalrat
(8875-8878) Judiciary
see KKW283-KKW288
Political rights. Citizenship. Political
participation
8901 General works
(8911-8915) Naturalization
see KKW2440
Elections. Voting. Suffrage. Right to vote
8931 General works
(8935-8939) Election law
see KKW2506

Europe
Switzerland
Government. Public administration -- Continued
8961 Political corruption
Political parties
8971.A1 General works
8971.A2-Z Special parties, A-Z
Cantonal government
9015 General and comparative
By canton
For local government, see JS6421+
9100-9119 Aargau (Table J9)
9120-9139 Appenzell-Ausser Rhoden (Table J9)
9140-9149 Appenzell Inner Rhoden (Table J9)
9160-9179 Baselland (Table J9)
9180-9199 Basel-Stadt (Table J9)
9200-9219 Bern (Table J9)
9220-9239 Fribourg (Table J9)
9240-9259 Geneva (Table J9)
9260-9279 Glarus (Table J9)
9280-9299 Graubunden (Table J9)
9299.5 Jura (Table J11)
9300-9319 Lucerne (Table J9)
9320-9339 Neuchâtel (Table J9)
9340-9359 St. Gall (Table J9)
9360-9379 Schaffhausen (Table J9)
9380-9399 Schwyz (Table J9)
9400-9419 Solothurn (Table J9)
9420-9439 Thurgau (Table J9)
9440-9459 Ticino (Table J9)
9460-9479 Unterwalden nid dem Wald. Nidwalden (Table J9)
9480-9499 Unterwalden ob dem Wald. Obwalden (Table J9)
9500-9519 Uri (Table J9)
9520-9539 Valais (Table J9)
9540-9559 Vaud (Table J9)
9560-9579 Zug (Table J9)
9580-9599 Zurich (Table J9)
Balkan States
For the Balkan States in general, see JN97
9600-9609 Bulgaria (Table J10)
9610-9619 Montenegro (Table J10)
9620-9639 Romania (Table J9)
9640-9659 Serbia (Table J9)
9660-9679 Yugoslavia (Table J9)
9679.A6-Z By republic, province, etc.
9679.B6 Bosnia-Herzegovina
Croatia, see JN2202
9679.M3 Macedonia
Montenegro, see JN9610+
Serbia, see JN9640+

Europe
Balkan States
Yugoslavia
By republic, province, etc. -- Continued
(9679.S6) Slovenia
see JN2201
9680-9689 Albania (Table J10)
Turkey, see JQ1800+

Political institutions and public administration
Asia
(1) Periodicals. Societies. Serials
see JQ21.A1
(5) Constitutional history. Constitutional law. Constitutions
see KMO527
21.A1 Periodicals. Societies. Serials
21.A11-A19 Directories. Registers
21.A25 Dictionaries. Encyclopedias
(22) Constitutional history. Constitutional law. Constitutions
see KMO527
24 General works
26 Civil-military relations
29.5 Political corruption
Executive branch
31 General works
32 Civil service
33 Legislative branch
Political rights. Political participation. Practical politics
36 General works
38 Elections. Voting. Suffrage. Right to vote
39 Political parties
Regions
(94) Middle East. Southwest Asia
see JQ1758
(96) Southeast Asia
see JQ750
South Asia
98 General (Table J11)
India
200-298 General (Table J8)
States and union territories
298.8 States and union territories treated collectively
320-339 Assam (Table J9)
360-369 Bengal (Table J9)
(379.4) East Bengal
see JQ630-JQ639
379.5 West Bengal (Table J11)
400-419 Bombay (State) (Table J9)
(440-450) Burma
see JQ751
480-499 Madhya Pradesh. Central Provinces (Table J9)
520-539 Tamil Nadu. Madras (Table J9)
(540-559) Pakistan
see JQ629
560-579 Punjab (Table J9)
600-619 Uttar Pradesh. United Provinces of Agra and Oudh (Table J9)
620.A-Z Other states and union territories, A-Z

Asia
South Asia
India
States and union territories
Other states and union territories, A-Z -- Continued

620.A66 Andaman and Nicobar Islands (Table J12)
620.A69-A78 Andhra Pradesh (Table J12)
620.A782 Arunchal Pradesh (Table J12)
620.B52 Bihar (Table J12)
620.C48 Chandagarh (Table J12)
620.D2 Dadar and Nagar Haveli (Table J12)
620.D225 Daman and Diu (Table J12)
620.D4 Delhi (Table J12)
620.G6 Goa (Table J12)
620.G8 Gujarat (Table J12)
620.H3 Haryana (Table J12)
620.H5 Himachal Pradesh (Table J12)
Jammu and Kashmir, see JQ620.K3
620.K2 Karnataka. Mysore (Table J12)
620.K3 Kashmir. Jammu and Kashmir (Table J12)
620.K47 Kerala (Table J12)
620.L32 Ladshadweep (Table J12)
620.M26 Maharashtra (Table J12)
620.M29 Manipur (Table J12)
620.M45 Meghalaya (Table J12)
620.M58 Mizoram (Table J12)
(620.M7) Mysore
see JQ620.K2
620.N2 Nagaland (Table J12)
620.O7 Orissa (Table J12)
620.P6 Pondicherry (Table J12)
620.R28 Rajasthan (Table J12)
620.S48 Sikkim (Table J12)
620.T82 Tripura (Table J12)
Afghanistan, see JQ1760+
628 Nepal (Table J11)
628.5 Bhutan (Table J11)
629 Pakistan (Table J11)
630-639 Bangladesh (Table J10)
(640) Brunei
see JQ1064
650-659 Sri Lanka. Ceylon (Table J10)
(660-669) Cyprus
see JQ1811
(670-679) Hong Kong
see JQ1539.5
(710-719) Malaysia. Malaya
see JQ1062
(745) Singapore
see JQ1063
Southeast Asia. Indochina
750 General (Table J11)

	Asia
	Southeast Asia. Indochina -- Continued
751	Burma (Table J11)
760-779	Indonesia (Table J9)
	Philippines, see JQ1250+
800-899	Vietnam (Table J8)
930-939	Cambodia. Kampuchea (Table J10)
950-959	Laos (Table J10)
(960-969)	Pondicherry. French India see JQ620
(1050-1059)	Goa see JQ620
(1061)	Macao see JQ1519.5
	Thailand, see JQ1740+
1062	Malaysia. Malaya (Table J11)
1063	Singapore (Table J11)
1064	Brunei (Table J11)
	Central Asia
1070-1089	General (Table J9)
1090	Kazakhstan (Table J11)
1092	Kyrgyztan (Table J11)
1093	Tajikistan (Table J11)
1094	Turkmenistan (Table J11)
1095	Uzbekistan (Table J11)
1100-1199	Siberia (Russia) (Table J8)
	Philippines
1250-1269	Spanish regime, to 1898 (Table J9)
1300-1399	United States rule, 1898-1946 (Table J8)
1400-1419	Republic, 1946- (Table J9)
	East Asia. Far East
1499	General (Table J11)
1500-1519	China (Table J9)
1519.5	Macao (Table J11)
1520-1539	Taiwan (Table J9)
1539.5	Hong Kong (Table J11)
1600-1699	Japan (Table J8)
1720-1729	Korea (Table J10) Including South Korea
1729.5	North Korea (Table J11)
1730	Mongolia. Outer Mongolia (Table J11)
1740-1749	Thailand (Table J10)
	Middle East. Near East. Southwest Asia. Islamic Empire
1758	General (Table J11)
	Caucasus
1759	General (Table J11)
1759.3	Armenia (Table J11)
1759.5	Azerbaijan (Table J11)
1759.7	Georgia (Republic) (Table J11)
1760-1769	Afghanistan (Table J10)
1780-1789	Iran (Table J10)
1800-1809	Turkey (Table J10)

Asia
Middle East. Near East.
Southwest Asia. Islamic Empire -- Continued
1811 Cyprus (Table J11)
(1825) Other
see JQ1826-JQ1848
1826 Syria (Table J11)
1828 Lebanon (Table J11)
1830 Israel. Palestine (Table J11)
1833 Jordan (Table J11)
Arabian Peninsula. Arabia. Persian Gulf States
1840 General works
1841 Saudi Arabia (Table J11)
1842 Yemen (Table J11)
1843 Oman. Muscat and Oman (Table J11)
1844 United Arab Emirates. Trucial States (Table J11)
1845 Qatar (Table J11)
1846 Bahrain (Table J11)
1848 Kuwait (Table J11)
1849 Iraq (Table J11)
Iran, see JQ1780+
1850 Arab countries
1852 Islamic countries
Africa
1870-1879 General (Table J10)
English-speaking Africa
1880-1899 General (Table J9)
South Africa. Republic of South Africa
1900-1999 General (Table J8)
(2000-2699) Provinces. Self-governing territories. Homelands
see JQ1999
Southern Africa. Central Africa
2720 General (Table J11)
2721 Swaziland (Table J11)
2740 Lesotho. Basutoland (Table J11)
2760 Botswana. Bechuanaland (Table J11)
2780-2789 Rhodesia. Federation of Rhodesia and Nyasaland. British Central African Protectorate (Table J10)
2800-2899 Zambia. Northern Rhodesia (Table J8)
2920-2929 Zimbabwe. Southern Rhodesia (Table J10)
2941 Malawi (Table J11)
Namibia. Southwest Africa, see JQ3540+
East Africa
2945 General (Table J11)
2947 Kenya (Table J11)
Tanganyika, see JQ3510+
Zanzibar, see JQ3510+
2951 Uganda (Table J11)
West Africa
2998 General (Table J11)
3001 Gambia (Table J11)

	Africa
	English-speaking Africa
	West Africa -- Continued
	Liberia, see JQ3920+
3020-3039	Ghana. Gold Coast (Table J9)
3080-3099	Nigeria (Table J9)
3121	Sierra Leone (Table J11)
(3141-3151)	Atlantic Ocean islands see JQ3982-JQ3986.7
	Indian Ocean islands
3158	General (Table J11)
3159	Maldive Islands (Table J11)
3160-3179	Mauritius (Table J9)
3185	Seychelles (Table J11)
	Comoro Islands, see JQ3494
	Reunion, see JQ3480+
3188	Kerguelen Islands (Table J11)
	North Africa
3198	General (Table J11)
	Morocco, see JQ3940+
3200-3299	Algeria (Table J8)
3320-3339	Tunisia (Table J9)
3340-3349	Libya (Table J10)
	Egypt, see JQ3800+
	Sudan, see JQ3981
	French-speaking Africa
3349.5	General works
	French-speaking West Africa
3350-3369	General (Table J9)
3376	Benin. Dahomey (Table J11)
	Togo, see JQ3530+
3381	Guinea (Table J11)
3386	Cote d'Ivoire. Ivory Coast (Table J11)
3389	Mali. French Sudan (Table J11)
3391	Mauritania (Table J11)
3394	Niger (Table J11)
3396	Senegal (Table J11)
3398	Burkina Faso. Upper Volta (Table J11)
	French-speaking Equatorial Africa
3403	General (Table J11)
	Zaire, see JQ3600+
3404	Central African Republic. Ubangi Shari (Table J11)
3405	Chad (Table J11)
	Cameroon, see JQ3520+
3406	Congo (Brazzaville). Middle Congo (Table J11)
3407	Gabon (Table J11)
3421	Djibouti. French Territory of the Afars and Issas. French Somaliland (Table J11)
3450-3469	Madagascar. Malagasy Republic (Table J9)
3480-3489	Reunion (Table J10)
3494	Comoro Islands (Table J11)
3500-3509	German East Africa (Table J10)

Africa -- Continued
3510-3519 Tanzania. Tanganyika. Zanzibar (Table J10)
3520-3529 Cameroon (Table J10)
3530-3539 Togo (Table J10)
3540-3549 Namibia. Southwest Africa (Table J10)
3566 Burundi (Table 11)
3567 Rwanda (Table 11)
3580 Italian East Africa (Table 11)
3583 Eritrea (Table 11)
3585 Somalia. Italian Somaliland (Table J11)
Djibouti, see JQ3421
(3590-3599) Libya
see JQ3340-JQ3349
3600-3619 Zaire. Congo (Democratic Republic). Belgian Congo (Table J9)
3651 Angola. Portuguese West Africa (Table J11)
3661 Cape Verde Islands (Table J11)
3671 Mozambique. Portuguese West Africa (Table J11)
3681 Guinea-Bissau. Portuguese Guinea (Table J11)
3685 Sao Tome and Principe (Table J11)
3701 Western Sahara. Spanish Sahara (Table J11)
3702 Equatorial Guinea (Table J11)
3750-3769 Ethiopia. Abyssinia (Table J9)
3800-3899 Egypt. United Arab Republic (Table J8)
3920-3929 Liberia (Table J10)
3940-3949 Morocco (Table J10)
3981 Sudan (Table J11)
Atlantic Ocean islands
3981.5 General (Table J11)
3982 Azores (Table J11)
Bermuda, see JL590+
3983 Madeira Islands (Table J11)
3984 Canary Islands (Table J11)
Cape Verde Islands, see JQ3661
3986 Saint Helena (Table J11)
3986.5 Tristan da Cunha (Table J11)
3986.7 Falkland Islands (Table J11)
Indian Ocean islands, see JQ3158+
3995 Australasia (Table J11)
Australia
4000-4099 General (Table J8)
4400-4499 Australian Capital Territory (Table J8)
4500-4599 New South Wales (Table J8)
4640-4659 Northern Territory (Table J9)
4700-4799 Queensland (Table J8)
4900-4999 South Australia (Table J8)
5100-5199 Tasmania (Table J8)
5300-5399 Victoria (Table J8)
5500-5599 Western Australia (Table J8)
5800-5899 New Zealand (Table J8)
Pacific Area. Pacific Ocean islands
5995 General works
6000-6019 Guam (Table J9)

Pacific Area. Pacific Ocean islands -- Continued

(6080-6199) Hawaii
see JK9301-JK9395

6220-6239 Samoan Islands. American Samoa (Table J9)
Western Samoa, see JQ6651

6240 Trust Territory of the Pacific. Micronesia (Table J9)

6241 Marshall Islands (Table J9)

6242 Marianas (Table J9)
Including Northern Marianas

6301 Fiji (Table J9)

6311 Papua New Guinea (Table J9)

6312 Kiribati. Gilbert Islands (Table J9)

6313 Tuvalu. Ellice Islands (Table J9)

6321 Tonga (Table J9)

6340 Cook Islands (Table J9)

6341 Solomon Islands (Table J9)

6400 Vanuatu. New Hebrides (Table J9)

6401 New Caledonia (Table J9)

6431 French Polynesia (Table J9)

(6500-6519) New Guinea
see JQ6311

6591 Palau (Table J9)

(6601) Solomon Islands
see JQ6341

6651 Western Samoa (Table J11)

Local government. Municipal government
Official gazettes, codes, charters
see class K
(3-37) Serial documents
see JS300-JS8500
Periodicals. Serials
Class here general periodicals by place of imprint
39 American
40 British
41 Other
42 Societies (International)
43 Museums. Exhibitions
44 Congresses
48 Dictionaries. Encyclopedias
49 Study and teaching. Training of local and municipal employees
50 Theory. Method. Scope. Relations to other subjects
(51) City and central government
see JS113
History
55 General
58 Ancient
61 Medieval
64 Modern to 1800
66 Nineteenth century
67 Twentieth century
78 General works
(85) Legal works
see K3428-K3431
(91) Social and economic aspects
see HT101-HT384
100 Electronic data processing
105 Public relations
113 Federal-city relations. State-local relations. Municipal home rule
Executive branch. Mayor
141 General works
(145) Administration
see JS141
Civil service
Cf. HD8001+, State labor
148 General works
Study and teaching, see JS49
153 Salaries. Pensions. Retirement
163 Public records management
171 Legislative branch
(185-188) Municipal courts
see K2100
211 Political participation. Neighborhood government
Elections. Local elections. Municipal elections
221 General works
(227) Election law
see K3299

231 Political corruption
Local government other than municipal
241 General works
251 Intermediate levels of government. State government. Provincial government. Departmental government
261 County government
271 Village government. Rural public administration
United States
Local and municipal government
300 Periodicals. Serials
(301) Yearbooks
see JS39
Societies
302 National
303.A-W State, A-W
303.5 Citizens' associations
For individual associations, see JS451.A+
304 Congresses
305 Museums. Exhibitions
(308) Collections
see JS331
History
309 General works
By period
Colonial to 1800
311 General works
(315) Local
see JS431-JS451
319 19th century to 1880
323 Recent, 1880-
331 General works
(335) Compends
see JS331
(338) Legal
see KF5304-KF5305
(341) Social and economic aspects
see HT123-HT123.5
Commission government. Municipal government by commission
342 General works
343.A3A-Z By state, A-Z
(343.A4-Z) By city
see JS504-JS1583
344.A-Z Other topics, A-Z
344.A5 Annexation
344.C5 City manager
Commission government, see JS342+
344.E5 Electronic data processing
(344.F4) Federal-city relations
see JS348-JS349
(344.P6-P63) Police power
see KF5399
344.P77 Public records management

JS

United States
Local and municipal government
Other topics, A-Z -- Continued
344.P8 Public relations
344.R4 Recall
344.T45 Telecommunication systems
(345) Pamphlets, lectures, etc.
see JS331
346 Juvenile works
Federal-city relations. State-local relations. Municipal home rule
348 General works
349.A-W By state, A-W
(351) Law
see KF5304-KF5305
(354) Incorporation. Charters
see KF5313
Executive branch. Mayor
356 General works
Civil service
Cf. HD8001+, State labor
358 General works
(359) Study and teaching. Training of local and municipal employees
see JK716-JK717
361 Salaries. Pensions. Retirement
362 Consultants. Government consultants
362.3 Incentive awards. Merit increases. Performance awards
362.5 Minorities. Affirmative action programs
363 Productivity. Labor productivity
364 Selection and appointment. Recruiting. Dismissal
371 Legislative branch. City councils
(381-385) Judiciary. Municipal courts
see subclasses KFA-KFW
388 Government property. Government purchasing
391 Political participation. Neighborhood government
Elections. Local elections. Municipal elections
395 General works
(397) Election law
see KF4916
401 Political corruption
Local government other than municipal
408 General works
State government, see JK2403+
411 County government
418 Township government
422 Metropolitan government
425 Rural public administration. Village government
426 Special districts. Public authorities
Local
By region

United States
Local
By region -- Continued
431 Northeastern States. New England
434 Middle West
437 South. Southern States
440 West
451.A-W By state, A-W
For District of Columbia, see JK2701+
Under each:
.x1 *Periodicals. Serials*
.x2-.x5 *General works*
.x8-.x9 *Local*
By city, see JS504 JS1583
.x8A-.x8Z *By metropolitan area, A-Z*
.x9A-.x9Z *By county, township, parish, A-Z*
By city
504 A to Akron (Table J17)
505 Akron, Ohio (Table J16)
506 Akron to Alameda (Table J17)
507 Alameda, California (Table J16)
509 Alameda to Albany (Table J17)
511-519 Albany, New York (Table J15)
521 Albany to Alexandria (Table J17)
524 Alexandria, Virginia (Table J16)
525 Alexandria to Allegheny (Table J17)
531-539 Allegheny, Pennsylvania (Table J15)
541 Allegheny to Altoona (Table J17)
545 Altoona, Pennsylvania (Table J16)
546 Altoona to Annapolis (Table J17)
547 Annapolis, Maryland (Table J16)
548 Annapolis to Atlanta (Table J17)
551-559 Atlanta, Georgia (Table J15)
561 Atlanta to Auburn (Table J17)
562 Auburn, New York (Table J16)
563 Auburn to Augusta (Table J17)
565 Augusta, Georgia (Table J16)
566 Augusta, Maine to Austin (Table J17)
567 Austin, Texas (Table J16)
568 Austin to Baltimore (Table J17)
571-590 Baltimore, Maryland (Table J14)
591 Baltimore to Bangor (Table J17)
592 Bangor, Maine (Table J16)
593 Bangor to Berj. (Table J17)
594 Berkeley to Binghamton (Table J17)
595 Binghamton, New York (Table J16)
596 Binghamton to Birmingham (Table J17)
598 Birmingham, Alabama (Table J16)
599 Birmingham to Boston (Table J17)
601-620 Boston, Massachusetts (Table J14)
621 Boston To Bridgeport (Table J17)
623 Bridgeport, Connecticut (Table J16)

United States
Local
By city -- Continued

624 Bridgeport to Brockton (Table J17)
625 Brockton, Massachusetts (Table J16)
626 Brockton to Brooklyn (Table J17)
631-650 Brooklyn, New York (Table J14)
651 Brooklyn to Brunswick (Table J17)
656 Brunswick, Georgia (Table J16)
657 Brunswick to Buffalo (Table J17)
661-680 Buffalo, New York (Table J14)
681 Buffalo to Cambridge (Table J17)
683 Cambridge, Massachusetts (Table J16)
684 Cambridge to Camden (Table J17)
685 Camden, New Jersey (Table J16)
686 Camden to Canton (Table J17)
687 Canton, Ohio (Table J16)
688 Canton to Charleston (Table J17)
689 Charleston, South Carolina (Table J16)
690 Charleston, South Carolina to Charlestown, Massachusetts (Table J17)
693 Charlestown, Massachusetts (Table J16)
694 Charlestown to Chelsea (Table J17)
697 Chelsea, Massachusetts (Table J16)
698 Chelsea to Chicago (Table J17)
701-720 Chicago, Illinois (Table J14)
721 Chicago, Illinois to Chillicothe, Missouri (Table J17)
725 Chilicothe, Ohio (Table J16)
726 Chillicothe, Texas to Cincinnati, Iowa (Table J17)
731-750 Cincinnati, Ohio (Table J14)
751 Cincinnati, Ohio to Cleveland, North Carolina (Table J17)
761-780 Cleveland, Ohio (Table J14)
781 Cleveland, Ohio to Cohoes, New York (Table J17)
783 Cohoes, New York (Table J16)
784 Cohoes to Colorado (Table J17)
785 Colorado Springs, Colorado (Table J16)
786 Colorado Springs, Colorado to Columbia, South Carolina (Table J17)
787 Columbia, South Carolina (Table J16)
789 Columbia to Columbus (Table J17)
791-799 Columbus, Ohio (Table J15)
800 Columbus to Covington (Table J17)
801 Covington, Kentucky (Table J16)
802 Covington to Dallas (Table J17)
803 Dallas, Texas (Table J16)
804 Dallas to Dayton (Table J17)
805 Dayton, Ohio (Table J16)
806 Dayton to Decatur (Table J17)
807 Decatur, Illinois (Table J16)
808 Decatur to Denver (Table J17)

United States
Local
By city -- Continued

811-819 Denver, Colorado (Table J15)
821 Denver to Des Moines (Table J17)
823 Des Moines, Iowa (Table J16)
824 Des Moines to Detroit (Table J17)
831-849 Detroit, Michigan (Table J14)
849.5 Local. By district, ward, etc.
850 Detroit to Duluth (Table J17)
851 Duluth, Minnesota (Table J16)
852 Duluth to Easton (Table J17)
853 Easton, Pennsylvania (Table J16)
854 Easton to Elizabeth (Table J17)
855 Elizabeth, New Jersey (Table J16)
856 Elizabeth to Erie (Table J17)
861 Erie, Pennsylvania (Table J16)
862 Erie to Evansville (Table J17)
865 Evansville, Indiana (Table J16)
866 Evansville to Fall River (Table J17)
871-879 Fall River, Massachusetts (Table J15)
883 Fall River to Fort Wayne (Table J17)
885 Fort Wayne, Indiana (Table J16)
886 Fort Wayne to Galveston (Table J17)
888 Galveston, Texas (Table J16)
889 Galveston to Grand Forks (Table J17)
891 Grand Forks, North Dakota (Table J16)
892 Grand Forks to Grand Rapids (Table J17)
893 Grand Rapids, Michigan (Table J16)
894 Grand Rapids to Harrisburg (Table J17)
895 Harrisburg, Pennsylvania (Table J16)
896 Harrisburg to Hartford (Table J17)
901-909 Hartford, Connecticut (Table J15)
910 Hartford to Haverhill (Table J17)
911 Haverhill, Massachusetts (Table J16)
912 Haverhill to Hoboken (Table J17)
915 Hoboken, New Jersey (Table J16)
916 Hoboken to Holyoke (Table J17)
921-929 Holyoke, Massachusetts (Table J15)
931 Holyoke to Houston (Table J17)
935 Houston, Texas (Table J16)
936 Houston to Indianapolis (Table J17)
941-949 Indianapolis, Indiana (Table J15)
953 Indianapolis to Jacksonville, Florida (Table J17)
954 Jacksonville, Florida (Table J16)
955 Jacksonville, Illinois (Table J16)
956 Jacksonville to Jefferson (Table J17)
957 Jefferson City, Missouri (Table J16)
961-969 Jersey City, New Jersey (Table J15)
970 Jersey City to Joliet (Table J17)
971 Joliet, Illinois (Table J16)
972 Joliet to Joplin (Table J17)

United States
Local
By city -- Continued

973 Joplin, Missouri (Table J16)
974 Joplin to Kalamazoo (Table J17)
975 Kalamazoo, Michigan (Table J16)
976 Kalamazoo to Kansas City (Table J17)
979 Kansas City, Kansas (Table J16)
981-989 Kansas City, Missouri (Table J15)
990 Kansas City to Lancaster (Table J17)
991 Lancaster, Pennsylvania (Table J16)
992 Lancaster to Lawrence (Table J17)
993 Lawrence, Massachusetts (Table J16)
994 Lawrence to Lem (Table J17)
995 Len to Lincoln (Table J17)
996 Lincoln, Nebraska (Table J16)
997 Lincoln to Little Rock (Table J17)
998 Little Rock, Arkansas (Table J16)
999 Little Rock to Los Angeles (Table J17)
1001-1009 Los Angeles, California (Table J15)
1011 Los Angeles to Louisville (Table J17)
1021-1040 Louisville, Kentucky (Table J14)
1041 Louisville to Lowell (Table J17)
1051-1059 Lowell, Massachusetts (Table J15)
1061 Lowell to Lynn (Table J17)
1071-1079 Lynn, Massachusetts (Table J15)
1080 Lynn to McKeesport (Table J17)
1081 McKeesport, Pennsylvania (Table J16)
1082 McKeesport to Madison (Table J17)
1083 Madison, Wisconsin (Table J16)
1084 Madison to Manchester (Table J17)
1085 Manchester, New Hampshire (Table J16)
1086 Manchester to Marquette (Table J17)
1087 Marquette, Michigan (Table J16)
1088 Marquette to Memphis (Table J17)
1091-1099 Memphis, Tennessee (Table J15)
1101 Memphis to Middletown (Table J17)
1105 Middletown, Connecticut (Table J16)
1106 Middletown to Mill (Table J17)
1108 Mill to Milwaukee (Table J17)
1111-1119 Milwaukee, Wisconsin (Table J15)
1131-1150 Minneapolis, Minnesota (Table J14)
1151 Minneapolis to Mobile (Table J17)
1155 Mobile, Alabama (Table J16)
1156 Mobile to Montgomery (Table J17)
1157 Montgomery, Alabama (Table J16)
1159 Montgomery to Nashville (Table J17)
1161-1169 Nashville, Tennessee (Table J15)
1185 Nashville to New Bedford, Indiana (Table J17)
1193 New Bedford, Massachusetts (Table J16)
1194 New Bedford, New Jersey to New Haven, Connecticut (Table J17)
1195 New Haven, Connecticut (Table J16)

United States
Local
By city -- Continued

1198 New Haven to New Orleans (Table J17)
1201-1209 New Orleans, Louisiana (Table J15)
1211 New Orleans to New York (Table J17)
1221-1240 New York, New York (Table J14)
1241 New York to Newark (Table J17)
1242 Newark, New Jersey (Table J16)
1243 Newark to Norfolk (Table J17)
1245 Norfolk, Virginia (Table J16)
1246 Norfolk to North (Table J17)
1247 North Adams to Oakland (Table J17)
1248 Oakland, California (Table J16)
1249 Oakland to Omaha (Table J17)
1251 Omaha, Nebraska (Table J16)
1252 Omaha to Paterson (Table J17)
1253 Paterson, New Jersey (Table J16)
1254 Paterson to Pawtucket (Table J17)
1255 Pawtucket, Rhode Island (Table J16)
1256 Pawtucket to Peoria (Table J17)
1258 Peoria, Illinois (Table J16)
1259 Peoria to Philadelphia (Table J17)
1261-1280 Philadelphia, Pennsylvania (Table J14)
1281 Philadelphia, Pennsylvania to Pittsburgh, New Hampshire (Table J17)
1291-1310 Pittsburgh, Pennsylvania (Table J14)
1311 Pittsburgh, Pennsylvania to Pittsfield, Massachusetts (Table J17)
1312 Pittsfield, Massachusetts (Table J16)
1313 Pittsfield, Michigan to Portland, Iowa (Table J17)
1315 Portland, Maine (Table J16)
1316 Portland, Michigan to Portland, North Dakota (Table J17)
1318 Portland, Oregon (Table J16)
1319 Portland, Pennsylvania to Providence, Pennsyslvania (Table J17)
1321-1329 Providence, Rhode Island (Table J15)
1330 Providence, South Carolina to Quincy, Florida (Table J17)
1331 Quincy, Illinois (Table J16)
1332 Quincy, Indiana to Reading, Ohio (Table J17)
1335 Reading, Pennsylvania (Table J16)
1339 Reading, Vermont to Richmond, Vermont (Table J17)
1341-1349 Richmond, Virginia (Table J15)
1351 Richmond, Virginia to Rochester (Table J17)
1361-1369 Rochester, New York (Table J15)
1370 Rochester to Rockland (Table J17)
1371 Rockland, Maine (Table J16)
1372 Rockland to Saginaw (Table J17)
1373 Saginaw, Michigan (Table J16)

United States
Local
By city -- Continued

1374 Saginaw to St. Joseph (Table J17)
1376 St. Joseph, Missouri (Table J16)
1377 St. Joseph to St. Louis (Table J17)
1381-1400 St. Louis, Missouri (Table J14)
1401 St. Louis to St. Paul (Table J17)
1411-1419 St. Paul, Minnesota (Table J15)
1420 St. Paul to Salem (Table J17)
1421 Salem, Massachusetts (Table J16)
1422 Salem to Salt Lake (Table J17)
1423 Salt Lake City, Utah (Table J16)
1424 Salt Lake City to San Antonio (Table J17)
1425 San Antonio, Texas (Table J16)
1426 San Antonio to San Diego (Table J17)
1427 San Diego, California (Table J16)
1428 San Diego to San Francisco (Table J17)
1431-1449 San Francisco, California (Table J14)
1449.5 Local. By district, ward, etc.
1450 San Francisco to Savannah (Table J17)
1451 Savannah, Georgia (Table J16)
1452 Savannah to Scranton (Table J17)
1453 Scranton, Pennsylvania (Table J16)
1454 Scranton to Seattle (Table J17)
1455 Seattle, Washington (Table J16)
1456 Seattle to Shz (Table J17)
1457 Si to Somerville (Table J17)
1458 Somerville, Massachusetts (Table J16)
1459 Somerville to Springfield (Table J17)
1460 Springfield, Illinois (Table J16)
1461 Springfield, Kentucky to Springfield, Maine (Table J17)
1462 Springfield, Massachusetts (Table J16)
1464 Springfield, Missouri (Table J16)
1466 Springfield to Steubenville (Table J17)
1467 Steubenvile, Ohio (Table J16)
1468 Steubenville to Superior (Table J17)
1469 Superior, Wisconsin (Table J16)
1470 Superior to Syracuse (Table J17)
1471-1479 Syracuse, New York (Table J15)
1480 Syracuse to Tacoma (Table J17)
1481 Tacoma, Washington (Table J16)
1482 Tacoma to Taunton (Table J17)
1485 Taunton, Massachusetts (Table J16)
1486 Taunton to Terre Haute (Table J17)
1487 Terre Haute, Indiana (Table J16)
1488 Terre Haute to Toledo (Table J17)
1491-1499 Toledo, Ohio (Table J15)
1500 Toledo to Topeka (Table J17)
1501 Topeka, Kansas (Table J16)
1502 Topeka to Trenton (Table J17)
1503 Trenton, New Jersey (Table J16)

United States
Local
By city -- Continued
1504 Trenton to Troy (Table J17)
1505 Troy, New York (Table J16)
1507 Troy to Utica (Table J17)
1508 Utica, New York (Table J16)
1509 Utica to Washington (Table J17)
(1511-1530) Washington, District of Columbia
see JK2701-JK2795
1531 Washington to Waterbury (Table J17)
1535 Waterbury, Connecticut (Table J16)
1536 Waterbury to Wheeling (Table J17)
1538 Wheeling, West Virginia (Table J16)
1539 Wheeling to Wichita (Table J17)
1540 Wichita, Kansas (Table J16)
1541 Wichita to Wilkes-Barre (Table J17)
1543 Wilkes-Barre, Pennsylvania (Table J16)
1544 Wilkes-Barre to Wilmington (Table J17)
1545 Wilmington, Delaware (Table J16)
1546 Wilmington to Winston (Table J17)
1547 Winston-Salem, North Carolina (Table J16)
1548 Winston to Wom (Table J17)
1549 Won to Worcester (Table J17)
1551-1559 Worcester, Massachusetts (Table J15)
1561 Worcester to Yonkers (Table J17)
1563 Yonkers, New York (Table J16)
1564 Yonkers to Youngstown (Table J17)
1565 Youngstown, Ohio (Table J16)
1566 Youngstown to Ypsilanti (Table J17)
1568 Ypsilanti, Michigan (Table J16)
1579 Ypsilanti to Zanesville (Table J17)
1581 Zanesville, Ohio (Table J16)
1583 Zanesville to Zz (Table J17)
Canada
1701-1719 General (Table J14)
1721.A-Z Local. By province, A-Z (Table J17)
Local. By city
1726 A
1728 B
1731 Calgary
1733 Calgary to Charlottetown
1734 Charlottetown to Dawson
1738 Dawson
1741 Dawson to Edmonton
1742 Edmonton
1743 Edmonton to Fredericton
1744 Fredericton
1747 Fredericton to Halifax
1749 Halifax
1750 Halifax to Hamilton
1751 Hamilton
1756 Hamilton to London

Canada
Local. By city -- Continued
1757 London
1760 London to Montreal
1761 Montreal
1762 Montreal to Moosejaw
1763 Moosejaw
1765 Moosejaw to Ottawa
1766 Ottawa
1770 Ottawa to Quebec
1771 Quebec
1773 Quebec to Regina
1775 Regina
1776 Regina to St. John
1779 St. John
1780 St. John to Saskatoon
1781 Saskatoon
1784 Saskatoon to Sydney
1785 Sydney
1788 Sydney to Toronto
1789 Toronto
1790 Toronto to Vancouver
1791 Vancouver
1792 Vancouver to Victoria
1793 Victoria
1795 Victoria to Winnipeg
1797 Winnipeg
1800 Winnipeg to Z
(1811-1819) Newfoundland
see JS1721
1830 Bermuda
West Indies. Caribbean Area
1840 General works
1841 Bahamas
1851-1852 British West Indies. English-speaking Caribbean (Table J15)
Cuba, see JS2001+
Haiti, see JS2051
Dominican Republic, see JS2055
1861-1866 Jamaica (Table J15)
Puerto Rico, see JS2021+
Virgin Islands of the United States, see JS2058
British West Indies. English-speaking Caribbean, see JS1851+
1869 Barbados
Leeward Islands
1870 General works
1871 Anguilla
1871.5 Antigua and Barbuda
1872 Montserrat
1873 Saint Kitts and Nevis
Windward Islands
1874 General works

	West Indies. Caribbean Area
	Windward Islands -- Continued
1875	Dominica
1876	Grenada
1877	Saint Lucia
1877.5	Saint Vincent and the Grenadines
1878	Trinidad and Tobago
	Danish West Indies, see JS2058
	Netherlands Antilles. Dutch West Indies
1911	General works
1913	Aruba
1915	Bonaire
1918	Curaçao
1920	Saba
1921	Saint Eustatius
1922	Saint Martin
	French West Indies
1941	General works
1942	Guadeloupe
1943	Martinique
2001-2020	Cuba (Table J14)
2021-2040	Puerto Rico (Table J14)
2051	Haiti (Table J16)
2055	Dominican Republic (Table J16)
2058	Virgin Islands of the United States (Table J16)
2061	Latin America
	Mexico
2101-2119	General (Table J14)
2119.5.A-Z	Local. By state, A-Z
	Local. By city, A-Z
2120	A to M
2121-2140	Mexico City (Table J14)
2143	M to Z
	Central America
2145	General works
2151-2159	Belize (Table J15)
2161-2169	Costa Rica (Table J15)
2171-2179	Guatemala (Table J15)
2181-2189	Honduras (Table J15)
2191-2199	El Salvador (Table J15)
2201-2209	Nicaragua (Table J15)
2211-2219	Panama (Table J15)
	South America
2300	General works
	Argentina
2301-2319	General (Table J14)
2325.A-Z	Local. By province, A-Z
2328.A-Z	Local. By city, A-Z
2351-2370	Bolivia (Table J14)
	Brazil
2401-2419	General (Table J14)
2423.A-Z	Local. By state, etc., A-Z
2425.A-Z	Local. By city, A-Z

South America -- Continued
Chile
2451-2469 General (Table J14)
2475.A-Z Local. By province, etc., A-Z
2478.A-Z Local. By city, A-Z
2501-2520 Colombia (Table J14)
2551-2570 Ecuador (Table J14)
Guianas
2573 Guyana
2575 Surinam. Dutch Guiana
2577 French Guiana
2601-2620 Paraguay (Table J14)
Peru
2651-2669 General (Table J14)
2675.A-Z Local. By region or province, etc., A-Z
2678.A-Z Local. By city, A-Z
2701-2720 Uruguay (Table J14)
Venezuela
2751-2769 General (Table J14)
2775.A-Z Local. By state, etc., A-Z
2778.A-Z Local. By city, A-Z
Europe
3000 General (Table J16)
Including European Union countries discussed collectively
3000.3 European Community countries (Table J16)
3000.7 Eastern Europe (Table J16)
Great Britain. England
3001 Periodicals. Societies. Serials
(3003) Annuals
see JS3001
3008 Congresses
3011 Museums. Exhibitions
(3013-3020) Collections
see JS3025-JS3095
History
3025 General works
3029 Early to 1066
3041 Norman Conquest to William and Mary (1066-1689)
3051 1689 to 1835
3065 Nineteenth century
3095 Twentieth century
3111 General works
(3113) Compends, textbooks, etc.
see JS3111
(3115-3125) Municipal government
see JS3111
Federal-city relations. Central-local government relations. Municipal home rule
(3134) Law
see KD4765
3137 General works

Europe
Great Britain. England
Federal-city relations. Central-local government relations. Municipal home rule -- Continued
(3141) Local taxation
see HJ9425-HJ9428
3152.A-Z Other topics, A-Z
3152.E4 Electronic data processing
3152.L5 Limits, Territorial. Local and administrative divisions. Administrative and political divisions
Executive branch. Mayor
3158 General works
Civil service
(3169) Law
see KD4805-KD4818
3173 General works
3175 Salaries. Pensions. Retirement
3185 Legislative branch. City councils
3200 Government property. Government purchasing
3209 Political participation
Elections. Local elections. Municipal elections
3215 General works
(3218) Election law
see KD4347
3225 Political corruption
Local government other than municipal
3251 General works
3260 County government
3265 Boroughs
3270 District government
3275 Parish government
3325.A-Z Local. By country, shire, etc., A-Z
Local. By city
3341-3360 Birmingham (Table J14)
3365 Birmingham to Bradford (Table J17)
3371-3379 Bradford (Table J15)
3385 Bradford to Bristol (Table J17)
3401-3420 Bristol (Table J14)
3425 Bristol to Hull (Table J17)
3451-3459 Hull (Table J15)
3465 Hull to Liverpool (Table J17)
3481-3500 Liverpool (Table J14)
London
3551 Periodicals. Societies. Serials
3553 Directories. Registers
(3557) Laws, ordinances, etc.
see KD8866-KD8872
History
3559 General works
3562 Early to 1699
3566 18th century

	Europe
	Great Britain. England
	Local. By city
	London
	History -- Continued
3571	19th century
3600	20th century
3605	General works
3611	Central-local government relations. Municipal home rule
3613	Relations to the City of London
	Greater London Council. London County Council
3624	Directories. Registers
3625	General works
	Corporation of the City of London
3658	General works
3661	Lord Mayor
3663	Aldermen
	Civil Service
3668	General works
3674	Salaries. Pensions. Retirement
3675	Civil service examinations
3681	Political participation
3693	Elections
3705	Political corruption
3711	Local. By borough, parish, etc.
3731-3750	Manchester (Table J14)
3758	Newcastel-under-Lyme (Table J16)
3759	Newcastel-upon-Tyne (Table J16)
3781-3789	Norwich (Table J15)
3801-3820	Nottingham (Table J14)
3841-3860	Portsmouth (Table J14)
3865	Portsmouth to Rochester (Table J17)
3875	Rochester (Table J16)
3880	Rochester to Salford (Table J17)
3891-3899	Salford (Table J15)
3911-3930	Sheffield (Table J14)
3930.5	Sheffield to Sunderland (Table J17)
3931-3939	Sunderland (Table J15)
3940	Sunderland to West Ham (Table J17)
3961-3969	West Ham (Table J15)
3970	West Ham to York (Table J17)
3971-3979	York (Table J15)
	Wales
4001-4019	General (Table J14)
	Local
4025.A-Z	By country, shire, etc., A-Z
	By city
4030	A - Cardiff (Table J17)
4031-4039	Cardiff (Table J15)
4045	Merthyr-Tydfil (Table J16)
4051	Swansea (Table J16)
	Scotland

Europe
Great Britain. England
Scotland -- Continued
4101-4195 General (Table J13)
4206.A-Z By country, shire, etc., A-Z
By city
4211-4219 Aberdeen (Table J15)
4225 Dundee (Table J16)
4231-4250 Edinburgh (Table J14)
4261-4280 Glasgow (Table J14)
4290.A-Z Other cities, A-Z
4295 Northern Ireland (Table J16)
Ireland. Irish Republic
4301-4395 General (Table J13)
(4403) Northern Ireland
see JS4295
4411.A-Z Local. By county, shire, etc., A-Z
Local. By city
4441-4449 Dublin (Table J15)
4461-4469 Limerick (Table J15)
4490.A-Z Other cities, A-Z
Austria
4501-4595 General (Table J13)
4605.A-Z Local. By state, etc., A-Z
Local. By city
4607 A - Vienna (Table J17)
4631-4650 Vienna (Table J14)
4655 Vienna - Z (Table J17)
Hungary
4661-4680 General (Table J14)
4682.A-Z Local. By county, etc., A-Z
Local. By city
4685 A - Budapest (Table J17)
4686-4695 Budapest (Table J14)
4696 Budapest - Z (Table J17)
Czechoslovakia. Czech Republic. Bohemia
4721-4740 General (Table J14)
4742.A-Z Local. By region, province, etc., A-Z (Table J17)
Local. By city
4745 A - Prague (Table J17)
4746-4755 Prague (Table J15)
4756 Prague - Z (Table J17)
4760 Slovakia (Table J16)
4770 Leichtenstein (Table J16)
France
4801 Periodicals. Societies. Serials
4803 Directories. Registers
4807 Museums. Exhibitions
History
General works, see JS4881
By period
Ancien Régime (To 1789)
4821 General works

JS

Europe
France
History
Ancien R egime (To 1789)
By period -- Continued
Provincial government
4842 Administrative and political divisions
4843 Intendants
4845.A-Z Local. By province, etc., A-Z
4851 1789-1900
4874 Twentieth century
4881 General works
4895 Central-local government relations. Municipal home rule
Local government other than municipal
4901 General works
4902 Regional government
Départmental government
4903 General works
4905 Prefect. Commissaire de la République
4907 Conseil-Général
4912 Arrondissement
4917 Canton
4922 Commune
For municipalities, see JS5000+
Municipal government specifically
(4931-4944) General works
see JS4821-JS4895
4947 Executive branch. Mayor
4953 Municipal council
4965 Government property. Government purchasing
4965.5.A-Z Other topics, A-Z
4965.5.B6 Boundaries
4966 Political participation
4975 Elections. Local elections. Municipal elections
4981 Political corruption
4990.A-Z Local. By region, A-Z
4991.A-Z Local. By department, A-Z
For Seine (Dept.), see JS5101+
Under each:
.xA1-.xA4 Periodicals. Serials
.xA5 General works
.xA6-.xZ Local. By arrondisement, commune, etc.
Local. By city
5000 A - Bordeaux (Table J17)
5001-5009 Bordeaux (Table J15)
5015 Bordeaux to Lille (Table J17)
5021-5029 Lille (Table J15)
5035 Lille to Lyons (Table J17)
5041-5049 Lyons (Table J15)
5061-5069 Marseilles (Table J15)
5075 Marseilles to Paris (Table J17)

Europe
France
Local. By city -- Continued
5101-5199 Paris (Table J13)
Including Département of the Seine
5205 Paris to Toulouse (Table J17)
5241-5249 Toulouse (Table J15)
5250 Toulouse to Z (Table J17)
Germany
5301 Periodicals. Societies. Serials
5303 Directories. Registers
5305 Congresses
5307 Museums. Exhibitions
History
5321 General works
By period
5324 To 1800
5371 Nineteenth century
5390 Twentieth century
5395 General works
For municipal government, see JS5431+
Central-local government relations. Municipal home rule
5409 General works
(5411) Law
see KK5876-KK5882
Local government other than municipal
5415 General works
5417 Provinz. Provincial government
5419 Regierungsbezirk
5421 Kreis. Landkreis. Stadtkreis. Ämter
5425 Gemeinde
Municipal government
5431 General works
5437 Executive branch. Mayor
5441 City councils. Stadtverordnetenersammlung
5445 Government property. Government purchasing
5448 Political participation
Elections. Local elections. Municipal elections
(5457) Election law
see KK5295
5459 General works
5463 Political corruption
5471.A-Z Local. By state or province, A-Z
For government at the state or province level, see JN4000+
Under each:
.xA1-.xA4 Periodicals. Serials
.xA5 General works
.xA6-.xZ Local. By Regierungsbezirk, Kreis, Ämter, etc.

JS

Europe
Germany -- Continued
5472 German Democratic Republic (1949-1990) (Table J16)
Class here works on the government of the Bezirke and Kreise of the former East Germany
For works on the government of the cities located in East Germany, see JS5474+
Local. By city
5474 Aachen (Aix-la-Chapelle) (Table J16)
5475 Aachen to Altona (Table J17)
5476 Altona (Table J16)
5477 Altona to Barmen (Table J17)
5478 Barmen to Berlin (Table J17)
5481-5500 Berlin (Table J14)
5501 Berlin to Bielefeld (Table J17)
5502 Bielefeld (Table J16)
5503 Bielefeld to Bonn (Table J17)
5506 Bonn (Table J16)
5507 Bonn to Bremen (Table J17)
5508 Bremen (Table J16)
5509 Bremen to Breslau (Table J17)
5511-5519 Breslau (Table J15)
5520 Breslau to Charlottenburg (Table J17)
5521 Charlottenburg (Table J16)
5522 Charlottenburg to Chemnitz (Table J17)
5523 Chemnitz (Table J16)
5524 Chemnitz to Cologne (Table J17)
5525 Cologne (Table J16)
5526 Cologne to Crefeld (Table J17)
5527 Crefeld (Table J16)
5528 Crefeld to Danzig (Table J17)
5529 Danzig (Table J16)
5530 Danzig to Dresden (Table J17)
5531-5539 Dresden (Table J15)
5541 Dresden to Düsseldorf (Table J17)
5543 Düsseldorf (Table J16)
5545 Düsseldorf to Essen (Table J17)
5546 Essen (Table J16)
5547 Essen to Frankfurt a. M. (Table J17)
5548 Frankfurt a. M. (Table J16)
5549 Frankfurt a. M. to Hamburg (Table J17)
5551-5559 Hamburg (Table J15)
5560 Hamburg to Kiel (Table J17)
5561 Kiel (Table J16)
5562 Kiel to Königsberg i. Pr. (Table J17)
5563 Königsberg i. Pr. (Table J16)
5564 Königsberg i. Pr. to Leipzig (Table J17)
5565 Leipzig (Table J16)
5566 Leipzig to Lübeck (Table J17)
5567 Lübeck (Table J16)
5568 Lübeck to Magdeburg (Table J17)
5569 Magdeburg (Table J16)
5570 Magdeburg to Munich (Table J17)

Europe
Germany
Local. By city -- Continued
5571-5579 Munich (Table J15)
5581 Munich to Nuremberg (Table J17)
5585 Nuremberg (Table J16)
5586 Nuremberg to Posen (Table J17)
5587 Posen (Table J16)
5588 Posen to Rostock (Table J17)
5589 Rostock (Table J16)
5590 Rostock to Stettin (Table J17)
5591 Stettin (Table J16)
5592 Stettin to Strassburg i. E. (Table J17)
5593 Strassburg i. E. (Table J16)
5594 Strassburg i. E. to Stuttgart (Table J17)
5595 Stuttgart (Table J16)
5596 Stuttgart to Wiesbaden (Table J17)
5597 Wiesbaden (Table J16)
5598 Wiesbaden to Z (Table J17)
Greece
5601-5619 General (Table J14)
Local
5621-5629 Athens (Table J15)
5638.A-Z Other cities, A-Z (Table J17)
Italy
5701-5795 General (Table J13)
5796.A-Z Local. By region, province, A-Z
For government of the individual regions or provinces at the regional or provincial level, see JN5690.A+
Local. By city
5811-5819 Florence (Table J15)
5831-5839 Milan (Table J15)
5851-5859 Naples (Table J15)
5871-5879 Rome (Table J15)
5881-5889 Trieste (Table J15)
5891-5899 Turin (Table J15)
5911-5919 Venice (Table J15)
5925.A-Z Other cities, A-Z (Table J17)
5927 Malta (Table J16)
Benelux Countries. Low Countries
5928 General works
Netherlands
5931-5949 General (Table J14)
5950.A-Z Local. By province, A-Z
Local. By city
5961-5969 Amsterdam (Table J15)
5981-5989 The Hague (Table J15)
5995 Rotterdam (Table J16)
5998.A-Z Other cities, A-Z (Table J17)
Belgium
6001-6019 General (Table J14)
6020.A-Z Local. By province, etc., A-Z

Europe
Benelux Countries. Low Countries
Belgium -- Continued
Local. By city
6021-6029 Antwerp (Table J15)
6031-6039 Brussels (Table J15)
6043 Ghent (Table J16)
6047 Liege (Table J16)
6048.A-Z Other cities, A-Z (Table J17)
6049 Luxembourg (Table J16)
Russia. Soviet Union. Former Soviet republics
For individual cities, other than Moscow and St. Petersburg, see the successor states to the Soviet Union
6051-6069 General (Table J14)
6081-6089 Moscow (Table J15)
6101-6109 St. Petersburg. Leningrad. Petrograd (Table J15)
Soviet Central Asia, see JS7261+
Siberia, see JS7281+
(6112) Armenia
see JS7437
(6113) Azerbaijan
see JS7438
6114 Belarus (Table J16)
(6115) Georgia
see JS7439
6116 Moldova (Table J16)
6117 Russia (Federation) (Table J16)
6118 Ukraine (Table J16)
Autonomous republics of the former Russian S.F.S.R, see JS6117
Finland, see JS6291+
6130.2 Estonia (Table J16)
6130.3 Latvia (Table J16)
6130.5 Lithuania (Table J16)
6131-6139 Poland (Table J15)
Scandinavia
6141-6149 General (Table J15)
Denmark
6151-6169 General (Table J14)
Local
6170.A-Z By region, province, county, etc., A-Z
By city
6171-6179 Copenhagen (Table J15)
6185.A-Z Other, A-Z (Table J17)
6187 Greenland (Table J16)
6189 Iceland (Table J16)
Norway
6201-6219 General (Table J14)
Local
6220.A-Z By region, province, county, etc., A-Z
By city
6221-6229 Oslo. Kristiania (Table J15)

Europe
Scandinavia
Norway
Local
By city -- Continued
6235.A-Z Other, A-Z (Table J17)
Sweden
6251-6269 General (Table J14)
Local
6270.A-Z By region, province, county, etc., A-Z
By city
6271-6279 Stockholm (Table J15)
6285.A-Z Other, A-Z (Table J17)
6291-6299 Finland (Table J15)
Spain
6301-6319 General (Table J14)
Local
6320.A-Z By region, province, etc., A-Z
By city
6321-6329 Madrid (Table J15)
6335.A-Z Other, A-Z (Table J17)
Portugal
6341-6359 General (Table J14)
Local (Table J14)
6360.A-Z By region, district, etc., A-Z
By city
6361-6369 Lisbon (Table J15)
6375.A-Z Other, A-Z (Table J17)
Switzerland
6401-6419 General (Table J14)
Local. By canton
For government of the individual cantons at the canton level, see JN9100+
6421-6429 Aargau (Table J15)
6441-6449 Appenzell Ausserrhoden (Table J15)
6461-6469 Appenzell Innerrhoden (Table J15)
6481-6489 Baselland (Table J15)
6491-6499 Basel-Stadt (Table J15)
6501-6509 Basel (City) (Table J15)
6511-6519 Bern (Table J15)
6521-6529 Bern (City) (Table J15)
6531-6539 Fribourg (Table J15)
6541-6549 Fribourg (City) (Table J15)
6551-6559 Geneva (Table J15)
6561-6569 Geneva (City) (Table J15)
6571-6579 Glarus (Table J15)
6591-6599 Grisons (Graubunden) (Table J15)
6611-6619 Lucerne (Table J15)
6621-6629 Lucerne (City) (Table J15)
6631-6639 Neuchâtel (Table J15)
6641-6649 Neuchâtel (City) (Table J15)
6651-6659 St. Gall (Table J15)
6661-6669 St. Gall (City) (Table J15)

Europe
Switzerland
Local. By canton -- Continued
6671-6679 Schaffhausen (Table J15)
6681-6689 Schaffhausen (City) (Table J15)
6691-6699 Schwyz (Table J15)
6711-6719 Solothurn (Table J15)
6721-6729 Solothurn (City) (Table J15)
6731-6739 Thurgau (Table J15)
6751-6759 Ticino (Table J15)
6771-6779 Unterwalden (Table J15)
6791-6799 Uri (Table J15)
6811-6819 Valais (Wallis) (Table J15)
6821-6829 Vaud (Table J15)
6831-6839 Lausanne (City) (Table J15)
6851-6859 Zug (Table J15)
6871-6879 Zurich (Table J15)
6881-6889 Zurich (City) (Table J15)
Balkan States
6899.5 General works
6900 Albania (Table J16)
6901-6909 Bulgaria (Table J15)
6921-6929 Romania (Table J15)
6931-6939 Serbia (Table J15)
6941-6949 Yugoslavia (Table J15 nos. 1-8)
6949.2 Bosnia Herzegovina (Table J16)
6949.5 Croatia (Table J16)
6949.7 Macedonia (Republic) (Table J16)
Serbia, see JS6931+
6949.8 Slovenia (Table J16)
Asia
6950 General works
6951-6959 Turkey (Table J15)
Middle East. Southwest Asia, see JS7435+
South Asia
6970 General works
India
7001-7019 General (Table J14)
7025.A-Z Local. By state, union territory, etc., A-Z
Local. By city
7030 A - Bombay (Table J17)
7031-7039 Bombay (Table J15)
7040 Bombay - Calcutta (Table J17)
7051-7059 Calcutta (Table J15)
7065 Calcutta - Madras (Table J17)
7081-7089 Madras (Table J15)
7090 Madras - Z (Table J17)
Afghanistan, see JS7441+
Nepal, see JS7180
7090.5 Bhutan (Table J16)
7091-7099 Pakistan (Table J15)
7100 Bangladesh (Table J16)
7111-7119 Burma (Table J15)

Asia
South Asia -- Continued
7121-7129 Sri Lanka. Ceylon (Table J15)
(7135) Local
see JS7129
Southeast Asia. Indochina
7139 General works
(7141-7149) Hong Kong
see JS7367
Burma, see JS7111+
Sri Lanka, see JS7121+
7150 Cambodia. Kampuchea (Table J16)
7151 Laos (Table J16)
7152 Vietnam (Table J16)
7153 Thailand (Table J16)
7161-7169 Malaysia. Malaya (Table J15)
7171-7179 Singapore (Table J15)
7180 Nepal (Table J16)
7185 Brunei (Table J16)
Indonesia
7191-7198 General (Table J15)
7205.A-Z Local. By province, district, etc., A-Z
7206.A-Z Local. By city, A-Z (Table J17)
Philippines, see JS7301+
(7225) Vietnam
see JS7152
Central Asia
7261 General works
7265 Kazakhstan (Table J16)
7267 Kyrgyztan (Table J16)
7271 Tajikistan (Table J16)
7275 Uzbekistan (Table J16)
7281-7289 Siberia (Russia) (Table J15)
Including Siberian republics and autonomous areas
(7295) Local
see JS7289
Philippines
7301-7308 General (Table J15)
Local
7321-7329 Manila (Table J15)
7335.A-Z Other, A-Z (Table J17)
East Asia. Far East
7350 General works
China
7351-7358 General (Table J15)
7365.A-Z Local, A-Z (Table J17)
7365.5 Macao (Table J16)
7366 Taiwan (Table J16)
7367 Hong Kong (Table J16)
Japan
7371-7378 General (Table J15)
7384.A-Z Local. By prefecture, etc., A-Z
7385.A-Z Local. By city, A-Z (Table J17)

JS

Asia
East Asia. Far East -- Continued
7391-7399 Korea (Table J15)
Including South Korea
7400 North Korea (Table J16)
7400.5 Mongolia. Outer Mongolia (Table J16)
(7401-7415) Thailand
see JS7150
Middle East. Near East. Southwest Asia. Islamic Empire
7435 General works
Caucasus
7436 General works
7437 Armenia (Table J16)
7438 Azerbaijan (Table J16)
7439 Georgia (Republic) (Table J16)
Turkey, see JS6951+
Afghanistan
7441-7449 General (Table J15)
(7455) Local
see JS7449
Iran
7461-7469 General (Table J15)
(7475) Local
see JS7469
(7499) Other
see JS7500-JS7509
7500 Cyprus (Table J16)
7501 Syria (Table J16)
7501.5 Lebanon (Table J16)
7502 Israel. Palestine (Table J16)
7503 Jordan (Table J16)
Arabian Peninsula. Arabia. Persian Gulf States
7504 General works
7506 Saudi Arabia (Table J16)
7506.3 Yemen (Table J16)
7506.5 Oman. Muscat and Oman (Table J16)
7506.7 United Arab Emirates. Trucial States (Table J16)
7506.8 Qatar (Table J16)
7507 Bahrain (Table J16)
7508 Kuwait (Table J16)
7509 Iraq (Table J16)
Iran, see JS7461+
7510 Arab countries
7520 Islamic countries
Africa
7525 General works
English-speaking Africa
7528 General works
South Africa
7531-7539 General (Table J15)

Africa
English-speaking Africa
South Africa -- Continued
Local
see JS7539
Southern Africa. Central Africa
7637 General works
7638 Botswana. Bechuanaland (Table J16)
7639 Lesotho. Basutoland (Table J16)
7640 Swaziland (Table J16)
7641 Rhodesia. Federation of Rhodesia and Nyasaland. British Central African Protectorate (Table J16)
7642 Zambia. Northern Rhodesia (Table J16)
7643 Zimbabwe. Southern Rhodesia (Table J16)
7644 Malawi (Table J16)
7645 Namibia. Southwest Africa (Table J16)
East Africa
7647 General works
7648 Kenya (Table J16)
Tanganyika, see JS7697
Zanzibar, see JS7697
7649 Uganda (Table J16)
West Africa
7653 General works
7654 Gambia (Table J16)
Liberia, see JS7799
7655 Ghana. Gold Coast (Table J16)
7656 Nigeria (Table J16)
7657 Sierra Leone (Table J16)
7660 French-speaking Africa
North Africa
7660.5 General works
Morocco, see JS7809
7661-7669 Algeria (Table J15)
7670 Tunisia (Table J16)
7670.5 Libya (Table J16)
Egypt, see JS7761+
Sudan, see JS7819
French-speaking West Africa
7671 General works
7672 Benin. Dahomey (Table J16)
7672.5 Togo (Table J16)
7673 Guinea (Table J16)
7674 Côte d'Ivoire. Ivory Coast (Table J16)
7675 Mali. French Sudan (Table J16)
7676 Mauritania (Table J16)
7677 Niger (Table J16)
7678 Senegal (Table J16)
7679 Burkina Faso. Upper Volta (Table J16)
French-speaking Equatorial Africa
7681 General works
Zaire, see JS7715

Africa
French-speaking Equatorial Africa -- Continued
7682 Central African Republic. Ubangi Shari (Table J16)
7683 Chad (Table J16)
Cameroon, see JS7692
7684 Congo (Brazzaville). Middle Congo (Table J16)
7685 Gabon (Table J16)
7687 Djibouti. French Territory of the Afars and Issas. French Somaliland (Table J16)
7688 Madagascar. Malagasy Republic (Table J16)
7690 German East Africa (Table J16)
7692 Cameroon (Table J16)
7694 Burundi (Table J16)
7695 Rwanda (Table J16)
(7696) Namibia
see JS7645
7697 Tanzania. Tanganyika. Zanzibar (Table J16)
(7698) Togo
see JS7672.5
7703 Italian East Africa (Table J16)
(7705) Libya
see JS7670.5
7707 Somalia. Italian Somaliland
Djibouti, see JS7687
7715 Zaire. Congo (Democratic Republic). Belgian Congo (Table J16)
7723 Angola. Portuguese West Africa (Table J16)
7725 Cape Verde Islands (Table J16)
7727 Guinea-Bissau. Portuguese Guinea (Table J16)
7729 Mozambique. Portuguese East Africa (Table J16)
7731 Sao Tome and Principe (Table J16)
7735 Spanish West Africa (Table J16)
7736 Equatorial Guinea (Table J16)
7755 Ethiopia. Abyssinia (Table J16)
Egypt. United Arab Republic
7761-7769 General (Table J15)
(7781-7790) Local
see JS7769
7799 Liberia (Table J16)
7809 Morocco (Table J16)
7819 Sudan (Table J16)
Atlantic Ocean islands
7820 Azores (Table J16)
7821 Bermuda (Table J16)
7822 Madeira Islands (Table J16)
7823 Canary Islands (Table J16)
Cape Verde Islands, see JS7725
7825 Saint Helena (Table J16)
7826 Tristan da Cunha (Table J16)
7827 Falkland Islands (Table J16)
Indian Ocean islands
7900 Maldives (Table J16)

	Indian Ocean islands -- Continued
7901	Seychelles (Table J16)
7902	Comoro Islands (Table J16)
7904	Mauritius (Table J16)
7905	Reunion (Table J16)
7906	Kerguelen Islands (Table J16)
	Australia
8001-8095	General (Table J13)
	Local. By state
8131-8139	Australian Capital Territory (Table J15)
8141-8149	New South Wales (Table J15)
8150	North Australia. Northern Territory (Table J16)
8151-8159	Queensland (Table J15)
8161-8169	South Australia (Table J15)
8171-8179	Tasmania (Table J15)
8181-8189	Victoria (Table J15)
8191-8199	Western Australia (Table J15)
	Local. By city
8241-8249	Adelaide (Table J15)
8253	Adelaide to Brisbane (Table J17)
8261-8269	Brisbane (Table J15)
8273	Brisbane to Hobart (Table J17)
8275	Hobart (Table J16)
8278	Hobart to Melbourne (Table J17)
8281-8289	Melbourne (Table J15)
8293	Melbourne to Perth (Table J17)
8295	Perth (Table J16)
8298	Perth to Sydney (Table J17)
8301-8309	Sydney (Table J15)
8310	Sydney to Z (Table J17)
	New Zealand
8331-8349	General (Table J14)
8350.A-Z	Local. By territorial local authority, regional authority, district, etc., A-Z
	Local. By city
8351-8359	Auckland (Table J15)
8371-8379	Christchurch (Table J15)
8391-8399	Wellington (Table J15)
	Pacific Area. Pacific Ocean islands
(8401-8408)	Hawaii see JS451
8450	General works
(8455)	By island see JS8460+
8460	Melanesia (Table J16)
8462	Trust Territory of the Pacific. Micronesia (Table J16)
8463	Marshall Islands (Table J16)
8464	Marianas (Table J16) Including Northern Marianas
8465	Palau (Table J16)
8466	Guam (Table J16)
8467	Papua New Guinea (Table J16)

Pacific Area. Pacific Ocean islands -- Continued
8468 Kiribati. Gilbert Islands (Table J16)
8469 Tuvalu. Ellice Islands (Table J16)
8470 Solomon Islands (Table J16)
8471 New Caledonia (Table J16)
8472 Vanuatu. New Hebrides (Table J16)
8473 Fiji Islands (Table J16)
8474 Tonga (Table J16)
8475 Cook Islands (Table J16)
Samoan Islands
8480 General works
8481 American Samoa (Table J16)
8482 Western Samoa (Table J16)
8490 French Polynesia (Table J16)
Arctic regions
8495 General works
8496 Greenland (Table J16)
8499 Antarctic regions (Table J16)
8500 Developing countries

Colonies and colonization
Periodicals. Serials
Class here general periodicals by place of imprint
1 American
2 British
3 Dutch
4 French
5 German
6 Italian
7 Spanish
9 Other
Societies
For periodical publications with distinctive titles and not limited to proceedings or transactions, see JV1+
10 International
11 American
12 British
13 Dutch
14 French
15 German
16 Italian
17 Spanish
19 Other
21 Congresses
22 Dictionaries. Encyclopedias
23 Museums. Exhibitions
(31-37) Documents
see JV500-JV5399
51 Theory. Philosophy
Study and teaching
55 General works
57.A-Z By region or country, A-Z
60 Biography
For individual biography and collective biography by country, see JV500+
History
61 General works
By period
Ancient
71 General
Special countries
75 Egypt
81 Phoenicia
85 Carthage
93 Greece
98 Rome
Modern
105 General
121 Medieval to 1500
125 15th-16th century
131 17th century
135 18th century

History
By period
Modern -- Continued
141 19th century to 1870
145 1870 to 1900
151 20th century
185 General works
By region, hemisphere, continent
201 Tropics
America. Western hemisphere
221 General works
226 North America
231 South America. Latin America
Eastern hemisphere
236 General works
241 Asia and Pacific Area
246 Africa
Relations with indigenous peoples
305 General works
(308) Administration of colonies
see JV412
321 Colonization and Christianity
331 Colonization and education
341 Colonization and economics
Cf. JV420, Economic policy
(365) Colonial companies
see HF481-HF491
(373) Penal colonies
see HV8935-HF8962
(406-407) Law
see K3375
Administration. Colonial administration
412 General works
420 Economic policy
Executive
Including Viceroy, governor
431 General works
443 Civil service
461 Legislative bodies
Including Colonial assemblies
Colonizing nations
500-599 United States (Table J18)
1000-1099 Great Britain (Table J18)
1800-1899 France (Table J18)
2000-2099 Germany (Table J18)
2200-2299 Italy (Table J18)
2500-2599 Netherlands. Holland (Table J18)
2800-2899 Belgium (Table J18)
3000-3099 Russia. Soviet Union (Table J18)
3300-3399 Denmark (Table J18)
3500-3599 Sweden (Table J18)
4000-4099 Spain (Table J18)
4200-4299 Portugal (Table J18)

Colonizing nations -- Continued

5200-5299 Japan (Table J18)

5300-5399 Australia (Table J18)

Emigration and immigration. International migration
Cf. HB1951+, Population geography
Periodicals. Serials
Class here general periodicals by place of imprint
6001 American
6002 English
6003 French
6004 German
6005 Italian
6006 Other
6008 Societies
6011 Congresses
6012 Dictionaries. Encyclopedias
6013 Psychological aspects
6013.5 Study and teaching
Statistics
6019 Collections of statistics
6020 Theory. Statistical methods
History
6021 General
By period
6026 To 1800
6029 19th century
6032 20th century
6035 General works
6038 Government policy
(6045-6049) Law
see K3275
Emigration
(6061-6081) History
see JV6021-JV6032
6091 General works
Causes of emigration
6098 Economic
6101 Social
6104 Political
6107 Religious
Effects of emigration
6118 Economic
6121 Social
6124 Political
(6135-6149) Emigration to and from special regions or countries
see JV6350-JV9480
Immigration
History, see JV6021+
6201 General works
(6214) Immigration and labor. Alien labor
see HD6300
6217 Economic aspects
6217.5 Return migration
Social aspects
6225 General works

Immigration
Social aspects -- Continued
(6228) Illiteracy
see LC149+
(6231) Crime
see HV6181
6255 Political aspects
(6268) Inspection and registration
see K3275
6271 Government policy
(6325-6337) Services for immigrants. Social work with immigrants
see HV4005-HV4013
6342 Assimilation of immigrants
6346 Refugees
6347 Women immigrants
(6348) By ethnic group,
see classes D, E, F
America. Western Hemisphere
6350 General works
North America
6351 General works
United States
Periodicals, see JV6001
Manuals, guides for immigrants, see JV6543+
6403 Societies
For immigrant relief societies, see HV4010+
For societies at the state level, see JV6905+
6405 Congresses
Documents
(6409-6416) Federal documents
see JV6435
(6419) State documents
see JV6905-JV7127
(6421-6429) Laws. Regulations
see KF4801-KF4848
6435 Emigration
Immigration
History
6450 General
6451 Early to 1880
6453 1880-1900
6455 1900-
6461 Statistics
6465 General works
6471 Economic aspects
(6473) Immigration and labor, alien labor
see HD8081
6475 Social aspects
6477 Political aspects
(6479) Medical aspects
see RA448.5.I44
Immigration policy. Government policy

America. Western Hemisphere
North America
United States
Immigration policy.
Government policy -- Continued
(6481) Documents
see JV6483
6483 General works
6484 Ellis Island Immigration Station. Ellis Island Museum
(6485) Inspection and registration
see KF4840
6487 Fees. Poll tax
Cf. HJ4930, Taxation
(6491-6495) Regulation and control
see KF4801-KF4848, Law, JV6483, Government policy
(6501-6509) Restriction and exclusion
see JV6483
(6525-6533) Services for immigrants. Social work with immigrants
see HV4010-HV4012
(6535) Padrone system
see HV4871-HV4875
Handbooks, manuals, etc. for immigrants
6543 General works
6545.A-Z Manuals in foreign languages. By language, A-Z
Local
By section
6554 New England. Northeastern States
6556 Middle States. Middle Atlantic States
6559 Southern States
6565 West
6567 Middle West
6569 Northwestern States
6571 Pacific States
By state, see JV6905+
Local, see JV6905+
Special groups of immigrants
6600 Children
6601 Refugees
6602 Women immigrants
(6606) Occupational groups
see HD8039
(6611-6895) By race or ethnic origin
see E184.A1-Y7
By state
6905-6907 Alabama (Table J19)
6908-6910 Alaska (Table J19)
6912-6914 Arizona (Table J19)
6916-6918 Arkansas (Table J19)
6920-6921 California (Table J19)
6923-6925 San Francisco (Table J19)

	America. Western Hemisphere
	North America
	United States
	By state
	California -- Continued
6926.A-Z	Other local, A-Z
6928-6930	Colorado (Table J19)
6932-6934	Connecticut (Table J19)
6936-6938	Delaware (Table J19)
6940-6942	District of Columbia (Table J19)
6944-6946	Florida (Table J19)
6947-6949	Georgia (Table J19)
6950.5-7	Hawaii (Table J19)
6951-6953	Idaho (Table J19)
6954-6955	Illinois (Table J19)
6957-6959	Chicago (Table J19)
6960.A-Z	Other local, A-Z
6965-6967	Indiana (Table J19)
6968-6970	Iowa (Table J19)
6972-6974	Kansas (Table J19)
6975-6977	Kentucky (Table J19)
6979-6980	Louisiana (Table J19)
6982-6984	New Orleans (Table J19)
6985.A-Z	Other local, A-Z
6987-6989	Maine (Table J19)
6991-6992	Maryland (Table J19)
6994-6996	Baltimore (Table J19)
6997.A-Z	Other local, A-Z
7001-7002	Massachusetts (Table J19)
7004-7006	Boston (Table J19)
7007.A-Z	Other local, A-Z
7009-7011	Michigan (Table J19)
7012-7014	Minnesota (Table J19)
7016-7018	Mississippi (Table J19)
7019-7021	Missouri (Table J19)
7023-7025	Montana (Table J19)
7027-7029	Nebraska (Table J19)
7031-7033	Nevada (Table J19)
7034-7036	New Hampshire (Table J19)
7037-7039	New Jersey (Table J19)
7041-7043	New Mexico (Table J19)
7045-7046	New York (Table J19)
7048-7050	New York City (Table J19)
7051.A-Z	Other local, A-Z
7053-7055	North Carolina (Table J19)
7057-7059	North Dakota (Table J19)
7061-7063	Ohio (Table J19)
7065-7067	Oklahoma (Table J19)
7070-7072	Oregon (Table J19)
7075-7076	Pennsylvania (Table J19)
7078-7080	Philadelphia (Table J19)
7081.A-Z	Other local, A-Z
7083-7085	Rhode Island (Table J19)

America. Western Hemisphere
North America
United States
By state -- Continued
7087-7089 South Carolina (Table J19)
7091-7093 South Dakota (Table J19)
7095-7097 Tennessee (Table J19)
7098-7100 Texas (Table J19)
7102-7104 Utah (Table J19)
7106-7108 Vermont (Table J19)
7109-7111 Virginia (Table J19)
7114-7116 Washington (Table J19)
7117-7119 West Virginia (Table J19)
7121-7123 Wisconsin (Table J19)
7125-7127 Wyoming (Table J19)
Canada, Latin America, etc.
7200-7299 Canada (Table J20)
7310-7319 Bermuda (Table J21)
Mexico, see JV7400+
Central America, see JV7412+
West Indies. Caribbean Area
7320-7329 General (Table J21)
7329.3 Bahamas
Cuba, see JV7370+
Haiti, see JV7393
7329.5 Jamaica
Dominican Republic, see JV7395
Puerto Rico, see JV7380+
Virgin Islands of the United States, see JV7397
British West Indies. English-speaking Caribbean
7330-7339 General (Table J21)
7341 Barbados
Guyana, see JV7499.3
Leeward Islands
7341.5 General works
7341.6 Anguilla
7341.7 Antigua and Barbuda
7341.8 Montserrat
7341.9 Saint Kitts and Nevis
Windward Islands
7345 General works
7345.3 Dominica
7345.4 Grenada
7345.5 Saint Lucia
7345.6 Saint Vincent and the Grenadines
7352 Trinidad and Tobago
(7353) Danish West Indies
see JV7397
Netherlands Antilles. Dutch West Indies
7356 General works
7356.2 Aruba
7356.3 Bonaire
7356.4 Curaçao

America. Western Hemisphere
Canada, Latin America, etc.
West Indies. Caribbean Area
Netherlands Antilles.
Dutch West Indies -- Continued
7356.5 Saba
7356.6 Saint Eustatius
7356.7 Saint Martin
Surinam, see JV7499.5
French West Indies
7359 General works
French Guyana, see JV7499.7
7360 Guadeloupe
7361 Martinique
7370-7379 Cuba (Table J21)
7380-7389 Puerto Rico (Table J21)
7393 Haiti
7395 Dominican Republic
7397 Virgin Islands of the United States
Latin America
7398 General works
7400-7409 Mexico
Central America
7412 General works
7412.5 Belize. British Honduras
7413 Costa Rica
7416 Guatemala
7419 Honduras
7423 El Salvador
7426 Nicaragua
7429 Panama
7432 Panama Canal Zone
South America
7433 General works
7436 Southern Cone of South America
7440-7449 Argentina (Table J21)
7450-7459 Bolivia (Table J21)
7460-7469 Brazil (Table J21)
7470-7479 Chile (Table J21)
7480-7489 Colombia (Table J21)
7490-7499 Ecuador (Table J21)
Guianas
7499.2 General works
7499.3 Guyana. British Guiana
7499.5 Surinam. Dutch Guiana
7499.7 French Guiana
7500-7509 Paraguay (Table J21)
7510-7519 Peru (Table J21)
7520-7529 Uruguay (Table J21)
7530-7539 Venezuela (Table J21)
Europe

Europe -- Continued
7590 General works
Including European Union countries discussed collectively
7595 European Community countries
7597 Eastern Europe
7600-7699 Great Britain. England (Table J20)
7700-7709 Scotland (Table J21)
7709.5 Northern Ireland
7710-7719 Ireland. Irish Republic (Table J21)
7720-7729 Wales (Table J21)
7800-7899 Austria (Table J20)
7899.15 Czechoslovakia. Czech Republic
7899.2 Slovakia
7899.3 Hungary
7899.5 Liechtenstein
7900-7999 France (Table J20)
8000-8099 Germany (Table J20)
8110-8119 Greece (Table J21)
8130-8139 Italy (Table J21)
8141 Malta
Benelux countries. Low countries
8149 General works
8150-8159 Netherlands (Table J21)
8160-8169 Belgium (Table J21)
8175 Luxembourg
8180-8189 Russia. Soviet Union. Former Soviet republics (Table J21)
8190 Russia (Federation)
8191 Estonia
8192 Finland
Baltic States
8192.5 General works
Estonia, see JV8191
8193 Latvia
8194 Lithuania
8195 Poland
8195.2 Belarus
8195.5 Moldova
8196 Ukraine
Scandinavia
8198 General works
8200-8209 Denmark (Table J21)
8209.5 Iceland
8210-8219 Norway (Table J21)
8220-8229 Sweden (Table J21)
8250-8259 Spain (Table J21)
8259.5 Andorra
8259.7 Gibraltar
8260-8269 Portugal (Table J21)
8280-8289 Switzerland (Table J21)
Balkan States
8295 General works

Europe
Balkan States -- Continued
8296 Albania
8300-8309 Bulgaria (Table J21)
8320-8329 Romania (Table J21)
8330-8339 Yugoslavia. Serbia (Table J21)
8339.2 Slovenia
8339.4 Croatia
8339.5 Bosnia and Hercegovina
8339.7 Macedonia (Republic)
Greece, see JV8110+
(8340-8349) Turkey
see JV8745
Asia
8490 General works
8500-8509 India (Table J21)
8510 Nepal
(8515-8635) Former colonies in Asia
see JV8500-JV8762
8685 Philippines
8700-8709 China (Table J21)
8710-8719 Taiwan (Table J21)
8720-8729 Japan (Table J21)
Middle East. Near East
8739 General works
Caucasus
8739.5 General works
8739.6 Armenia
8739.7 Azerbaijan
8739.8 Georgia (Republic)
8741 Iran
8745 Turkey
8746 Cyprus
8747 Syria
8748 Lebanon
8749 Israel. Palestine
8749.5 Jordan
Arabian Peninsula. Arabia. Persian Gulf States
8750 General works
8750.3 Saudi Arabia
8750.5 Yemen (Yeman Arab Republic)
8750.55 Yemen (People's Democratic Republic). Southern Yemen. Aden (Colony and Protectorate)
8750.6 Oman. Muscat and Oman
8750.65 United Arab Emirates. Trucial States
8750.7 Qatar
8750.75 Bahrain
8750.8 Kuwait
8751 Iraq
Iran, see JV8741
South Asia
8752 General works
8752.3 Afghanistan

Asia
South Asia -- Continued
8752.5 Burma
8752.7 Sri Lanka. Ceylon
Nepal, see JV8510
India, see JV8500+
8752.8 Bhutan
8753 Pakistan
8753.5 Bangladesh
Southeast Asia. Indochina
Including French Indochina
8753.7 General works
Burma, see JV8752.5
8754 Cambodia. Kampuchea
8754.3 Laos
8754.5 Vietnam
8754.7 Thailand
8755 Malaysia. Malaya
8755.5 Singapore
8755.7 Brunei
8756 Indonesia
Philippines, see JV8685
East Asia. Far East
8756.5 General works
Japan, see JV8720+
8757 Korea
Including South Korea
8757.5 North Korea
China, see JV8700+
8757.7 Macao
Taiwan, see JV8710+
8758 Hong Kong
8760 Arab countries (Collective)
8762 Islamic countries
Africa
8790 General works
8800-8895 South Africa. Republic of South Africa (Table J20)
(8900-8969) Provinces, cities, etc.
see JV8890-JV8895
(8975) Former British colonies
see JV8800-JV9023.5
North Africa
8977 General works
8978 Morocco
8980 Algeria
8981 Tunisia
8983 Libya
8989 Egypt. United Arab Republic
8991 Sudan
(8995) Former French colonies
see JV8977-JV9021.8
Northeast Africa
8996 General works

Africa
Northeast Africa -- Continued
8997 Ethiopia
8998 Somalia
8998.5 Djibouti. French Territory of the Afars and Issas
Southeast Africa
Including East Africa
8998.7 General works
8999 Kenya
9001 Uganda
9001.5 Rwanda
9001.7 Burundi
9002 Tanzania. Tanganyika. Zanzibar
9003 Mozambique
9004 Madagascar. Malagasy Republic
(9005) Former German colonies
see JV9001.5, Rwanda 9001.7 Burundi; JV9007.5, Namibia; JV9018, Cameroon; JV9020.7, Togo
Southern Africa
9006 General works
South Africa, see JV8800+
9006.15 Rhodesia
Including Zimbabwe (Southern Rhodesia)
9006.3 Zambia. Northern Rhodesia
9006.7 Lesotho. Basutoland
9007 Swaziland
9007.2 Botswana. Bechuanaland
9007.3 Malawi. Nyasaland
9007.5 Namibia. Southwest Africa
(9009) Former Italian Colonies
see JV8983, Libya; JV8998, Somalia
Central Africa. Equatorial Africa
9010 General works
9011 Angola
9015 Zaire. Congo (Democratic Republic)
9015.3 Equatorial Guinea
9015.5 Sao Tome and Principe
9015.7 French-speaking Equatorial Africa
9016 Gabon
9016.5 Congo (Brazzaville). Middle Congo
9016.8 Central African Republic. Ubangi Shari
9017 Chad
9018 Cameroon
(9019) Former Portuguese colonies
see JV9003, Mozambique; JV9010, Angola; JV9015.5, Sao Tome e Principe; JV9024, Guinea-Bissau
West Africa. West Coast
9020 General works
9020.15 Sahel
9020.3 French-speaking West Africa
9020.5 Benin. Dahomey
9020.7 Togo
9020.8 Niger

	Africa
	West Africa. West Coast -- Continued
9021	Côte d'Ivoire. Ivory Coast
9021.2	Guinea
9021.4	Mali
9021.6	Burkina Faso. Upper Volta
9021.7	Senegal
9021.8	Mauritania
9022	Nigeria
9022.3	Ghana
9023	Sierra Leone
9023.5	Gambia
9023.6	Liberia
9024	Guinea-Bissau. Portuguese Guinea
9024.5	Spanish Sahara
(9025)	Independent African States see JV8790-JV9024
	Atlantic Ocean islands
9029	General works
	Iceland, see JV8209.5
9030	Azores
	Bermuda, see JV7310+
9031	Madeira Islands
9032	Canary Islands
9033	Cape Verde
9034	Saint Helena
9035	Tristan da Cunha
9036	Falkland Islands
	Indian Ocean islands
9040	General works
9041	Maldives
9042	Seychelles
9043	Comoro Islands
9045	Mauritius
9046	Reunion
9047	Kerguelen Islands
	Australia
9100-9199	General (Table J20)
(9200-9299)	States, cities, etc. see JV9190-JV9195
9260-9269	New Zealand (Table J21)
	Pacific Area. Pacific Ocean islands
9290	General works
(9300-9445)	Former colonies see JV9290-JV9470
9446	Melanesia
9447	Trust Territory of the Pacific. Micronesia
9448	Marshall Islands
9449	Marianas
9450	Palau
(9451)	Hawaii see JV6950.5-7
9452	Guam

Pacific Area. Pacific Ocean islands -- Continued

9453 Papua New Guinea
9455 Kiribati. Gilbert Islands
9456 Tuvalu. Ellice Islands
9457 Solomon Islands
9458 New Caledonia
9459 Vanuatu. New Hebrides
9460 Fiji
9461 Tonga
9462 Cook Islands
Samoan Islands
9465 General works
9466 American Samoa
9467 Western Samoa
9470 French Polynesia
Arctic regions
9472 General works
9473 Greenland
9475 Antarctica
9480 Developing countries

International law
Periodicals
(1) American and English
(3) French and Belgian
(5) German
(7) Italian
(9) Spanish, Portuguese and Latin American
(18) Other
(21) Yearbooks
For Annuaire de la vie internationale, see JX1904
For Annuaire de l'Institut de droit international, see JX24
Societies
(24) International
(27) American
(31) English
(32) French, etc.
(33) German
(34) Italian
(35) Spanish, etc.
(38) Other
Congresses and conferences
(41) General works. Organization. History
(54.A-Z) Special congresses. By name, A-Z
For Hague Conferences, see JX1912+
Collections. Documents. Cases
General. Selections, sources, etc.
For collections limited to particular countries, see JX221+
Polyglot editions
(63) Early
(64) Recent
(65) Latin
(68) English
(71) Dutch
(74) French, etc.
(77) German
(81) Italian
(84) Spanish, etc.
(91.A-Z) Other, A-Z
(97) Pamphlets, lectures, etc.
Diplomatic relations (Universal collections)
(101) Latin (and polyglot)
(103) English
(105) French
(107) German
(109) Italian
(111) Spanish
(115) Other

Collections. Documents. Cases -- Continued
Treaties (General collections)
Including publications started within the period although extending into later periods
Including collections contemporary or later limited in content to the period
For collections of treaties of one particular country with other countries, see JX236, and JX350-JX1200, (subdivision (6) under each country)
For collections of arbitration treaties, see JX1985+

(118) Ancient
see JX2001
To 1700
(120) Latin (and polyglot)
Subarranged by title or editor
(121) English
Subarranged by title or editor
(122) French
Subarranged by title or editor
(123) German
Subarranged by title or editor
(124) Italian
Subarranged by title or editor
(125) Spanish
Subarranged by title or editor
(128.A-Z) Other, A-Z
Subarranged by title or editor
1700-1789
(130) Latin (and polyglot)
Subarranged by title or editor
(131) English
Subarranged by title or editor
(132) French
Subarranged by title or editor
(133) German
Subarranged by title or editor
(134) Italian
Subarranged by title or editor
(135) Spanish
Subarranged by title or editor
(138.A-Z) Other, A-Z
Subarranged by title or editor
1789-1815
(140) Latin (and polyglot)
Subarranged by title or editor
(141) English
Subarranged by title or editor
(142) French
Subarranged by title or editor
(143) German
Subarranged by title or editor

Collections. Documents. Cases
Treaties (General collections)
1789-1815 -- Continued
(144) Italian
Subarranged by title or editor
(145) Spanish
Subarranged by title or editor
(148.A-Z) Other, A-Z
Subarranged by title or editor
1815-1860
(150) Latin (and polyglot)
Subarranged by title or editor
(151) English
Subarranged by title or editor
(152) French
Subarranged by title or editor
(153) German
Subarranged by title or editor
(155) Spanish
Subarranged by title or editor
(158.A-Z) Other, A-Z
Subarranged by title or editor
1860-1900
(160) Latin (and polyglot)
Subarranged by title or editor
(161) English
Subarranged by title or editor
(162) French
Subarranged by title or editor
(163) German
Subarranged by title or editor
(164) Italian
Subarranged by title or editor
(165) Spanish
Subarranged by title or editor
(168.A-Z) Other, A-Z
Subarranged by title or editor
1900-
(170) Latin (and polyglot)
Subarranged by title or editor
(171) English
Subarranged by title or editor
(172) French
Subarranged by title or editor
(173) German
Subarranged by title or editor
(174) Italian
Subarranged by title or editor
(175) Spanish
Subarranged by title or editor
(178.A-Z) Other, A-Z
Subarranged by title or editor

Collections. Documents. Cases -- Continued
(191) Separate treaties
Class here only treatises of general character or miscellaneous provisions, and treaties "of amity and commerce", to which the United States is not a party
To be arranged by date (year and month of signature or, if better known, by date of ratification)
For boundary treaties and treaties of peace, see classes D-F
For arbitration treaties, see JX1985+
For extradition treaties, see JX4301+
For tariff treaties, see HF1721+
For United States treaties (amity and commerce, etc.), see JX235+
Subarranged as follows:
1 *Original text, including editions in language of party of the first part if identical*
2 *Text in language of party of the second part*
3.A-3.Z *Text in language of third and fourth parties (in case of tripartite or quadripartite treaties) and translations into other languages. By language, A-Z*
4 *Preliminaries, negotiations, etc. (Official documents)*
5 *History, etc.; Pamphlets (Nonofficial)*
Collections. By country
(221-230) America (Table JX2)
United States
(231) General collections
Foreign relations and diplomatic correspondence
Secretary of state
(232) Report
Including bureau reports and documents
Diplomatic correspondence
Class here general collections, routine correspondence
For correspondence covering special affairs, negotiations, wars, etc., to be classified, see D; E; F
(233.A1-A4) Serial (in chronological order of series)
(233.A5-A59) Special (not limited to special countries)
(233.A6-Z) Relations with particular countries
(234.A1) President's messages and other executive documents
Legislative documents
Senate
(234.A2) Collected
(234.A3) Special. By date

Collections. By country
United States
Foreign relations and diplomatic correspondence
Legislative documents -- Continued
House
(234.A4) Collected
(234.A5) Special. By date
(234.A8-Z) Other documents
Treaties and conventions
(235) Separate treaties. By date
(235.9) Series
Main official series, .A3 by number
(236) Collections. By date of first volume (or if period covered)
(237) Digests of decisions, opinions, etc.
Including United States Attorney-general's opinions on international law questions
(238.A-Z) Cases, claims, etc. By name, A-Z
(238.A2) Collections
(238.A4-A7) Alabama claims
(238.A4) Documents, correspondence, etc. prior to Treaty of Washington. By date
Treaty of Washington, see JX235+
(238.A42) The Arbitration. Correspondence, etc.
The American case
(238.A43-A47) Collections. General statement, and other documents (American editions)
(238.A48-A49) Foreign editions
Special documents
(238.A5) 1872 dated
Chronologically
(a) *American official edition*
(b)-(x) *Foreign editions and translations*
(238.A51) 1872 undated
(238.A53) After 1872
The British case
(238.A54-A57) Collections (English editions)
(238.A58-A59) Foreign editions
Special documents
(238.A6) 1872 dated
(238.A61) 1872 updated
(238.A63) After 1872
The Tribunal
(238.A64) Collections
(238.A65) Documents prior to the award
(238.A66) Decision and award
(238.A67) Other
(238.A687) United States Court of Commissioners, 1874
United States Court of Commissioners, 1882
(238.A69) Proceedings
(238.A692) Rules, opinions (etc.), 1882-1885

Collections. By country
United States
Cases, claims, etc. By name, A-Z
Alabama claims
United States Court of Commissioners, 1882 -- Continued
(238.A695) Separate documents. By date
(238.A7) Semiofficial and nonofficial. By date
Mixed Commission on British and American claims under Article XII of the Treaty of Washington, 1871
British claims
(238.A8) Memorials, briefs, decisions
(238.A8a) Testimony
American claims
(238.A81) Memorials, briefs, decisions
(238.A81a) Testimony
(238.A83) List of claims
(238.A85) Other documents, and nonofficial matter. By date
(238.A9-Z) Other cases. By country of name
(238.F4-F77) French and American claims
(238.F6-F7) Claims originating 1860-1871
Including Mexican intervention 1860-1866, Franco-German war, 1870-1871
(238.F72-F75) French spoliation claims
Including spoliations prior to July, 1801 (treaties and awards, etc. under conventions of 1803; 1831; treaty with Spain, 1819; etc.)
(238.F72) General collections
United States
(238.F73) Documents. By date
(238.F74A-Z) Special claims. By name
(238.F743-F746) French documents
(238.F75) Nonofficial (pamphlets, etc.). By date
(238.F77A-Z) Other special, A-Z
(238.F8-F9) Fur seal arbitration
(238.N6-N69) Northeastern fisheries
(238.P5-P6) Pious Fund cases
(238.S7-S8) Spanish treaty claims
To include all Spanish claims
(239) Other cases. By date
(245.A-W) States, A-W
e. g.
(245.T4) Texas (Republic)
Confederate States diplomatic documents, etc.
see KFZ8600-KFZ9100
Other countries
(351-360) Canada (Table JX2)
(355.9.A3) Treaty series. By number
(361-370) Mexico (Table JX2)
(371-380) Central America (Table JX2)

Collections. By country
Other countries
Central America -- Continued
(381-390) Belize (Table JX2)
(391-400) Costa Rica (Table JX2)
(401-410) Guatemala (Table JX2)
(411-420) Honduras (Table JX2)
(421-430) Nicaragua (Table JX2)
(431-440) Panama (Table JX2)
(441-450) El Salvador (Table JX2)
West Indies
(451-460) Cuba (Table JX2)
(461-470) Haiti (Table JX2)
(471-480) Dominican Republic (Table JX2)
(483) Puerto Rico (Table JX1)
(484) U.S. Virgin Islands (Table JX1)
Cf. JX491+, Danish West Indies
British West Indies
(485) General
(486.A-Z) Local, A-Z
Danish West Indies
Cf. JX484, U.S. Virgin Islands
(491) General
(492.A-Z) Local, A-Z
Dutch West Indies
(493) General
(493.A-Z) Local, A-Z
French West Indies
(495) General
(496.A-Z) Local, A-Z
(501-510) South America (Table JX2)
(511-520) Argentina (Table JX2)
(521-530) Bolivia (Table JX2)
(531-540) Brazil (Table JX2)
(541-550) Chile (Table JX2)
(551-560) Colombia (Table JX2)
(561-570) Ecuador (Table JX2)
(571) Guyana (Table JX1)
(574) Surinam (Table JX1)
(577) French Guiana (Table JX1)
(581-590) Paraguay (Table JX2)
(591-600) Peru (Table JX2)
(611-620) Venezuela (Table JX2)
(621-630) Europe (Table JX2)
(631-640) Great Britain (Table JX2)
(671-680) Austria-Hungary (Table JX2)
Czechoslovakia
(680.C9) Collections and serial documents
(680.C92) Treaties and conventions
(680.C93) Cases, claims, etc.
(681-690) France (Table JX2)
(691-700) Germany (Table JX2)
(701-710) Greece (Table JX2)

Collections. By country
Other countries
Europe -- Continued
(711-720) Italy (Table JX2)
(721-730) Netherlands (Table JX2)
(731-740) Belgium (Table JX2)
(741-750) Holland (Table JX2)
(751-760) Russia. Soviet Union (Table JX2)
(761-770) Scandinavia (Table JX2)
(771-780) Denmark (Table JX2)
Iceland, see JX899.I3
(791-800) Norway (Table JX2)
(801-810) Sweden (Table JX2)
(811-820) Spain (Table JX2)
(821-830) Portugal (Table JX2)
Turkey and Balkan States
(841-850) Turkey (Table JX2)
Albania
(850.A4) Collections and serial documents
(850.A5) Treaties and conventions
(850.A6) Cases, claims, etc.
(851-860) Bulgaria (Table JX2)
(861-870) Montenegro (Table JX2)
(871-880) Romania (Table JX2)
(881-890) Yugoslavia. Serbia (Table JX2)
Other European
(893) Luxembourg (Table JX1)
(895) Monaco (Table JX1)
(899.A-Z) Other, A-Z
e. g.
Under each:
1 *Collections and serial documents*
2 *Treaties and conventions*
3 *Cases, claims, etc.*
(899.I3) Iceland
(899.S3) San Marino
Asia
(900) General works
(901-910) Philippines (Table JX2)
British possessions
(911-920) India (Table JX2)
(920.5.A-Z) Other special, A-Z
Under each:
1 *Collections and serial documents*
2 *Treatises and conventions*
3 *Cases, claims, etc.*
(921-930) China (Table JX2)
(931-940) Dutch East Indies. Indonesia (Table JX2)
French possessions
(943) General and Indo-China (Table JX1)

JX

Collections. By country
Other countries
Asia
French possessions -- Continued
(945.A-Z) Local, A-Z
Apply table at JX(920.5.A-Z)
German possessions
(947) General
(948.A-Z) Local, A-Z
(951-960) Japan (Table JX2)
(961-970) Korea (Table JX2)
(970.15) Korea (Democratic People's Republic) (Table JX1)
(970.5) Pakistan (Table JX1)
(971-980) Iran (Table JX2)
(981-990) Russia in Asia. Soviet Union in Asia (Table JX2)
(991-1000) Thailand (Table JX2)
(1001-1010) Turkey in Asia (Table JX2)
(1015.A-Z) Other, A-Z
e.g.
Apply table at JX(920.5.A-Z)
(1015.A72) League of Arab States
(1015.U5) United Arab Republic
(1021-1030) Africa (Table JX2)
(1031-1039) Egypt (Table JX2)
British Africa and South Africa
(1040) General works (Table JX1)
(1041) Cape of Good Hope (Table JX1)
(1042) Natal (Table JX1)
(1043) Orange Free State (Table JX1)
(1044) South African Republic (Table JX1)
(1045) Transvaal (Table JX1)
(1046) Zimbabwe (Table JX1)
(1050.A-Z) Other, A-Z (Table JX1)
French possessions
(1059) General
(1060.A-Z) Local, A-Z
German possessions
(1069) General
(1070.A-Z) Local, A-Z
Italian possessions
(1079) General
(1080.A-Z) Local, A-Z
(1085) Zaire (Table JX1)
Portuguese possessions
(1089) General
Spanish possessions
(1099) General
(1100.A-Z) Local, A-Z
(1101-1110) Ethiopia (Table JX2)
(1121-1130) Liberia (Table JX2)
(1131-1140) Morocco (Table JX2)
(1145.A-Z) Other, A-Z (Table JX1)

Collections. By country
Other countries -- Continued
(1161-1170) Australia (Table JX2)
(1171-1179) New Zealand (Table JX2)
Pacific islands
(1180) General works (Table JX1)
American
(1181) Hawaii (Table JX1)
Philippines, see JX901+
(1182.A-Z) Other, A-Z
Apply table at JX(920.5.A-Z)
(1184-1185) British
Under each:
1 *General*
2 *Local, A-Z*
(1187-1188) French
Apply table at JX(1184-1185)
(1191-1192) German
Apply table at JX(1184-1185)
(1195.A-Z) Other, A-Z
Apply table at JX(920.5.A-Z)
Digests of cases, e. g. Snow, Wharton, Moore, etc, see JX63+
(1226) Dictionaries
Theory, scope, relations, sources
For collections of "sources", see JX63+
(1245) General
Cf. JC362, Internationalism
Cf. JX1995, International unions, bureaus, etc.
(1246) General special
Including sanctions: compulsion, enforcement in public international law (Power to enforce treaties, etc.)
Cf. JX1975.6, League of Nations
Cf. JX1977.8.S3, United Nations
Cf. JX4161+, Treaties and convention
(1248) Relation to municipal law
(1249-1253) Relation to the social sciences
(1250) Relation to political science
(1251) Relation to sociology
(1252) Relation to economics
(1253) Relation to history
(1255) Other
Codification of International law
(1261) Collections. Congresses. Societies
Codes
(1265) Official. By date (issued by official bodies as documents, etc.)
(1268) Nonofficial. By editor
Including Field, Bluntschli, etc.
Treaties and other general works
(1270) Early, to 1860

Codification of International law
Treaties and other general works -- Continued
Recent
(1271) American and English
(1273) French and Belgian
(1275) German
(1277) Italian
(1279) Spanish, Portuguese, and Latin American
(1280.A-Z) Other, A-Z
e. g.
(1280.R8) Russian
(1281) Addresses, essays, lectures
(1283) Special topics
(1287) Procedure
see JX1901-JX1991
Study and teaching
Cf. JX1904.5, International organization
(1291) General works
(1293.A-Z) By region or country, A-Z
(1295.A-Z) By school, A-Z
(1297) Outlines. Syllabi
(1299) Quizzes and examination questions
Textbooks, compends, see JX2001 +
Foreign relations
Class here international questions treated as sources of or contributions to the theory of international law
For histories of events, diplomatic history of wars, etc., see History. (In case of doubt, favor classes D - F)
History of international relations and the development of international law
(1305) Comprehensive works
e. g. Laurent
(1308) Treatises. Textbooks
e. g. Nys, E. Etudes
(1311) Addresses, essays, lectures
By period
Ancient, see JX2001 +
Medieval, see JX2041 +
Modern
(1315) Comprehensive works
(1318) Balance of power
(1319) Balkan question
(1321) Far Eastern question
By period
Peace of Westphalia to the Treaty of Utrecht (1648-1713)
(1325) General
(1328) Peace of Westphalia
(1331) Spanish succession
Treaty of Utrecht, see D283.5
(1333) Addresses, essays, lectures

Foreign relations
History of international relations and the development of international law
By period
Modern
By period -- Continued
Treaty of Utrecht to the French Revolution (1713-1789)
(1335) General
(1336) Treaty of Paris, 1763
see D297
(1338.A-Z) Special. By subject, A-Z
e. g. League of the Neutrals
(1341) Contemporary works
French Revolution to the Congress of Vienna (1789-1815)
(1345) General
(1346) Congress of Rastatt
(1347) Treaty of Ghent
(1349) Holy Alliance
(1351) Congress of Vienna
(1352.A-Z) Other, A-Z
(1353) Contemporary works
Congress of Vienna to the American Civil War (1815-1861)
(1358) General
(1361) Congress of Troppau (1820)
(1363) Congress of Laibach (1821)
(1365) Congress of Verona (1822)
(1366) Congress of Panama
see F1404
(1367) Treaty of Paris (1856)
Class here publications of the English Maritime League
Including works on the Declaration of Paris
(1369) Contemporary works
American Civil War to the First Conference on the Hague (1861-1899)
General
(1375) Geneva Conference, 1864, etc.
see JX5136-JX5144, JX5243
(1377) St. Petersburg Convention, 1868
(1379) London Conference, 1871
(1381) Brussels Conference, 1875
(1383) Berlin Conference, 1878
(1385) Congo Conference, 1884-1885
Cf. DT31+, Partition of Africa
Cf. DT652, Congo question
(1386.A-Z) Other, A-Z
(1387) Contemporary works
Twentieth century

Foreign relations
History of international relations and the development of international law
By period
Twentieth century -- Continued
(1391) General
(1392) World War I
Cf. D610+, Diplomatic history of the war
(1392.5) World War II
Cf. D748+, Diplomatic history of the war
(1393.A-Z) Other special. By subject, A-Z
(1393.A8) Atlantic Union
(1393.B74) British Honduras question
(1393.C65) Conference on Security and Cooperation in Europe
(1393.D46) Detente
(1393.D8) Drago doctrine
(1393.E8) Exterritoriality
(1393.I53) Indian Ocean region
(1393.I8) Italo-Ethiopian War, 1935-1936
(1393.K6) Korean War, 1950-1953
(1393.L3) Latin America
London Declaration (Laws of naval war), 1909, see JX5203+
(1393.M43) Mediterranean region
(1393.N54) Nonalignment
(1393.N57) North Atlantic region
North Atlantic Treaty Organization (NATO). North Atlantic Assembly
Cf. D845.2, Twentieth century history
(1393.N58-N62) Official serials
(1393.N63) Official monographs. By date of publication
(1393.N67A-Z) General works
(1393.P3) Pacific islands
(1393.R4) Rhine River and Valley
(1393.R8) Russo-Japanese War, 1904-1905
(1393.S5) Sino-Japanese Conflict, 1937-1945
(1393.S6) South African War, 1899-1902
(1393.S63) South Atlantic region
(1393.S65) Spanish Civil War, 1936-1939
(1393.S8) Straits question
Strategic Arms Limitation Talks, see JX1974.75
(1393.W2) Warsaw Pact Organization
(1395) Contemporary works
Interoceanic canals
Class here diplomatic history only
Cf. HE532, Interoceanic canals
Cf. TC773+, Hydraulic engineering
For treatises, see JX4155

Foreign relations
Interoceanic canals -- Continued
(1398-1398.8) Panama Canal (and Isthmian canals in general)
Cf. HE537+, Traffic and tolls
Cf. TC774+, Construction and maintenance
(1398) General
(1398.2) Early to 1876/1879
(1398.3) French companies (1876/1879 - ca. 1903)
United States
(1398.5) Documents
(1398.6) Clayton-Bulwer Treaty, 1850
(1398.7) Hay-Pauncefote Treaties, 1901-1902
Panama Canal Treaties, 1977
(1398.72) Text of treaties. By date of publication
(1398.73) General works
Panama Republic, see F1566
(1398.8) Nonofficial
(1400) Nicaragua Canal
(1401) Other American Isthmian canal projects
(1403) Suez Canal
Foreign relations. By country
(1404) America
United States
(1405) Collections
(1406) History of international law in the United States
History of foreign relations, diplomatic questions, etc.
(1407) General
By period
(1411) Colonial to 1776
(1412) 1776-1800/1815
(1413) 1800/1815-1861
(1414) 1861-1880
Including Trent affair
(1415) 1880-1900
(1416) 1900-1945
(1417) 1945-
Special topics
Boundary questions
see class E
(1421) Eastern policy
(1423) Great Lakes
(1425) Monroe Doctrine
Class here works on general theory only
For Cuban intervention, see E723
For Mexican intervention, see F1233
(1426) Philippine annexation, etc. Spanish-American War
Fisheries question, see JX238.A+
Oregon question, see F880
Panama Canal, see JX1398+
(1427.A-Z) Other topics, A-Z
(1427.E5) Embargo
(1427.M5) Military influence

Foreign relations. By country
United States -- Continued
(1428.A-Z) Relations with special countries, A-Z
Cf. E183.7+, Diplomatic history (U.S.)
Cf. F1418, Relations (general) of the United States and Latin America, Pan-Americanism
Confederate States
see E488
(1429) General
(1430) Contemporary. By date
(1431.A-Z) Special topics. By subject, A-Z
Other countries
(1515) Canada. British America (Table JX3)
(1515.5) Latin America
(1516) Mexico (Table JX3)
Central America
(1517) General works
(1517.5) Belize (Table JX3)
For the British Honduras question, see F1449.B7
(1518) Costa Rica (Table JX3)
(1519) Guatemala (Table JX3)
(1520) Honduras (Table JX3)
(1521) Nicaragua (Table JX3)
(1522) Panama (Table JX3)
(1522.5) Panama Canal (Table JX3)
(1523) El Salvador (Table JX3)
West Indies
(1524) General works
(1524.5) Bahamas (Table JX3)
(1525) Cuba (Table JX3)
(1526) Haiti (Table JX3)
(1526.5) Dominican Republic (Table JX3)
(1527) Jamaica (Table JX3)
(1528) Puerto Rico (Table JX3)
(1528.5) U.S. Virgin Islands (Table JX3)
(1529.A-Z) Other, A-Z (Table JX3)
South America
(1530) General works
(1531) Argentina (Table JX3)
(1532) Bolivia (Table JX3)
(1533) Brazil (Table JX3)
(1534) Chile (Table JX3)
(1535) Colombia (Table JX3)
(1536) Ecuador (Table JX3)
Guianas
(1537) General works
(1537.1) Guyana (Table JX3)
(1537.3) Surinam (Table JX3)
(1537.5) French Guiana (Table JX3)
(1538) Paraguay (Table JX3)
(1539) Peru (Table JX3)
(1540) Uruguay (Table JX3)

Foreign relations. By country
Other countries
South America -- Continued
(1541) Venezuela (Table JX3)
Europe
(1542) General works
European communities, see KJE5105
Great Britain. England
(1543) General (Table JX3)
(1545) Scotland (Table JX3)
(1546) Ireland (Table JX3)
(1547) Austria (Table JX3)
(1547.3) Czechoslovakia (Table JX3)
(1548) France (Table JX3)
(1548.3) Monaco (Table JX3)
Germany
(1549) General works
(1549.Z7A2) International relations of the German states to one another
(1549.3) Danzig
(1549.5) Saar
(1550) Greece (Table JX3)
(1550.5) Hungary (Table JX3)
Italy
(1551) General works
(1552) Papacy. States of the Church. Vatican (City) (Table JX3)
Yugoslavia, see JX1564.5
(1552.5) Latvia (Table JX3)
(1553) Belgium (Table JX3)
(1554) Holland (and Netherlands in general) (Table JX3)
(1554.5) Luxembourg (Table JX3)
Russia. Soviet Union
(1555) General (Table JX3)
(1555.7) Poland (Table JX3)
(1555.8) Ukraine (Table JX3)
(1555.9) White Russia (Table JX3)
Scandinavia
(1556) General works
(1557) Denmark (Table JX3)
(1558) Iceland (Table JX3)
(1559) Norway (Table JX3)
(1560) Sweden (Table JX3)
(1562) Portugal (Table JX3)
(1563) Switzerland (Table JX3)
Turkey and the Balkan states
(1564) Bulgaria (Table JX3)
(1564.5) Yugoslavia (Table JX3)
(1565) Montenegro (Table JX3)
(1566) Romania (Table JX3)
(1567) Serbia (Table JX3)

Foreign relations. By country
Other countries
Europe
Turkey and the Balkan states -- Continued
(1568) Turkey and Islamic countries in general (Table JX3)
Including capitulations
Cf. JX841+, Turkey
Asia
(1569) General works
(1570) China (Table JX3)
India
(1571) General (Table JX3)
(1571.5.A-Z) Other British possessions, A-Z (Table JX3)
Indochina
(1572) General works
(1573) French Indochina (Table JX3)
Indonesia
(1574) General (Table JX3)
(1575) Dutch East Indies. Indonesia (Table JX3)
(1576) Philippines (Table JX3)
(1577) Japan (Table JX3)
(1577.5) Korea (Table JX3)
(1578) Iran (Table JX3)
(1579) Soviet Union in Asia (Table JX3)
(1579.5) Thailand (Table JX3)
(1579.7) Taiwan (Table JX3)
(1580) Turkey in Asia (Table JX3)
(1581.A-Z) Other divisions in Asia, A-Z (Table JX3)
Africa
(1582) General works
(1584.A-Z) British possessions, A-Z (Table JX3)
(1584.S7) South Africa
(1584.T8) Transvaal
(1585.A-Z) French possessions, A-Z (Table JX3)
(1586.A-Z) German possessions, A-Z (Table JX3)
(1586.5.A-Z) Italian possessions, A-Z (Table JX3)
(1586.7) Zaire (Table JX3)
(1587.A-Z) Portuguese possessions, A-Z (Table JX3)
(1587.5.A-Z) Spanish possessions, A-Z (Table JX3)
(1588.A-Z) Other divisions of Africa. Native states, A-Z (Table JX3)
Morocco
(1588.M5) Collections
General works. History
(1588.M55) To 1800
(1588.M6) 1800-
For Morocco question, see DT317
(1588.M65) Contemporary works. By date
(1588.M7A-Z) Special topics, A-Z
(1588.M8) Relations with special countries
Australia and New Zealand
(1589) General (Table JX3)

Foreign relations. By country
  Other countries
    Australia and New Zealand -- Continued
(1590) New South Wales
(1591) New Zealand (Table JX3)
(1592) North Australia. Northern Territory
(1593) Queensland
(1594) South Australia
(1595) Tasmania
(1596) Victoria
(1597) Western Australia
(1598.A-Z) Pacific islands, A-Z (Table JX3)
Diplomacy. The Diplomatic Service
(1621) Periodicals
  see JX1-JX18
(1625) Yearbooks, etc.
  Class here general works only
(1628) Societies
(1631) Collections
  Class here general works only
(1632) Codes
(1634) Study and teaching. Schools
  History. Treatises. General works
(1635) Comprehensive
  By period
(1638) Ancient
  Medieval (to 1600)
(1641) Treatises
(1643) Contemporary works
  Modern
(1648) Comprehensive works
  By period
  17th century
(1651) Histories
(1652) Contemporary works, etc.
  18th century
(1654) Histories
(1655) Contemporary works, etc.
  19th century
(1658) Histories
(1659) Contemporary works, etc.
  20th century
(1661) Histories
(1662) Contemporary works, etc.
(1664) Addresses, pamphlets, etc.
  The Diplomatic Service
  Appointment
(1665) Cases, documents, sources
(1666) Treatises
  Credentials
(1668) Cases, documents, sources
(1669) Treatises

JX

Diplomacy. The Diplomatic Service
The Diplomatic Service -- Continued
(1670) Unauthorized negotiations
Including works on their criminal aspects
Powers and privileges. Immunities
(1671) Cases, documents, sources
(1672) Treatises
Duties. Functions
(1674) General works
(1675) To the home government
(1676) To the foreign government
(1677) Diplomatic language, style, etc.
Cf. CD70+, Practice of special chancelleries
Ceremonials. Precedence
(1678) Cases, documents, sources
(1679) Treatises
Dress
(1681) Cases, documents, sources
(1682) Treatises
(1683.A-Z) Other topics, A-Z
(1683.F6) Foreign interests
(1683.G5) Gifts
(1683.P7) Protection of foreign missions
Organization. Administration
Cf. JX1648+, History of the diplomatic service
(1684) General works
Department of foreign affairs. The minister of state or foreign affairs
(1686) Cases, documents, sources
(1687) Treatises
Ambassadors, plenipotentiaries, envoys, etc.
(1691) Cases, documents, sources
(1692) Treatises
Special
Consuls
(1694) General works
History
(1695) Cases, documents, sources
(1696) Treatises
(1698.A-Z) Special topics, A-Z
(1698.A4) Administration of estates
Subarrangement:
1 Treatises
2 Cases, etc.
Invoices, requirements for exporters and importers, see HF5773.C7
(1698.J8) Jurisdiction
Apply table at JX(1698.A4)
(1698.P7) Police
Apply table at JX(1698.A4)
(1698.P8) Priveleges and immunities
Apply table at JX(1698.A4)

Diplomacy. The Diplomatic Service
Organization. Administration
Special
Consuls
Special topics, A-Z -- Continued
(1698.T8) Trade and the consular service
Apply table at JX(1698.A4)
(1699) Other
By country
United States
(1705-1706) General (Table JX6)
(1725.A-W) States, A-W
(1729-1730) Canada (Table JX6)
(1731-1732) Mexico (Table JX6)
Central America
(1733-1734) General
(1735-1736) Belize and Honduras (Table JX6)
(1737-1738) Costa Rica (Table JX6)
(1739) Guatemala (Table JX4)
Honduras, see JX1735+
(1741) Nicaragua (Table JX4)
(1742-1743) Panama (Table JX6)
(1743.5) Panama Canal (Table JX4)
(1744) El Salvador (Table JX4)
West Indies
(1745) General works
(1749-1750) Cuba (Table JX6)
(1751) Haiti (Table JX4)
(1752) Dominican Republic (Table JX4)
(1753) Jamaica (Table JX4)
(1755-1756) Puerto Rico (Table JX6)
(1756.5) U.S. Virgin Islands (Table JX4)
(1757.A-Z) Other, A-Z (Table JX5)
South America
(1758) General works
(1759-1760) Argentina (Table JX6)
(1761-1762) Bolivia (Table JX6)
(1763-1764) Brazil (Table JX6)
(1765-1766) Chile (Table JX6)
(1767-1768) Colombia (Table JX6)
(1769-1770) Ecuador (Table JX6)
Guianas
(1771) General works
(1772) Guyana (Table JX4)
(1772.5) Surinam (Table JX4)
(1772.7) French Guiana (Table JX4)
(1773-1774) Paraguay (Table JX6)
(1775-1776) Peru (Table JX6)
(1777-1778) Uruguay (Table JX6)
(1779-1780) Venezuela (Table JX6)
Europe
(1781) General works
Great Britain. England

Diplomacy. The Diplomatic Service
By country
Europe
Great Britain. England -- Continued
(1783-1784) General (Table JX6)
(1787-1788) Scotland (Table JX6)
(1789-1790) Ireland (Table JX6)
(1791-1792) Austria-Hungary (Table JX6)
(1792.5) Czechoslovakia (Table JX4)
(1793-1794) France (Table JX6)
(1794.5) Monaco (Table JX4)
(1795-1796) Germany (Table JX6)
(1797-1798) Greece (Table JX6)
(1798.5) Hungary (Table JX4)
Italy
(1799-1800) General (Table JX6)
(1801-1802) Papacy. States of the Church. Vatican (City) (Table JX6)
Yugoslavia, see JX1828.5
(1802.5) Latvia
e.g. JX1808.5
(1802.7) Malta (Table JX4)
Netherlands
(1803-1804) Belgium (Table JX6)
(1805-1806) Holland (and Netherlands in General) (Table JX6)
(1806.5) Luxembourg (Table JX4)
Soviet Union. Russia
(1807-1808) General (Table JX6)
(1808.2) Estonia (Table JX4)
(1808.3) Finland (Table JX4)
(1808.5) Latvia (Table JX4)
(1808.6) Lithuania (Table JX4)
(1808.7) Poland (Table JX4)
Scandinavia
(1809-1810) General (Table JX6)
Denmark
(1811-1812) General (Table JX6)
(1813-1814) Iceland (Table JX6)
(1815-1816) Norway (Table JX6)
(1817-1818) Sweden (Table JX6)
(1819-1820) Spain (Table JX6)
(1821-1822) Portugal (Table JX6)
(1823-1824) Switzerland (Table JX6)
Turkey (and Balkan states)
(1825-1826) General (Table JX6)
(1826.5) Albania (Table JX4)
(1827-1828) Bulgaria (Table JX6)
(1828.5) Yugoslavia (Table JX4)
(1829) Montenegro (Table JX4)
(1831-1832) Romania (Table JX6)
(1833-1834) Serbia (Table JX6)
Yugoslavia, see JX1828.5

Diplomacy. The Diplomatic Service
By country -- Continued
Asia
(1835) General works
(1837-1838) China (Table JX6)
(1838.5) Taiwan (Table JX4)
(1839-1840) India (Table JX6)
Indochina
(1841-1842) General (Table JX6)
(1843-1844) French Indochina (Table JX6)
Indonesia
(1845) General works (Table JX4)
(1847-1848) Dutch East Indies. Indonesia (Republic) (Table JX6)
(1849-1850) Philippines (Table JX6)
(1851-1852) Japan (Table JX6)
(1853-1854) Iran (Table JX6)
(1855-1856) Soviet Union in Asia (Table JX6)
(1857-1858) Turkey in Asia (Table JX6)
(1859.A-Z) Other divisions of Asia, A-Z (Table JX5)
Africa
(1861) General works
(1865.A-Z) British possessions, A-Z (Table JX5)
(1867.A-Z) French possessions, A-Z (Table JX5)
(1869.A-Z) German possessions, A-Z (Table JX5)
(1870.A-Z) Italian possessions, A-Z (Table JX5)
(1871.A-Z) Portuguese possessions, A-Z (Table JX5)
(1872.A-Z) Spanish possessions, A-Z (Table JX5)
(1873.A-Z) Other divisions, A-Z (Table JX5)
e.g.
(1873.L4-L6) Liberia
(1873.S5-S7) South African Republic
(1875-1876) Australia and New Zealand (Table JX6)
Pacific islands
(1891) General works
(1893) Hawaii (Table JX4)
(1894.A-Z) Others, A-Z (Table JX5)
(1896) Agents of foreign principals
International arbitration, organization, etc.
Periodicals
(1901) English and American
(1902) French and Belgian
(1903) Other
(1904) Annuals
(1904.5) Study and teaching. Research
(1905) Handbooks, manuals, etc.
Societies, institutions, etc., for the promotion of peace
For publication on special subjects, see the subject
For publications relating to conferences, see JX1930+
(1905.5) Directories
International

International arbitration, organization, etc.
Societies, institutions, etc., for the promotion of peace
International -- Continued
Carnegie endowment for International peace
(1906.A1-A3) Serial publications, collections, etc.
(1906.A5) Charter, etc.
(1906.A6) Announcements, circulars, etc.
(1906.A63-A65) United States public documents
(1906.A63) Collections. By earliest date
(1906.A65) Separate documents. By date
(1906.A7-Z) History
(1906.Z5) Pamphlets
(1907.A-Z) Other, A-Z
For Interparliamentary Union and similar conferences, see JX1930+
(1908.A-Z) Local. By country, A-Z
(1909) Celebrations, festivals, "Peace day", see JX1936.5
Congresses and conferences
(1910) General works. Organization. History
International
The Hague Conferences
(1912) Collections
Including official reports of 1st and 2d conferences
1st Conference (1899)
Official publications
(1913.A1) Preliminary correspondence, etc.
(1913.A13) Acts, proceedings
(1913.A16) Rules, etc.
(1913.A2A-Z) Official publications by countries taking part, A-Z
e.g.
Under each:

1	*Preliminary (Correspondence, etc.)*
2	*Acts, proceedings (Reports of delegates)*
3	*Other (Announcements, etc.)*

Great Britain
(1913.A2G6) Preliminary
(1913.A2G8) Other
(1913.A3-A4) 2d Conference (1907)
Official publications
(1913.A31) Preliminary correspondence, etc.
(1913.A33) Acts, proceedings
(1913.A36) Rules, etc.
(1913.A4A-Z) Official publications by countries taking part, A-Z
Apply table at JX(1913.A2A-Z)
Nonofficial works on the conferences

International arbitration, organization, etc.
Congresses and conferences
International
The Hague Conferences
Nonofficial works
on the conferences -- Continued
(1916) Texts (partial), analyses, commentaries, and other general works
(1918) Popular works
(1919) General special
Special, by subject
see the subject
Permanent Court of Arbitration
Cf. JX1971.5, Hague Permanent Court of International Justice
Cf. JX1990+, International courts
Documents
(1925.A2) Preliminary (Treaties, etc.), by date of issue
(1925.A5) Sessions
(1925.C2) Cases
For special, see the subject or country e. g. JX238.P5, The Pious fund case, United States vs. Mexico
For collections, see JX1991
(1928) General works. Legal, etc.
Other international congresses
(1930.A-1930) Congresses with permanent organization. By name, A-Z
Under each:
1 *Acts, proceedings*
2 *History*
(1931) Other. By date
National congresses
United States
(1932.A-Z) Permanent. By name, A-Z
(1933) Other. By date
(1935.A-Z) Other countries, A-Z
Under each:
1 *By name*
2 *By date*
(1936) Exhibitions. Museums
(1936.5) Celebrations, festivals, "Peace day," etc.
History and other general works
Including popular ethical "peace literature"
Cf. U21+, Ethics of war
(1937) Collections
Including digests
(1938) Comprehensive
By period
(1941) Ancient
(1942) Medieval
Modern
(1944) General works

International arbitration, organization, etc.
History and other general works
By period
Modern -- Continued
(1945) 17th century
(1946) 18th century
19th century
International arbitration, world peace, etc.
(1948) Treatises
(1949) Popular works
(1950) International organization
Cf. JC362, Internationalism
20th century
International arbitration, world peace, etc.
(1952) Treatises
(1953) Popular works
(1953.5) Juvenile literature
(1954) International organization
Cf. JC362, Internationalism
(1961.A-Z) By country, A-Z
Cf. JX1515+, Foreign relations
(1961.A3) America
(1962.A-Z) Biography, A-Z
(1962.A2) Collected
(1964) Illustrative material. Fiction, etc.
Including imaginary wars (works written to show the horrors of war)
Each imaginary wars may also be classed as follows:
1 *Works illustrating tactical problems in Class U*
2 *Works showing weakness of national defense in Class U*
3 *Works illustrating wolrd politics: D445*
4 *Works chiefly notable as Literature in Class P*
5 *General tactical works in U313; to which place reference should be made for all books*
(1964.3) Labor and war
(1964.4) Moving pictures and peace
(1964.5) Press and peace movements
(1964.7) Radio broadcasting and peace
(1965) Woman and peace movements
Cf. HQ1399, Women and civilization
(1965.5) Youth and peace movements
(1966) Theory, Philosophy
see U21
Special topics
(1968) Compromisory clause
(1970) Compulsory arbitration

	International arbitration, organization, etc.
	Special topics -- Continued
	Courts of international arbitration
	Cf. JX1925+, Hague Permanent Court of Arbitration
	Cf. JX1990+, International courts
(1971)	General works
(1971.5)	Permanent Court of International Justice
(1971.6)	International Court of Justice
	Disarmament. Arms control
	Cf. HC79.D4, Economic impact of defense and disarmament
	Cf. UA17, Army budgets
(1974)	General works
	Conference on the limitation of armament, Washington, D.C., 1921-1922
(1974.5)	General works
	Documents
(1974.5.A15)	Collections of preliminary documents
(1974.5.A2)	1st-3d plenary sessions
(1974.5.A3)	Proposal of the United States for the limitation of naval armament
(1974.5.A5)	Address of the President at concluding session
(1974.5.A6A-Z)	Documents. By country, A-Z
(1974.5.A7A-Z)	Special missions. By country, A-Z
(1974.5.A9-Z)	Works. By author (or title), A-Z
	Nuclear weapons
(1974.7)	General works
(1974.73)	Nuclear nonproliferation
	Nuclear-weapon-free-zones
(1974.735)	General works
(1974.74.A-Z)	By region or country, A-Z
(1974.74.L38)	Latin America
(1974.75)	Strategic Arms Limitation Talks, I, 1969. Strategic Arms Limitation Talks II, 1979
(1974.76)	Strategic Arms Reduction Talks
(1974.8)	Nuclear crisis control
	League of nations
(1975.A1)	Periodicals. Societies. Yearbooks
	Documents
	Collected sets
(1975.A2)	By "Official number"
(1975.A25)	By "Sales number"
	Including Series of League of Nations Publications
(1975.A3)	Official journal
(1975.A37)	Monthly summary
	Texts of the covenant
(1975.A39)	English. By date
(1975.A392A-11975.	Other languages, A-Z
(1975.A393)	Amendments to the covenant. By date
(1975.A395)	Proposed amendments. By date

International arbitration, organization, etc.
Special topics
League of nations
Documents
Texts of the covenant -- Continued
(1975.A397) Reports on application of the covenant. By date
Assembly
Records (Actes)
Committees
(1975.A42) General works
(1975.A422) Index to the records
Including Plenary meetings and committees
(1975.A423) Plenary meetings
(1975.A425) Journal
(1975.A43) Special reports of Assembly meetings. By date
(1975.A433) List of delegates
(1975.A435) Guide officiel. Official guide
(1975.A437) Miscellaneous documents. By date
(1975.A438) Rules of procedure. By date
(1975.A439A-Z) Reports of national delegates or delegations. By country, A-Z
Council
(1975.A44) Procès-verbaux. Minutes
Report on the work of the League
(1975.A4415) English edition
(1975.A4416) French edition
(1975.A45) Special reports of Council meetings. By date
(1975.A455) Miscellaneous documents. By date
(1975.A46A-Z) Council reports of special representatives. By country, A-Z
(1975.A465) Rules of procedure. By date
Secretariat. Secretary-General
(1975.A488) Serials
(1975.A49) Nonserial documents. By date
(1975.A5-Z) General works
(1975.5.A-Z) League of Nations in relation to individual countries, A-Z
(1975.5.A2) Collective
(1975.6) Sanctions
Including enonomic and military
(1975.7) Geneva protocol
Including protocol for the pacific settlement of international disputes
High Commission for Refugees
(1975.8.A1) General works
(1975.8.A3-Z) By country
e. g.
(1975.8.G3) Refugees from Germany
(1975.9) Miscellaneous
Class here drama, juvenile works, cartoons, women's work, etc.

International arbitration, organization, etc.
Special topics -- Continued
United Nations
(1976) Genesis of the United Nations
Including preliminary congresses in general
(1976.3) Dunbarton Oaks Conversations, 1944
(1976.4) San Francisco Conference, 1945
(1976.5) Preparatory Commission of the United Nations
(1976.8.A-Z) Ratification of the United Nations Charter. By country, A-Z
United Nations, 1946-
(1977.A1) Periodicals. Societies, etc.
Documents
Texts of the charter
(1977.A15) English. By date
(1977.A16.A-Z) Other languages, A-Z
Collected set
(1977.A2) English edition
(1977.A212) French edition
(1977.A213) Spanish edition
(1977.A22) Journal
Bulletin
(1977.A3) English edition
(1977.A314) French edition
(1977.A315) Spanish edition
(1977.A3155.A-Z) Resolutions. By editor or compiler, A-Z
Secretariat. Secretary-General
Including subordinate departments, committees, and library
(1977.A316-A359) Serials
Arranged alphabetically by subheading
(1977.A36) Nonserial documents. By date
(1977.A362.A-Z) Nonofficial publications. By author, A-Z
(1977.A365) Administrative tribunal
General handbooks, manuals, etc.
(1977.A37.A-Z) Serial. By title, A-Z
(1977.A38) Nonserial. By date
(1977.A39) Other documents. By date
Including advisory groups, committees, etc., of the United Nations
General Assembly
(1977.A4) General works
Official records
(1977.A41) English edition
(1977.A417) French edition
(1977.A418) Spanish edition
Journal
(1977.A42) English edition
(1977.A422) French edition
(1977.A423-A46) Other serials
(1977.A47) Nonserial documents of individual sessions. By date

International arbitration, organization, etc.
Special topics
United Nations
United Nations, 1946-
Documents
General Assembly -- Continued

(1977.A48) Reports of national delegations accredited to the General Assembly
Subarranged by country, A-Z, using two successive Cutter numbers for serials and nonserials (by date)
(1977.A49) Miscellaneous documents. By date
(1977.A495.A-Z) Nonofficial publications. By author, A-Z
Security Council
(1977.A5) General works
(1977.A51) Journal
(1977.A515) Official records
(1977.A52) Report to the General Assembly
(1977.A54) Nonserial documents of meetings. By date
Prefer classification by subject in Classes, B-Z
(1977.A59) Miscellaneous documents. By date
(1977.A593.A-Z) Nonofficial publications. By author, A-Z
(1977.A595) Selected documents. By compiler
(1977.A6-Z7) General works
(1977.Z8) Popular and juvenile works
United Nations in relation to regional organizations
(1977.18.A2) General
(1977.18.A3-Z) By organization, A-Z
(1977.2.A-Z) United Nations in relation to individual countries, A-Z
e.g.
(1977.2.A1) Collective
(1977.25) Relations with non-member nations
For individual countries, see JX1977.2.A+
(1977.3) United Nations in relation to learned societies, universities, etc.
Class cooperation in special projects with the project
(1977.3.A2) General works
(1977.3.A3-Z) By society, university, etc.
(1977.8.A-Z) Special topics, A-Z
(1977.8.D6) Documentation
Employees, see JX1977.8.O35
(1977.8.F5) Finance
(1977.8.H4) Headquarters
(1977.8.L35) Languages. Translating
(1977.8.M4) Membership
(1977.8.O35) Officials and employees
(1977.8.P7) Police force
see JX1981.P7
(1977.8.P8) Postal administration

International arbitration, organization, etc.
Special topics
United Nations
United Nations, 1946-
Special topics, A-Z -- Continued
(1977.8.S3) Sanctions
(1977.8.T4) Technical assistance
Translating, see JX1977.8.L35
(1977.8.T7) Treaty-making power
(1977.8.V4) Veto
(1977.8.V6) Voting
(1979) Regional organization. Regionalism
(1981.A-Z) Other, A-Z
e. g.
(1981.A35) Air force (International)
Bible and war, see BS680.W2
(1981.B65) Boundary disputes
(1981.N8) Nullity
(1981.P3) Papacy
(1981.P7) Police, International
(1981.T45) Terrorism
Arbitration treaties
(1985) General collections
(1987-1987.Z) United States
(1987) General works
(1987.A1-Z3) Collections
Treaties with several countries collectively
(1987.A4) Documents. By date of signature (or if better known, date of ratification)
(1987.A42.A-Z) General works
(1987.A5-Z) Separate treaties. By country, A-Z
(1988.A-Z) Other countries, A-Z (Collections)
(1989) Other treaties (to which United States is not a party, by date (year and month)
International courts
Cf. JX1971+, Courts of international arbitration
Cf. JX5428, International criminal courts
(1990.A2) General works
(1990.A3-Z) Individual courts
(1990.C2) Cartago, Costa Rica. Corte de justicia centroamericana
Hague. Permanent Court of Arbitration, see JX1925+
Hague. Permanent Court of International Justice, see JX1971+

International arbitration, organization, etc.
International courts -- Continued
Arbitration cases
For collections, by country, and particular cases, see JX200-JX1195, subdivision 8 and 9, under each country
Under each:
.A2-.A28 *Collections of cases of the Hague Permanent Court of Arbitration, chronologically*
.A3-.Z *Other collections. By editor, A-Z*
(1995) International unions, bureaus, "conventions," congresses
Cf. JC362, Internationalism
Cf. JX1245+, Theory
International law
Treatises (History and theory)
Ancient
(2001) Collections. Sources. Documents
(2005) General works
Oriental states
(2008) General works
(2009.A-Z) Special, A-Z
e. g. Assyro-Babylonian Empire; Egypt; Hebrews; Phoenicia
Greece
(2011) General works
(2014.A-Z) Special topics, A-Z
(2014.R5) Rhodian law
(2014.T7) Treaties
Roman
(2021) General works
Special topics
(2025) Jus feciale
(2027) Jus gentium
(2029) Jus sacrum
(2035.A-Z) Other, A-Z
Medieval (To circa 1500)
(2041) General works
Consulate of the sea, see K1163.C6, K1163.O4
(2051.A-Z) Other special topics, A-Z
Laws of Trani, see K1163.T7
(2055) Islamic countries
see JX1568
(2060.A-Z) Individual publicists, A-Z
(2060.T4) Saint Thomas Aquinas
Modern
1500-1713
(2061) General works
(2066) Special topics

International law
Treatises (History and theory)
Modern
1500-1713 -- Continued
(2069) Treatises on the "Jus naturae et gentium"
Added entry to be made in the shelflist under this number; the works are in JC137-JC291, JX2072-JX2799, and Class K
Individual publicists
Class here collected works and works of general theoretical character only (including compends)
(2070-2071) Alonso de la Vera Cruz (Table JX7)
(2072-2073) Ayala (Table JX7)
(2075-2076) Bodin (Table JX7)
(2081-2082) Brunus (Table JX7)
(2083) Brunus to Cumberland (Table JX9)
(2084-2085) Cumberland (Table JX7)
(2086) Cumberland to Gentilisk (Table JX9)
(2087-2088) Gentilis (Table JX7)
(2091-2099) Grotius (Table JX8)
(2103-2104) Hobbes (Table JX7)
(2107) Hobbes-Leibnitz (Table JX9)
(2109-2110) Leibnitz (Table JX7)
(2112-2113) Loccenius (Table JX7)
(2115-2116) Machiavellii (Table JX7)
(2117) Machiavellii to Molloy (Table JX9)
(2118-2119) Malloy (Table JX7)
(2125-2126) Peckius (Table JX7)
(2131-2139) Pufendorf (Table JX8)
Cf. JC156, Political theory
(2141-2142) Rachel (Table JX7)
(2144-2145) Santerna (Table JX7)
(2147-2148) Selden (Table JX7)
(2155-2156) Suárez (Table JX7)
(2157) Suárez to Victoria (Table JX9)
(2158-2159) Vitoria (Table JX7)
(2161-2169) Wicquefort (Table JX8)
(2181-2182) Zouch (Table JX7)
18th century
(2206) General works
(2215) Special topics
English publicists
(2220) A to Bentham (Table JX9)
(2221-2222) Bentham (Table JX7)
(2223) Bentham to Fulbeck (Table JX9)
(2225-2226) Fulbeck (Table JX7)
(2227) Fulbeck to Rutherforth (Table JX9)
(2231-2232) Rutherforth (Table JX7)
(2233) Rutherforth to Z (Table JX9)
Dutch publicists
(2242) A to Bynkershoek (Table JX9)
(2243-2244) Bynkershoek (Table JX7)

International law
  Treatises (History and theory)
    Modern
      18th century
        Dutch publicists -- Continued
(2245) Bynershoek to Z (Table JX9)
        French publicists
(2260) A to Mably (Table JX9)
(2261-2262) Mably (Table JX7)
(2266) Mably to Montesquieu (Table JX9)
(2271-2272) Montesquieu (Table JX7)
(2273) Montesquieu to Neyron (Table JX9)
(2274-2275) Neyron (Table JX7)
(2276) Neyron to Z (Table JX9)
        German publicists
(2303-2304) Achenwall (Table JX7)
(2305) Achenwall to Glafey (Table JX9)
(2305.E5) Eggers
(2306-2307) Glafey (Table JX7)
(2308) Glafey to Günther (Table JX9)
(2311-2312) Günther (Table JX7)
(2313) Günther to Heineccius (Table JX9)
(2314-2315) Heineccius (Heinecke) (Table JX7)
(2316) Heineccius to Kant (Table JX9)
(2321-2322) Kant (Table JX7)
(2323) Kant to Martens (Table JX9)
(2323.K7) Köhler, H.
(2324-2325) Martens, G.F. von
see JX2814-JX2815
(2326) Martens to Moser (Table JX9)
(2328-2329) Moser, F.C. (Table JX7)
(2332-2333) Moser, J.J. (Table JX7)
(2334) Moser to Ompteda (Table JX9)
(2335-2336) Ompteda (Table JX7)
(2339) Ompteda to Thomasius (Table JX9)
(2339.R7) Römer, C.H. von
(2344-2345) Thomasius (Table JX7)
(2346) Thomasius to Wolff (Table JX9)
(2346.W2) Weidler
(2346.W3) Wenck
(2347-2348) Wolff, C. von (Table JX7)
(2349) Wolff to Z (Table JX9)
(2349.Z3) Zechin
        Italian publicists
(2370) A to Azuni (Table JX9)
(2371-2372) Azuni (Table JX7)
Cf. JX4410, Maritime law
(2373) Azuni to Lampredi (Table JX9)
(2374-2375) Lampredi (Table JX7)
(2379) Lampredi to Z (Table JX9)
(2388.A-Z) Spanish and Portuguese publicists, A-Z (Table JX9)
(2388.M8) Muriel, Domingo (Morelli)

International law
Treatises (History and theory)
Modern
18th century
Spanish and Portuguese publicists, A-Z -- Continued

(2388.05) Olmeda y Leon
(2388.07) Ortega y Cotes
Scandinavian publicists
(2391) A to Hübner (Table JX9)
Eggers, see JX2305.E5
(2393-2394) Hübner (Table JX7)
(2395) Hübner to Z (Table JX9)
Swiss publicists
(2400) A to Burlamaqui (Table JX9)
(2401-2402) Burlamaqui (Table JX7)
(2406) Burlamaqui to Vattel (Table JX9)
e.g.
(2406.F4) Félice, F.B.
(2411-2419) Vattel (Table JX8)
(2420) Vattel to Z (Table JX9)
(2435.A-Z) Other. By country, A-Z (Table JX9)
(2435.P7) Polish
19th century
(2441) General works
(2446) Special topics
American publicists
(2451) A to Davis, C. (Table JX9)
(2451.B6) Bowen, H.W.
(2455-2456) Davis, C.K. (Table JX7)
(2458-2459) Davis, G. B. (Table JX7)
(2460) Davis, G. B., to Field (Table JX9)
(2460.D7) Duane
(2464-2465) Field, D.D. (Table JX7)
(2467-2468) Gallaudet (Table JX7)
(2469) Gallaudet to Halleck (Table JX9)
(2469.G2) Gardner
(2469.G4) Glenn
(2475-2476) Halleck (Table JX7)
(2478-2479) Kent (Table JX7)
(2480) Kent to Lawrence, W.B. (Table JX9)
(2481-2482) Lawrence, W.B. (Table JX7)
(2483) Lawrence to Snow (Table JX9)
(2483.L6) Lieber
(2483.P7) Pomeroy
(2483.S3) Schuyler
(2486-2487) Snow (Table JX7)
(2489-2490) Story (Table JX7)
(2492-2493) Wharton (Table JX7)
(2495-2496) Wheaton (Table JX7)
(2499-2499) Woolsey (Table JX7)
(2500) Woolsey to Z (Table JX9)
(2502.A-Z) Dutch publicists, A-Z (Table JX9)

International law
Treatises (History and theory)
Modern
19th century -- Continued
English publicists
(2503) A to Amos (Table JX9)
(2505-2506) Amos (Table JX7)
Amos to Creasy (Table JX9)
(2514-2515) Creasy (Table JX7)
(2523) Creasy to Hall (Table JX9)
(2523.G6) Griffith, W.
(2524-2525) Hall, W.E. (Table JX7)
(2527-2528) Hertslet (Table JX7)
(2529) Hertslet to Holland (Table JX9)
(2531-2532) Holland (Table JX7)
(2533) Holland to Hosack (Table JX9)
(2538-2539) Hosack (Table JX7)
(2540) Hosack to Lawrence (Table JX9)
(2542-2543) Lawrence, T.J. (Table JX7)
(2545-2546) Levi (Table JX7)
(2548-2549) Lorimer (Table JX7)
(2550) Lorimer to Mackintosh (Table JX9)
(2552-2553) Mackintosh (Table JX7)
(2554) Mackintosh to Maine (Table JX9)
(2555-2556) Maine, Sir Henry (Table JX7)
(2558-2559) Manning (Table JX7)
(2564) Manning to Phillimore (Table JX9)
(2564.M5) Miller, William G.
(2565-2566) Phillimore (Table JX7)
(2567) Phillimore to Polson (Table JX9)
(2572-2573) Polson (Table JX7)
(2574) Polson to Stowell (Table JX9)
(2578-2579) Stowell (Table JX7)
(2580) Stowell to Twiss (Table JX9)
(2582-2583) Twiss (Table JX7)
(2584) Twiss to Ward (Table JX9)
(2584.W3) Walker
(2585-2586) Ward, Robert Plumer (Table JX7)
(2588-2589) Westlake (Table JX7)
(2590) Westlake to Wildman (Table JX9)
(2592-2593) Wildman (Table JX7)
(2594) Wildman to Z (Table JX9)
French and Belgian publicists
(2607) A to Bonfils (Table JX9)
(2608-2609) Bonfils (Table JX7)
(2613) Bonfils to Cauchy (Table JX9)
(2613.B8) Bry, Georges
(2614-2615) Cauchy (Table JX7)
(2616) Cauchy to Cussy (Table JX9)
(2616.C4) Chrétien
(2624-2625) Cussy (Table JX7)
(2626) Cussy to Despagnet (Table JX9)
(2641-2642) Despagnet (Table JX7)

International law
Treatises (History and theory)
Modern
19th century
French and Belgian publicists -- Continued
(2643) Despagnet to Fauchille (Table JX9)
(2651-2652) Fauchille (Table JX7)
(2656) Fauchille to Féraud (Table JX9)
(2658-2659) Féraud-Giraud (Table JX7)
(2660) Féraud to Funck (Table JX9)
(2668-2669) Funck-Bretano (Table JX7)
(2671-2672) Garden, Guillaume de, comte (Table JX7)
(2673) Garden to Laveleye (Table JX9)
(2673.G2) Gérard de Rayneval
(2673.G4) Gondon
(2687-2688) Laveleye (Table JX7)
(2701) Laveleye to Nys (Table JX9)
(2701.L3) Leseur
(2701.M3) Michel, C.L.S.
(2702-2703) Nys (Table JX7)
(2704) Nys to Piédelièvre (Table JX9)
(2714-2715) Piédelièvre (Table JX7)
(2716) Piédelièvre to Pradier (Table JX9)
(2725-2726) Pradie-Fodéré (Table JX7)
(2728-2729) Proudhon (Table JX7)
(2730) Proudhon to Renault (Table JX9)
(2735-2736) Renault (Table JX7)
(2737) Renault to Rivier (Table JX9)
(2739-2740) Rivier (Table JX7)
(2742-2743) Rolin-Jacquemnyns (Table JX7)
(2745-2746) Rouard de Card (Table JX7)
(2747) Rouard to Sorel (Table JX9)
(2751-2752) Sorel (Table JX7)
(2753) Sorel to Z (Table JX9)
German and Austrian publicists
(2774) A to Bluntschli (Table JX9)
(2775-2776) Bluntschli (Table JX7)
(2778-2779) Bulmerincq (Table JX7)
(2781-2782) Gagern (Table JX7)
(2783) Gagern to Gz (Table JX9)
(2783.G3) Gareis
(2786) H to Heffter (Table JX9)
(2786.H3) Hartmann
(2787-2788) Heffter (Table JX7)
(2789) Heffter to Holtzendorff (Table JX9)
(2789.H3) Heilborn
(2791-2792) Holtzendorff (Table JX7)
(2793) Holtzendorff to Kaltenborn (Table JX9)
(2797-2798) Kaltenborn von Strachau (Table JX7)
(2799) Kaltenborn to Kamptz (Table JX9)
(2801-2802) Kamptz (Table JX7)
(2804-2805) Klüber (Table JX7)
(2806) Klüber to Lasson (Table JX9)

International law
Treatises (History and theory)
Modern
19th century
German and Austrian publicists -- Continued
(2811-2812) Lasson, Adolf (Table JX7)
(2814-2815) Martens, G.F. von (Table JX7)
(2817-2818) Neumann (Table JX7)
(2819) Neumann to Oppenheim (Table JX9)
(2821-2822) Oppenheim, H.B. (Table JX7)
(2824) Oppenheim to Saafeld (Table JX9)
(2824.P7) Pölitz
(2824.Q3) Quaritsch
(2824.R3) Resch
(2826-2827) Saafeld (Table JX7)
(2828) Saafeld to Savigny (Table JX9)
(2831-2832) Savigny (Table JX7)
(2833) Savigny to Schmalz (Table JX9)
(2834-2835) Schmalz (Table JX7)
(2836) Schmalz to Schulze (Table JX9)
(2836.S4) Schmelzing
(2838-2839) Schulze (Table JX7)
(2841-2842) Stoerk (Table JX7)
(2843) Stoerk to Z (Table JX9)
(2843.U6) Ullmann
Greek publicists
(2844) A to Saripoulos (Table JX9)
(2845-2846) Saripoulos (Table JX7)
(2847) Saripoulos to Z (Table JX9)
Italian publicists
(2857) A to Carnazza (Table JX9)
(2858-2859) Carnazza-Amari (Table JX7)
(2860) Carnazza to Casanova (Table JX9)
(2862-2863) Casanova (Table JX7)
(2865-2866) Celli (Table JX7)
(2868-2869) Contuzzi (Table JX7)
(2870) Contuzzi to Del Bon (Table JX9)
(2872-2873) Del Bon (Table JX7)
(2875-2876) Esperson (Table JX7)
(2878-2879) Ferrero Gola (Table JX7)
(2881-2882) Fiore (Table JX7)
(2883) Fiore to Grasso (Table JX9)
(2887-2888) Grasso (Table JX7)
(2889) Grasso to Macri (Table JX9)
(2894-2895) Macri (Table JX7)
(2897-2898) Mamiani (Table JX7)
(2899) Mamiani to Morello (Table JX9)
(2904-2905) Morello (Table JX7)
(2910) Morello to Pertile (Table JX9)
(2910.O7) Olivi, Luigi
(2914-2915) Pertile (Table JX7)
(2917-2918) Pierantoni (Table JX7)
(2919) Pierantoni to Sandonà (Table JX9)

International law
Treatises (History and theory)
Modern
19th century
Italian publicists -- Continued
(2924-2925) Sandonà (Table JX9)
(2926) Sandonà to Schiattarella (Table JX9)
(2928-2829) Schiattarella (Table JX7)
(2930) Schiattarella to Z (Table JX9)
Russian publicists
(2940) A to Bergholm (Table JX9)
(2941-2942) Bergholm (Table JX7)
(2943) Bergholm to Martens (Table JX9)
Bulmerincq, see JX2778+
(2951-2952) Martens, F.F. (Table JX7)
(2953) Martens to Z (Table JX9)
Scandinavian publicists
(2954) A to Matzen (Table JX9)
(2955-2956) Matzen (Table JX7)
(2957) Matzen to Tetens (Table JX9)
(2961-2962) Tetens (Table JX7)
(2963) Tetens to Z (Table JX9)
Spanish, Portuguese, and Latin-American publicists
(2966) A to Alcorta (Table JX9)
(2967-2968) Alcorta (Table JX7)
(2969) Alcorta to Arenal (Table JX9)
(2975-2976) Arenal (Table JX7)
(2977) Arenal to Bello (Table JX9)
(2978-2979) Bello (Table JX7)
(2980) Bello to Calvo (Table JX9)
(2980.C3) Calcaño
(2984-2985) Calvo (Table JX7)
(2986) Calvo to Ferrater (Table JX9)
(2986.C7) Cruchaga Tocornal
(2986.D5) Diez de Medina
(2991-2992) Ferrater (Table JX7)
(2994-2995) Ferrater, R. (Table JX7)
(2996) Ferrater to Gestoso (Table JX9)
(3001-3002) Gestoso y Acosto (Table JX7)
(3003) Gestoso to Labra (Table JX9)
(3007-3008) Labra y Cadrana (Table JX7)
(3015) Labra to López Sánchez (Table JX9)
(3015.L5) López, José F.
(3017-3018) López Sánchez (Table JX7)
(3019) López to Madiedo (Table JX9)
(3021-3022) Madiedo, Manuel M. (Table JX7)
(3027) Madiedo to Mozo (Table JX9)
(3027.M5) Montúfar y Rivera Maestre
(3027.M6) Moreira de Almeida
(3028-3029) Mozo (Table JX7)
(3030) Mozo to Olivart (Table JX9)
(3034-3035) Olivart (Table JX7)

International law
Treatises (History and theory)
Modern
19th century
Spanish, Portuguese, and Latin-American publicists -- Continued

(3036) Olivart to Pando (Table JX9)
(3038-3039) Pando (Table JX7)
(3040) Pando to Pinheiro (Table JX9)
(3040.P4) Pérez Gomar, Gregorio
(3041-3042) Pinheiro-Ferreira (Table JX7)
(3043) Pinheiro to Riquelme (Table JX9)
(3045-3046) Riquelme (Table JX7)
(3047.R4) Rodríguez Saráchaga (Table JX9)
(3048-3049) Seijas (Table JX7)
(3050) Seijas to Torres Campos (Table JX9)
(3055-3056) Torres Campos (Table JX7)
(3058-3059) Tremosa y Nadal (Table JX7)
(3060) Tremosa to Z (Table JX9)
(3085.A-Z) Other. By nationality, A-Z (Table JX9)
(3085.H8) Hungarian

20th century
(3091) General works
(3096) Special topics

American publicists
(3110) A to Hershey (Table JX9)
(3110.F6) Foulke, R.R.
(3110.H3) Hall, A.B.
(3131-3132) Hershey, Amos S. (Table JX7)
(3140) Hershey to Maxey (Table JX9)
(3140.H8) Hyde, C.C.
(3151-3152) Maxey (Table JX7)
(3160) Maxey to Scott (Table JX9)
(3160.R4) Root, Elihu
(3178-3179) Scott, J. Brown (Table JX7)
(3180) Scott to Taylor (Table JX9)
(3180.S4) Singer, B.
(3180.S7) Stockton, C.H.
(3181-3182) Taylor, Hannis (Table JX7)
(3185) Taylor to Wilson (Table JX9)
(3191-3192) Wilson, George C. (Table JX7)
(3195) Wilson to Z (Table JX9)

English publicists
Including Canadian publicists
(3205) A to Baker (Table JX9)
(3211-3212) Baker, Sir George S. (Table JX7)
(3215) Baker to Birkenhead (Table JX9)
(3215.B3) Baty, Thomas
(3220-3221) Birkenhead, Frederick Edwin Smith, baron (Table JX7)
(3225) Birkenhead to Oppenehim (Table JX9)
(3225.B8) Burns, C.D.
(3264-3265) Oppenheim, Lassa F.L. (Table JX7)

International law
Treatises (History and theory)
Modern
20th century
English publicists -- Continued
(3275) Oppenheim to Smith (Table JX9)
(3275.P5) Plater, C.D.
(3281-3282) Smith, Frederick Edwin
see JX3220-JX3221
(3295) Smith to Z (Table JX9)
French and Belgian publicists
(3310) A to Mérignhac (Table JX9)
(3351-3352) Mérignhac (Table JX7)
(3375) Mérignhac to Z (Table JX9)
German, Austrian, etc., publicists
(3425) A to Liszt (Table JX9)
(3425.C9) Cybichowski
(3425.K7) Kohler
(3445-3446) Liszt, Franz von (Table JX7)
(3491) Liszt to Z (Table JX9)
(3491.P6) Pohl, H.
(3491.S5) Schucking, W.M.A.
(3491.Z5) Zorn
(3545.A-Z) Italian publicists, A-Z (Table JX9)
(3545.C3) Cavarreta
(3545.D4) Diena, G.
(3545.L5) Lomonaco
(3545.M3) Marino
(3651.A-Z) Spanish publicists, A-Z (Table JX9)
Including Portuguese and Latin American specialists
(3651.A6) Alvarez, A.
(3651.B3) Bevilagua, C.
(3651.C3) Cavalcanti
(3651.D4) Díaz de Medina
(3651.F3) Fernández Prida
(3651.F5) Flores y Flores
(3651.G2) García Alvarez
(3651.P7) Planos Suárez
(3651.R7) Romanos
(3651.S3) Sarmiento Laspiur
(3695.A-Z) Other. By nationality, A-Z (Table JX9)
Dutch
(3695.D8L5) Jitta
(3695.D8L6) Louter
Norwegian
Russian
(3695.R9K3) Kazanski
(3695.R9U4) Ulianitskii
Treatises on special topics
(4000) The individual as subject of international law
The state as subject of international law

International law
Treatises on special topics
International persons
The state as subject
of international law -- Continued
(4003) General special. The international community
Including fundamental rights of states from the standpoint of international law
Sovereign states
General, see JX4041+
(4005) Unions of sovereign states. Alliances. Federation (from the standpoint of international law)
Cf. JC11+, Political theory
Cf. JF5.2+, Constitutional history
(4008) Suzerain states
Semisovereign, dependent, and vassal states
Cf. JV1+, Colonies
(4011) General works
(4015) Mediatized states
Protected states. Protectorates. Spheres of influence. Mandates. International trusteeships
(4021) General works
(4023.A-Z) By region or country, A-Z
(4025) Vassal states
(4027) Colonies (from viewpoint of international law)
Servitudes, see JX4068.S5
Neutralized states. Neutralization
Cf. JX1305+, Neutrality policy
Cf. JX5355+, Neutrality in war
(4031) General works
(4033.A-Z) Special states, A-Z
e. g.
(4033.B4) Belgium
(4033.D4) Dominican Republic
(4033.L9) Luxemburg
(4033.S9) Switzerland
(4035) Regions: Rivers, canals, etc. (General)
Cf. HE385+, International waterways
Cf. JX1398+, Panama Canal
Cf. JX4122, Rivers
Cf. JX4150, International rivers and waterways
Cf. TC770, Ship canals
Sovereignty
Cf. JC11+, Political theory
(4041) General (from standpoint of international law)
(4044) Recognition of sovereignty
Cf. JX4574, Recognition of belligerency
Transfer of sovereignty. State succession
(4053) General works
(4054) International plebiscite

International law
Treatises on special topics
International persons
The state as subject of international law
Sovereignty -- Continued
Special
(4055) State dismemberment. Civil war
Cf. JC491, Change of form of the state
(4061) Dissolution of a state
(4068.A-Z) Other, A-Z
(4068.C7) Condominium
(4068.E92) Exclaves
Free cities, see JX4068.I6
(4068.G6) Governments in exile
(4068.I6) Internationalized territories. "Free cities"
(4068.S5) Servitudes
(4068.S8) State bankruptcy
Means of protecting independence.
Self-preservation. Noninterference
Cf. JX4001+, The state as a subject of international law
Cf. JX4481, Intervention
(4071) General works
(4077) Exterritorial self-defense
(4079.A-Z) Other special, A-Z
e.g.
(4079.N4) Necessity, Doctrine
(4079.P7) Propaganda
(4081) International courtesy. Comitas. Court-oisie. Precedence
(4084) International status of particular states, regions, organizations, etc.
(4084.A13) Aegean Islands (Greece and Turkey)
(4084.A15) Aland Islands
(4084.A34) Afghanistan
(4084.A43) Algeria
(4084.A45) Alsace
(4084.A5) Antartic regions
see KWX
Arabistan, see JX4084.K45
(4084.A68) Arctic regions
(4084.A7) Armenia
(4084.A8) Austria
(4084.A86) Aves Island
(4084.B3) Bali (Island)
(4084.B314) Baltic Sea
(4084.B3146) Baltic States
(4084.B315) Baltic Straits
Including Skagerrak, Kattegat and The Sound
(4084.B32) Bangladesh
(4084.B35) Barents Sea

JX

International law
Treatises on special topics
International persons
The state as subject of international law
International status of particular states, regions, organizations, etc. -- Continued

(4084.B38) Berlin
(4084.B4) Bessarabia
(4084.B55) Black Sea
(4084.B75) British West Indies
(4084.B8) Bukowina
(4084.C33) Cameroon
(4084.C34) Canary Islands
(4084.C5) China
(4084.C52) China (People's Republic of China, 1949-)
(4084.C6) Commonwealth of Nations
(4084.C63) Constance, Lake of
(4084.C86) Cyprus
(4084.C9) Czechoslovakia
(4084.D64) Dodecanese
(4084.D68) Dover, Strait of
(4084.E65) Epirus (Greece and Albania)
(4084.E9) Euphrates River
(4084.F34) Falkland Islands
Formosa, see JX4084.T25
(4084.G3) Germany (General) and Federal Republic, 1949-
(4084.G4) Germany (Democratic Republic, 1949-)
(4084.G5) Gibraltar
(4084.G52) Gibraltar, Strait of
(4084.H66) Hong Kong
(4084.I7) Irian Barat, Indonesia
(4084.I8) Israel. Palestine
(4084.J3) Japan
(4084.J4) Jerusalem
(4084.J67) Jordan (Territory under Israeli occupation, 1967-)
Kangwane (South Africa), see JX4084.S62
(4084.K34) Kashmir
Kattegat (Denmark and Sweden), see JX4084.B315
(4084.K45) Khuzistan, Iran. Arabistan
(4084.K48) Kiel Canal (Germany)
(4084.K55) Knights of Malta
(4084.K67) Korea
(4084.K673) Korea (Democratic People's Republic)
(4084.K82) Kuril Islands
(4084.K83) Kwantung, Leased Territory, China
(4084.M24) Maddalena Island (Italy)
Including Maddalena Archipelago (Italy)
(4084.M28) Magellan, Strait of
(4084.M3) Malacca, Strait of
Malta, Knights of, see JX4084.K55

International law
Treatises on special topics
International persons
The state as subject of international law
International status of particular states, regions, organizations, etc. -- Continued

(4084.M44) Memel (Klaipéda, Lith.)
(4084.M65) Montenegro (Yugoslavia)
Namibia, see JX4084.S68
(4084.N4) Near East
(4084.N45) Netherlands Antilles
(4084.N65) North Sea
(4084.P27) Pacific Islands (Ter.)
(4084.P28) Paracel Islands
Including Spratly Islands
(4084.P39) Persian Gulf
(4084.P4) Persian Gulf States
(4084.P65) Polar regions
(4084.P66) Pomerian Bay
(4084.P9) Puerto Rico
(4084.R5) Rhodesia, Southern
(4084.R65) Romania
(4084.R9) Ryukyu Islands
(4084.S3) Saarland
(4084.S32) Sabah
(4084.S36) San Andres y Providencia (Colombia)
(4084.S45) Senkaku Islands
(4084.S5) Silesia
Skagerrak (Denmark and Norway), see JX4084.B315
Sound, The (Denmark and Sweden), see JX4084.B315
(4084.S62) South Africa
(4084.S63) South China Sea islands
(4084.S65) South Moluccas
Southern Rhodesia, see JX4084.R5
(4084.S68) Southwest Africa. Namibia
(4084.S7) Spanish Sahara
Strait of Gibraltar, see JX4084.G52
(4084.S88) Sudetenland
(4084.S94) Svalbard
(4084.T25) Taiwan
(4084.T27) Tajikstan
(4084.T45) Tibet (China)
(4084.T5) Titicaca Lake
(4084.T62) Tok Island (Korea)
(4084.T67) Transkei
(4084.T7) Trentino-Alto Adige (Italy)
(4084.U4) Ukraine
(4084.V5) Vietnam
West Bank of the Jordan River, see JX4084.J67
(4084.W45) White Russia

Right of domain and property
Territory

International law
Treatises on special topics
Right of domain and property
Territory -- Continued
(4085) General works
Special
Acquisition of territory
Cf. JC11+, Political theory
(4088) General works
(4093) By occupation and possession
(4095) By discovery
(4098) By cession. Annexation
By conquest, see JX4093
(4099) Leased territories. Military bases
Cf. D - F, History
Boundaries
Cf. HE1+, Transportation and communications
(4111) General works (Collections, etc.)
Natural boundaries
(4115) General works
(4118) Mountains
(4122) Rivers
Cf. JX4150, International rivers and waterways
(4125) Lakes
Coast. Territorial waters
(4131) General works
(4135) Three-mile limit
(4137) Bays
(4138) Gulfs and harbors
(4141) Straits
Cf. HE386.A+, Sound tolls
Cf. JX1393.S8, Straits question
(4143) Continental shelf
(4144) Contiguous zones, Maritime
(4144.5) Economic zones, Maritime
(4145) Artificial boundaries
(4147) Adjoining territory. Nuisances
Cf. JX5405, Responsibility of the state for nuclear hazards
(4148) Islands
Cf. JX4427, Offshore structures
(4149) Archipelagoes
(4150) International rivers and waterways
Cf. HE387.A+, Special rivers
Cf. JX4122, Rivers as natural boundaries
(4155) Interoceanic canals
Cf. HE528+, Interoceanic canals
Cf. TC770, Ship canals
Right of legation and representation, see JX1621+

International law
Treatises on special topics -- Continued
Treaties and convention. Treaty making
For ancient Greek law, see JX2014.T7
For the effect of treaties on law of war, see JX4525
For the effect of war on treaties, see JX4171.W3
(4161) Early works to 1800
Treatises
(4165) English
(4166) French
(4167) German
(4169) Other
(4171.A-Z) Special topics. By subject, A-Z
Cf. HF1721+, "Favored nation clause", reciprocity
(4171.A3) Accession
(4171.C6) Clausula rebus sic stantibus
(4171.D8) Duration
(4171.G8) Guaranty treaties
(4171.I6) Interpretation
(4171.L3) Language
(4171.O3) Obligation
(4171.O32) Obsolescence
(4171.P3) "Pacta sunt servanda"
(4171.P4) Peace treaties
(4171.P77) Provisional application
(4171.R3) Ratification
(4171.R37) Reciprocity
(4171.R4) Reservations
(4171.R45) Revision
(4171.S72) State succession
(4171.T5) Termination
(4171.T6) Third parties
(4171.U5) Unequal treaties
(4171.V5) Violation
(4171.W3) War
Cf. JX4525, Effect of treaties
(4172) International legislation
Jurisdiction. Competence
Cf. JX1971+, Courts of international arbitration
Cf. JX1990+, International courts
Cf. JX5425+, International criminal jurisdiction
(4173) General works
(4175) Exterritoriality
(4185) Jurisdiction over property
(4190) Jurisdiction over shipping
(4195) Exterritorial crime

International law
Treatises on special topics -- Continued
Nationality and alienage. Allegiance. Citizenship
Cf. JC11+, Political theory
Cf. JF801, Citizenship
Cf. JK--JQ, Constitutional history and administration
History
(4203) General
Cf. JX1305+, Development of international law
Ancient
Cf. JX2009.A+, Treatises
(4204) General
(4205.A-Z) By state or nation, A-Z
(4205.H4) Hebrews
(4206) Medieval (General)
Cf. JX2041+, Treatises
(4207) Modern
Special countries, see JX4265+
Laws. Legislation
(4209) Collections of the laws of different countries
(4209.52) Special countries
see JK--JQ
(4211) General works
Nationality
(4215) General works
(4216) Naturalization
(4226) Expatriation
(4231.A-Z) Other special, A-Z
(4231.C5) Children
(4231.D5) Diplomatic and consular personnel
(4231.D7) Double allegiance
(4231.M3) Marriage and nationality
(4231.M5) Minorities
(4231.O7) Option of nationality
(4231.R5) Repatriation
(4231.S8) Statelessness
(4241) Domicile
Passports
Cf. JX5145+, Intercourse of belligerents
(4251) General works
(4253.A-Z) Special countries, A-Z
Aliens
Cf. JV6001+, Emigration and immigration
Aliens
Cf. JX5410.3+, Responsibility of the state for losses due to riots, etc.
(4255) General works
(4261) Expulsion. Deportation
Internationally protected persons
(4262) General works
(4262.5) Crimes against internationally protected persons

International law
Treatises on special topics
Nationality and alienage.
Allegiance. Citizenship -- Continued

(4263.A-Z) Other special topics, A-Z
For right of domicile, see JX4241
For taxation of aliens, see HJ2347+
(4263.A8) Arrest and imprisonment
For special cases, see JX4263.P8.A+
(4263.A9) Assistance to aliens
(4263.L2) Labor. Occupations. Professions
For right to employment see HD8081, United States; HD8101, Other regions or countries
(4263.M6) Military service
(4263.P6) Alien property
Including nationalization and valuation
Protection of nationals abroad by their home states
(4263.P7) General works
(4263.P8.A-Z) Special cases, A-Z
(4263.P8.W4) White affair
(4263.P82) Protection of stockholders abroad by their home state
(4263.T8) Travellers in foreign countries
For passports, see JX4251+

Special countries
United States
(4265.A1-A5) Collections. Documents
(4265.A7-Z) Monographs
(4270.A-Z) Other countries, A-Z
Under each country:
1 *Collections (Documents, etc.)*
2 *Other works*

Right of asylum. Extradiction
(4275) Collections
Treatises
(4280) Early works (prior to 1800)
(4281) English
(4282) French and Belgian
(4283) German
(4284) Italian
(4285) Spanish, Portuguese, and Latin American
(4286) Scandinavian
(4288.A-Z) Other, A-Z
(4292.A-Z) Special topics. By subject, A-Z
(4292.L5) Legations
(4292.P6) Political offenses
(4292.P8) Provisional arrest
(4292.R4) Refugees
(4292.S5) Ships
By country

International law
Treatises on special topics
Right of asylum. Extradiction
By country -- Continued
United States
(4301) Collections (Documents, etc.)
(4302) Separate documents. By date
(4305) Treatises and other general works
(4311) Addresses, essays, lectures
(4316.A-Z) Canada and other British American, A-Z
(4318.A-Z) West Indies other than British, A-Z
(4321) Mexico
(4326.A-Z) Central America, A-Z
(4335.A-Z) South America, A-Z
Europe
(4341) Great Britain
(4345.A-Z) Other European, A-Z
Asia
(4351) United States possessions (Philippines)
(4353.A-Z) British possessions, A-Z
(4357.A-Z) Other European possessions, A-Z
(4365.A-Z) Native states, A-Z
Africa
(4371.A-Z) Britsh possessions, A-Z
(4377.A-Z) Other European possessions, A-Z
(4384.A-Z) Native states, A-Z
(4387.A-Z) Australia, A-Z
(4391) New Zealand
Oceania
(4398.A-Z) Other, A-Z
(4399.A-Z) Cases. By name, A-Z
Jurisdiction over the high seas. Maritime law
Cf. JX4190, Jurisdiction over shipping
Cf. JX5203+, Maritime war
Cf. JX5239, Neutrality
Cf. JX5355+, Neutrality
(4408) Collections
Treatises
Cf. JX2041+, Medieval history
(4410) Early works (prior to 1800)
(4411) English
(4412) French and Belgian
(4413) German
(4414) Italian
(4415) Spanish, Portuguese, and Latin American
(4416) Scandinavian
(4418.A-Z) Other, A-Z
(4419) Addresses, essays, lectures
(4421) Codes
(4422.A-Z) By country, A-Z
Special topics
The open and closed sea
(4423) Early works to 1800

International law
Treatises on special topics
Jurisdiction over the high seas. Maritime law
Special topics
The open and closed sea -- Continued
(4425) Recent
(4426) Ocean bottom (Maritime law)
(4427) Offshore structures. Artificial islands
(4431) Navigation laws (Treatises only)
(4434) Collisions at sea
(4436) Shipwreck, salvage
(4437) Marine insurance
see Class K
Cf. HE961+, Marine insurance
Piracy
Cf. G535+, Pirates, buccaneers, etc.
Cf. Classes D-F, for works limited to one oregion or country, e. g. DT201, Barbary corsairs
(4444) General works. Treatises
(4446.A-Z) Cases, A-Z
(4447) Slavers, slave trade, etc.
Right of visit and search, see JX5268
(4449.A-Z) Other special, A-Z
(4449.A25) Access to the sea
(4449.A5) Airports (Floating)
(4449.A6) Angary
(4449.D4) Death on the high seas
Floating, see JX4449.A5
(4449.N3) Nationality of ships
(4449.R3) Responsibility of shipments
(4449.S4) Seizure of vessels and cargoes
Cf. JX5228, Capture (Maritime war)
(4449.S5) Shipmasters
(4449.W27) Warships
International disputes and collisions
Measures short of war
(4471) General works
(4472) Diplomatic protests
(4473) Diplomatic negotiations for pacific settlement
(4475) Mediation
(4478) Arbitration
see JX1901-JX1981
(4481) Intervention
(4484) Retorsion
(4486) Reprisals
For letters of marque, see JX5241
(4489) Boycott
(4491) Embargo
(4494) Pacific blockade
Law of War
(4505) Collections
(4507) Codes

International law
Treatises on special topics
International disputes and collisions
Law of War -- Continued
(4508) History
Treatises
(4510) Early works (prior to 1800)
(4511) English
(4512) French and Belgian
(4513) German
(4514) Italian
(4515) Spanish, Portugese, and Latin American
(4516) Scandinavian
(4518.A-Z) Other, A-Z
(4521) Addresses, essays, lectures
Philosophy and ethics of war, see U21+
Cf. HB195, Economics of war
(4525) Treaties, Effect of
(4530) Region of war
Kinds of war
Cf. JX5001+, Belligerent measures
(4541) Civil war
Declaration and outbreak
(4552) General works
(4556) Hostilities prior to declaration
Cf. JX4471+, Measures short of war
(4561) Declaration
(4564) Necessity for declaration
Belligerency
(4571) General works
(4574) Recognition of belligerency
Cf. JX4041+, Sovereignty
(4581) Alliance, succor, etc. (Specifically during state of war)
Cf. JX4004.62+, Unions of sovereign states
(4591) Belligerents and noncombatants
(4595) Martial law
Belligerent measures. Warfare
Cf. JX1381, Brussels Conference
(5001) General works
Special
Invasion. Belligerent occupation
Cf. JF1820, Military government
(5003) General works
(5003.5) Money. Occupation currency
(5005) Permissible violence
(5011) Devastation
Cf. JX5311, Property. Scientific collections
(5117) Bombardments and sieges
(5121) Deceit, spies, etc.
Cf. UB270+, Espionage

International law
Treatises on special topics
International disputes and collisions
Law of war
Belligerency
Special
Belligerent measures. Warfare
Special -- Continued
(5123) Guerrilla warfare
(5124) Air warfare
Cf. JX4093, Occupation and possession of territory
Cf. JX5397.A4, Infractions of neutrality
Arms and instruments of war
(5127) General works
(5131) Prohibited instruments and methods
(5133.A-Z) Special. By subject, A-Z
(5133.A7) Atomic bomb
Biological warfare, see JX5133.C5
(5133.C5) Chemical and biological warfare
(5133.D55) Directed energy weapons
(5133.G3) Gases (Asphyxiating and poisonous)
(5133.I5) Incendiary weapons
(5135.A-Z) Special topics, A-Z
(5135.C3) Cables
(5135.F7) Fortifications
(5135.M45) Mercenaries
(5135.M5) Military necessity
(5135.R3) Railroads
(5135.T5) Wireless telegraph
Treatment of the wounded. Geneva and Hague conventions
Including works on the Geneva and Hague conventions collectively
Cf. JX5141.A1+, Prisioners of war
Cf. JX5144.A1+, Protection of civilians
Cf. JX5243.A1+, Treatment of the wounded and shipwrecked (Maritime war)
Official publications
Geneva, 1864
(5136.A2) Preparatory conferences and committees. Preliminary drafts
(5136.A21) Preliminary correspondence
(5136.A22) Proceedings
(5136.A225) Resolutions. Final act
Text of convention
(5136.A23) English or French and English
(5136.A235.A-Z) Other languages, A-Z
(5136.A24A-Z) Other documents. Declaration of accession, etc. By country, A-Z

International law
Treatises on special topics
International disputes and collisions
Law of war
Belligerency
Special
Treatment of the wounded.
Geneva and Hague conventions
Official publications -- Continued
Hague (III), 1899
(5136.A25) Preparatory conferences and committees. Preliminary drafts
(5136.A26) Preliminary correspondence
(5136.A27) Proceedings
(5136.A2725) Resolutions. Final act
Text of convention
(5136.A28) English or French and English
(5136.A2835A-Z) Other languages, A-Z
(5136.A29A-Z) Other documents. Declaration of accession, etc. By country, A-Z
Geneva, 1906
(5136.A3) Preparatory conferences and committees. Preliminary drafts
(5136.A31) Preliminary correspondence
(5136.A32) Proceedings
(5136.A325) Resolutions. Final act
Text of convention
(5136.A33) English or French and English
(5136.A335A-Z) Other languages, A-Z
(5136.A34A-Z) Other documents. Declaration of accession, etc. By country, A-Z
Hague (X), 1907
(5136.A35) Preparatory conferences and committees. Preliminary drafts
(5136.A36) Preliminary correspondence
(5136.A37) Proceedings
(5136.A3725) Resolutions. Final act
Text of convention
(5136.A38) English or French and English
(5136.A3835A-Z) Other languages, A-Z
(5136.A39A-Z) Other documents. Declaration of accession, etc. By country, A-Z
Geneva, 1929
(5136.A4) Preparatory conferences and committees. Preliminary drafts
(5136.A41) Preliminary correspondence
(5136.A42) Proccedings
(5136.A425) Resolutions. Final act
Text of convention
(5136.A43) English or French and English
(5136.A435A-Z) Other languages, A-Z
(5136.A44A-Z) Other documents. Declaration of accession, etc. By country, A-Z

International law
Treatises on special topics
International disputes and collisions
Law of war
Belligerency
Special
Treatment of the wounded.
Geneva and Hague conventions
Official publications -- Continued
Geneva, 1949
(5136.A45) Preparatory conferences and committees. Preliminary drafts
(5136.A46) Preliminary correspondence
(5136.A47) Proceedings
(5136.A4725) Resolutions. Final act
Text of convention
(5136.A48) English or French and English
(5136.A4835A-Z) Other languages, A-Z
(5136.A49A-Z) Other documents. Declaration of accession, etc. By country, A-Z
Geneva, 1974-1977
(5136.A5) Preparatory conferences and committees. Preliminary drafts
(5136.A51) Preliminary correspondence
(5136.A52) Proceedings
(5136.A5225) Resolutions. Final act
Text of convention
(5136.A53) English or French and English
(5136.A5335A-Z) Other languages, A-Z
(5136.A54A-Z) Other documents. Declaration of accession, etc. By country, A-Z
(5136.A9-Z) Other works
Prisoners of war
(5141.A1) Texts of international conventions. By date
(5141.A2-Z) Other works
(5143) Hostages
Protection of civilians
(5144.A1) Text of international conventions
(5144.A2-Z) Other works
Intercourse of belligerents
(5145) General works
(5147) Protective signs
(5148) Flag of truce
(5151) Safe conduct
(5161) Deserters
Termination of belligerency
(5166) General works
(5169) Cartels
(5173) Truce and armistices
(5177) Capitulations

International law
Treatises on special topics
International disputes and collisions
Law of war
Belligerency
Special
Termination
of belligerency -- Continued
(5181) Treaties of peace
Cf. JX4165+, Treaty making
Cf. JX4525, Treaties, Effect of
Conquest of territory, see JX4093
Control of means of communication during war, see JX5135.A+
(5187) Postliminium
Maritime war
Collections
(5203) Congresses. Conferences
e. g. Declaration of London: JX5203 1909
(5205) Other
History
(5207) General works
(5208) Declaration of London, 1909
see JX5203
Treatises
(5210) Early works (prior to 1800)
(5211) English
(5212) French and Belgian
(5213) German
(5214) Italian
(5215) Spanish, Portuguese, and Latin American
(5216) Scandinavian
(5218.A-Z) Other, A-Z
(5221) Addresses, essays, lectures
(5225) Blockade
Cf. JX4491, Embargo
Cf. JX4494, Pacific blockade
(5228) Capture
Cf. JX4449.S4, Seizure of vessels and cargoes
Cf. JX5295+, Enemy property
Contraband
(5231) Theory
(5232.A-Z) Lists. By country, A-Z
(5234) Doctrine of continuous voyage
(5237) Innocent passage
(5239) War vessels in neutral ports
(5241) Privateers and letters of marque
Treatment of the wounded and shipwrecked.
Hospitals ships
(5243.A1) Texts of international conventions. By date
(5243.A2-Z) Other works
(5244.A-Z) Other, A-Z

International law
Treatises on special topics
International disputes and collisions
Law of war
Maritime war
Other, A-Z -- Continued
(5244.A7) Armed merchant ships
(5244.C6) Converted merchant ships
(5244.M6) Mines
(5244.S8) Submarines
Prize law
(5245) Collections
Treatises
(5250) Early works (prior to 1800)
(5251) English
(5252) French and Belgian
(5253) German
(5254) Italian
(5255) Spanish, Portuguese, and Latin American
(5256) Scandinavian
(5258.A-Z) Other, A-Z
(5261.A-Z) By country, A-Z
(5263) Prize courts
(5266) Procedure
(5268) Right of visit and search
Including Convoy
Cf. JX4408+, Jurisdiction over the High Seas
Cf. JX5316, Neutral property and trade
Effect on commerical relations of belligerents
Including trading with the enemy
(5270) General works
(5271.A-Z) Special topics, A-Z
(5271.C5) Contracts
(5271.L4) Licenses
(5271.M6) Moratorium
Enemy aliens
(5275) General works
(5276.A-Z) By region or country, A-Z
Property in war
(5278) Collections
Treatises
(5280) Early works (prior to 1800)
(5281) English
(5282) French and Belgian
(5283) German
(5284) Italian
(5285) Spanish, Portuguese, and Latin American
(5286) Scandinavian
(5288.A-Z) Other, A-Z
(5291) Addresses, essays, lectures
Enemy property
Including wartime control of alien property

International law
  Treatises on special topics
    International disputes and collisions
      Law of war
        Property in war
          Enemy property -- Continued
(5295) General works
(5298) Public property
(5305) Private property
(5311) Scientific collections, art treasures, libraries, churches, etc.
(5313.A-Z) By region or country, A-Z
(5316) Neutral property and trade
(5321) Requisitions
(5326) Damages. Claims, indemnity, etc.
            Right of visit and search, see JX5268
        Neutrality
            Cf. JX4031+, Neutralized states
(5355) Collections
          Treatises
(5360) Early works (prior to 1800)
(5361) English
(5362) French and Belgian
(5363) German
(5364) Italian
(5365) Spanish, Portuguese, and Latin American
(5366) Scandinavian
(5368.A-Z) Other, A-Z
(5371) Addresses, essays, lectures
(5383) Armed neutrality
              Class here theoretical discussions only
(5388) Asylum. Internment
(5390) Exportation of munitions of war
              Cf. HD9743+, Munitions industry
        Infractions of neutrality. Prohibited acts
              Cf. JX5231+, Contraband, etc.
(5391) General works
(5393) Fitting out of war vessels for belligerents
(5395) Foreign enlistment. Hostile military expeditions. Filibustering
(5397.A-Z) Other, A-Z
(5397.A4) Aerial warfare
(5397.L6) Loans
(5397.N5) Neutral trade with belligerents
(5397.P3) Passage of troops and goods
(5397.P7) Press
(5397.R4) Refueling of war ships
        Procedure in international disputes, see JX1901+

International law
Treatises on special topics -- Continued
International responsibility. International delinquencies
For responsibility or delinquency inherent in a particular subject listed elsewhere, see the subject, e. g. JX4263.P6, Alien property; JX4171.V5, Violations of treaties
(5401) General works
Responsibility of the state
Including responsibility for acts of organs and agents of the state
(5402) General works
Denial of justice to aliens, see JX4255+
(5404) Nonpayment of contract debts and damages
Cf. JX1393.D8, Drago doctrine
Cf. JX5485, Calvo doctrine and clause
(5405) Nuclear hazards and damages
(5407) Mass media
Cf. JX5397.P7, Press and infractions of neutrality
(5408) Acts of Unsuccessful insurgent governments
Acts of private persons
(5410) General works
(5410.2) Hostile acts against foreign states
Injuries and losses to aliens caused by mob violence, riots, etc.
(5410.3) General works
Riots against foreign missions, see JX1683.P7
Responsibility of international agencies
(5411) General works
League of Nations, see JX1975+
United Nations, see JX1976+
International unions, bureaus, etc, see JX1995
International offenses
Class here works on criminal law aspects of violations of international law
For noncriminal international delinquencies or noncriminal and criminal combined, see JX5401+
(5415) General works
(5417) Criminal responsibility of individuals
(5418) Crimes against humanity. Genocide
(5419) Offenses against peace. Aggression
(5419.5) War crimes
Cf. D625, History of World War I
Cf. D803, History of World War II
(5420) Terrorism
(5420.5) Vandalism
Class here works on destruction of cultural or artistic works of racial, religious, or social collectivities
Piracy at sea, see JX4444+

JX

International law
Treatises on special topics
International responsibility. International delinquencies
International offenses -- Continued
Piracy in the air, hijacking of aircraft, see JX5775.C7
Slave trade, see JX4447
International criminal jurisdiction and courts
(5425) General works
(5428) International criminal courts
Including proposed courts
For courts of temporary character, see JX5430+
Criminal trials
(5430) General works
War crime trials
(5433) General works
World War II
World War II
Cf. D803, History of World War II
(5433.5) Collected trials
(5434) General works
Trials by international military tribunals
(5436) General works
(5437) Nuremberg Trial of Major German War Criminals, 1945-1946 (Table JX10)
(5438) The Tokyo War Crimes Trial, 1946-1948 (Table JX10)
Trials by national courts other than those of the country of the defendant (sitting at home or abroad)
Collected trials
(5439) War crime trials, Nuremberg, 1946-1949 (subsequent proceedings) (Table JX10)
(5440) Other collected trials
(5441.A-Z) Particular trials. By first named defendant or best known (popular) name, A-Z (Table JX11)
e.g.
(5441.E3) Eichman trial
(5441.J8) Justice case
(5441.M3) Manila war crime trial, 1946
Yamashita, Tomoyuki, see JX5441.M3
Trials by the courts of defendant's own country
For trials by the courts of a particular country, see the country
For trials by the courts of countries in the same region, see the region

International law
Treatises on special topics
International
responsibility. International
delinquencies
International offenses
Criminal trials
War crime trials
World War II -- Continued
Trials by the courts of defendant's own country
For trials by courts of countries in different regions, see K545
(5445) Other wars
Piracy cases, see JX4446.A+
(5460.A-Z) Mock trials. By first named "defendant" or best known (popular) name, A-Z
Remedies
(5482) General works
(5482.5) Exhaustion of local remedies
Cf. JX4173+, Jurisdiction
Cf. JX4263.P7+, Protection of nationals abroad by their home states
Claims and reparation
Including restitution, recompensation, and satisfaction
Cf. JX1901+, Procedure in international disputes
Cf. JX5326, Property in war
Cf. JX5404, Nonpayment of contract debts
Claims and reparation
For collections of cases and claims, see JX238.A+
(5483) General works
(5485) Calvo doctrine and clause
Drago doctrine, see JX1393.D8
(5486.A-Z) By region or country, A-Z
(5501-5531) Finance
see class H
(5561-5681) Communication
see subclass HE
Transportation
(5701) Railways
Cf. HE1+, Transportation and communications
(5731) Maritime (commercial) law
see JX6311

International law
Treatises on special topics
International responsibility. International delinquencies
Transportation -- Continued
(5751) Waterways and water transport
Cf. HE386.A+, Harbors, straits
Cf. HE386.2+, Rivers
Cf. JX1398+, Panama Canal, etc.
Cf. JX4122, Rivers
Cf. JX4125, Lakes
Cf. JX4150, International rivers and waterways
Cf. TC770, Ship canals, etc.
Aeronautics
(5760) Periodicals. Societies
(5762) Congresses. Conferences
(5763) International public agencies
(5768) Collections
Treaties
(5769.A2) Collections
(5769.A3-Z) Separate treaties
(5770) History
(5771) General works
(5775.A-Z) Special topics, A-Z
(5775.C7) Crimes aboard aircraft. Hijacking of aircraft
Hijacking of aircraft, see JX5775.C7
(5775.L5) Licensing
(5775.S3) Salvage
(5775.T7) Traffic control
Space law
(6001-6650) Private international law. Conflict of laws
see K7051-K7054

	Governors' messages and other executive papers
	For messages on a specific subject, see the subject
.xA15	Collections covering more than one administration
.xA17	Collections covering one administration
	Veto messages
.xA18	Collections covering more than one administration
.xA19	Collections covering one administration
.xA2	Individual messages. By date of message
.xA25	Lieutenant Governors' messages
	Administrative papers
.xA3	Collections. Documents of several departments or agencies combined
.xA4	Secretary of State
(.xA5)	Other departments or agencies limited to a particular subject see the subject

.C General works
Legislative papers
For official gazettes, see class K
.G3 Joint sessions
.H Papers of a unicameral legislative body. Combined papers of a bicameral legislature
.H2 Debates. Proceedings. Sessional papers. Journals
(.H4) Calendars
see .H2
(.H45) Proceedings
see .H2
.H5 Bills
(.H6) Sessional papers
see .H2
.H7 Committee hearings, proceedings, reports
For committee papers on a special topic, see the topic
.J Upper House
.J2 Debates. Proceedings. Sessional papers. Journals
(.J4) Calendars
see .J2
(.J45) Proceedings
see .J2
.J5 Bills
(.J6) Sessional papers
see .J2
.J7 Committee hearings, proceedings, reports
For committee papers on a special topic, see the topic
.K Lower House
.K2 Debates. Proceedings. Sessional papers. Journals
(.K35) Calendars
see .K2
(.K4) Proceedings
see .K2
.K5 Bills
(.K6) Sessional papers
see .K2
.K7 Committee hearings, proceedings, reports
For committee papers on a special topic, see the topic
.M Indexes
.N Messages of heads of state and other executive papers
Class here official messages and documents only
For messages on a specific subject, see the subject
For the collected works of individual heads of state, see D - F
.N15 Collections
.N3 Individual messages. By date of message
(.N5) Executive orders
see class K
.R Administrative papers

Administrative papers -- Continued
Collections. Documents of several departments or agencies combined
.R1 Collected
(.R3) Department of the Interior
see JL - JQ
(.R7) Other departments or agencies limited to a particular subject
see the subject
(.T3) State, provincial documents
see JL - JS

1	Periodicals. Serials
2	Handbooks, manuals, etc.
3	Conventions. Congresses
4	Associations and clubs (National)
6	General works. History
	Local
	Including political clubs
8.A-W	By state
9.A-Z	By city

2 General works. History
Including periodicals, serials, handbooks, manuals, conventions, congresses, and national associations and clubs

Local
Including political clubs

4.A-W By state

5.A-Z By city

.A6A-Z	General works. History
	Including periodicals, serials, handbooks, manuals, conventions, congresses, and national associations and clubs
	Local
	Including political clubs
.A8A-.A8W	By state
.A9A-Z	By city

.xA5 General works. History
Including periodicals, serials, handbooks, manuals, conventions, congresses, and national associations and clubs

Local
Including political clubs

.x2A-.x2W By state

.x3A-Z By city

1	Periodicals. Serials
2	Societies
2.5	Museums. Exhibitions
(3)	Colonial period see JK99.A-Z
(5-6)	Constitution see KFC-KFZ
16	General works For Colonial period, see JK99
	Public administration
	Directories. Registers
30	Serials
31	Monographs
35	History
41	General works
45	Political corruption
49.A-Z	Other topics, A-Z
49.A8	Automatic data processing. Electronic data processing
49.C65	Communication systems
49.C7	Consultants. Executive advisory bodies
49.O4	Ombudsman
49.P36	Paperwork
49.P64	Political planning. Public policy
	Public policy, see 49.P64
49.P8	Publicity. Public relations
49.R4	Records. Public records management
49.W45	Whistle blowing
	Executive branch
50	General works
	Governor
51	General works
53.A-Z	Special. By subject, A-Z
53.L5	Lieutenant Governor
53.S8	Staff
53.V4	Veto
	Civil service
55	General works
(56)	Lists of officials. Registers see 30-31
57	Salaries. Fringe benefits Class here works dealing with service under the state in all branches; not limited to civil service proper Cf. 60.P4, Pensions
58	Appointments and removals
60.A-Z	Special. By subject, A-Z
60.A3	Accidents
60.A33	Affirmative action programs
60.A35	Alcoholism
60.D5	Discipline
60.E57	Employee assistance programs
60.F54	Flexitime. Hours of labor

	Public administration
	Executive branch
	Civil service
	Special. By subject, A-Z -- Continued
60.G7	Grievance procedures
60.H4	Health insurance
60.H68	Housing
60.I5	In-service training
60.I53	Interns
60.J63	Job sharing
60.L3	Labor productivity
60.L43	Leave
60.L5	Life insurance
60.P4	Pensions. Retirement
60.P44	Personnel management
60.P6	Political activity
60.P65	Positions
60.P7	Promotions
60.R3	Rating of employees
60.R4	Resignations
60.S5	Sick leave
60.S8	Suggestion awards. Incentive awards
60.T45	Temporary employment
(60.T7)	Travel regulations see KFA-KFZ
60.W6	Workers' compensation Cf. KFA-KFZ, Law
60.5.A-Z	Special classes of officials and employees, A-Z
60.5.A34	Afro-Americans. Blacks
60.5.A43	Aged. Older employees. Age and employment
60.5.E9	Executives
60.5.H3	Handicapped
60.5.H35	Mentally handicapped
60.5.M5	Minorities
	Older employees, see 60.5.A43
60.5.V64	Volunteer workers
60.5.W6	Women
60.6.A-Z	Special departments or agencies, A-Z For departments or agencies limited to a particular subject, see the subject
60.6.C65	Community Affairs
60.6.E94	Executive Department
60.6.S43	Secretary of State
	Legislative branch
(61)	Directories. Registers see J7 30-31
66	History For Colonial period, see JK83
68	Representation. Election districts
(69)	Powers see KFA-KFZ
71	Organization. Administration
74	Legislative reference bureaus

	Public administration
	Legislative branch -- Continued
74.4	Legislative internships
74.5	Lobbying. Pressure groups
74.7	Ethics
(74.8)	Investigations see KFA-KFZ
76	Upper House
78	Lower House
(79-80)	Contested elections see KFA-KFZ
(81-85)	Judiciary see KFA-KFZ
87	Capital. Seat of government. Site of the capital
	Public buildings see JK1651.A2-W
	Supplies. Government property. Government purchasing
88.A1	General
88.A2-Z	Special articles, A-Z
88.A4	Aircraft
88.C64	Computers
88.M7	Motor vehicles
88.P36	Paper
89	Political participation. Citizenship
	Elections. Voting. Suffrage. Right to vote
90	General works
91	Registered voters. Voter registration
	Election returns. Statistics. Voting behavior
92	General works
93	By date of election
	Campaign funds. Election finance. Political action committees. Campaign contributions see JK2295
	Political parties see JK2295

0	History
1	Periodicals. Societies. Serials
2	Directories. Registers
5	Dictionaries
(9-17)	Constitutional history. Constitutional law. Constitutions see class K
(18)	Treatises see 31 in this table
19	Separation of powers
20.A-Z	Special topics, A-Z
20.C58	Civil-military relations
	Federal and state relations, see 20.S8
	Language question see P119.32
20.M5	Minorities
20.R43	Regionalism
20.S8	State rights. Federal-state relations. Central-local relations
	Government. Public administration
(21)	Directories. Registers see 2 in this table
(24)	History see 31 in this table
29.A-Z	Special topics, A-Z
29.A8	Automatic data processing. Electronic data processing
(29.B8)	Business and politics. Pressure groups see 69.P7 in this table
29.C54	Communication systems
	Confidential information, see 29.S4
29.C55	Consultants
29.C57	Correspondence
29.C6	Corruption. Political corruption
29.C75	Crisis management
29.D42	Decentralization
29.D45	Decision making
	Electronic data processing, see 29.A8
29.E8	Ethics. Political ethics
29.I6	Intelligence service. Espionage
29.I63	Investigations
29.M37	Marketing
29.O35	Office practice
29.O4	Ombudsman
29.O73	Organizational change
29.P37	Paperwork
29.P64	Political planning. Public policy
29.P75	Productivity
29.R4	Records. Public records
29.S4	Secret and confidential information. Government information
29.T4	Telecommunication systems
29.T7	Transportation

Tables

Government. Public administration
Special topics, A-Z -- Continued
29.W55 Whistle blowing
(30) Administration law
see class K
31 General works
Executive branch
40 General works
Departments. Ministries
42 General works
Civil service
47 General works
49.A-Z1 Special topics, A-Z
49.A25 Accidents
49.A4 Alcoholism
49.A6 Appointments and removals
49.C53 Charitable contributions
49.C55 Classification
49.D4 Details. Transfers
49.D5 Discipline
49.D77 Drug abuse. Drug testing
49.E48 Employee assistance programs. Problem employees
49.E87 Examinations
49.E9 Executives. Government executives
49.F55 Financial disclosure
49.H35 Handicapped
49.H4 Health insurance
49.H6 Homosexuals. Gays. Lesbians
49.H65 Hours of labor
49.H68 Housing
49.I52 Incentive awards
49.I6 In-service training. Interns
49.J66 Job satisfaction
49.L53 Life insurance
49.M35 Mentally handicapped
49.M54 Minorities
49.O4 Older employees. Age and employment
49.P35 Part-time employment
(49.P4) Pensioners
see 49.Z2 in this table
49.P44 Personnel management
49.P64 Political activity
Problem employees, see 49.E48
49.P7 Promotions
Propaganda, see 49.P85
Public relations, see 49.P85
49.P85 Publicity and propaganda. Public relations. Government publicity
49.R3 Rating of employees
49.R47 Relocation of employees
Removals, see 49.A6

Government. Public administration
Executive branch
Departments. Ministries
Civil service
Special topics, A-Z -- Continued
Selection and appointment, see 49.A6
49.S56 Shift systems
49.T57 Titles of officials
49.T7 Travel
49.T85 Turnover of employees
49.V35 Vacations. Annual leave. Sick leave
49.V64 Volunteer workers
49.W6 Women in the civil service
49.W68 Work sharing
49.Z2 Salaries. Pensions. Retirement
Individual departments or ministries
50 Department of the Interior
Other departments or ministries limited to a particular subject
see the subject
Legislative branch
51 Directories. Registers
54 General works
(56) Constitution. Prerogatives. Powers
see class K
(59) Procedure
see class K
59.5 Legislative reference bureaus
Upper house
61.A4 Directories. Registers
61.A5 General works
Lower house
63.A4 Directories. Registers
65 General works
67 Election districts
69.A-Z Special topics, A-Z
69.B74 Broadcasting of proceedings
69.E45 Employees
69.E85 Ethics
69.F34 Filibusters
(69.L39) Legislative power
see class K
(69.L4) Legislative process
see class K
Lobbying, see 69.P7
69.O6 Opposition
69.P53 Political planning. Public policy
69.P7 Pressure groups. Lobbying
69.P8 Publication of proceedings
(69.R4) Reporters and reporting
see J8 69.P8
69.S65 Speaker. Presiding officer

Tables

Government. Public administration -- Continued

(70-76) Judiciary
see class K

79 Government property. Public buildings

Political rights. Political participation. Practical politics

81 General works

83 Citizenship

(86) Naturalization
see class K

Elections. Voting. Suffrage. Right to vote

92 General works

93.A-Z Local results of national elections. By place, A-Z

94 Election statistics. Election returns

(95) Election law
see class K

97 Election fraud. Corrupt practices

Political parties

98.A1 General works

98.A2-Z Special parties, A-Z

State, provincial, prefecture government (General and comparative)

98.8 General works

99.A-Z By state, province, prefecture, A-Z
For local government, see JS

0	History
1.A1	Periodicals. Societies. Serials
1.A11-A19	Directories. Registers
1.A25	Dictionaries
(1.A3-3)	Constitutional history. Constitutional law. Constitutions see class K
(4)	Treatises see 10.A4-Z in this table
5	Separation of powers
6.A-Z	Special topics, A-Z
6.C58	Civil-military relations
	Federal and state relations, see 6.S8
	Language question see P119.32
6.M5	Minorities
6.R43	Regionalism
6.S8	State rights. Federal-state relations. Central-local relations
	Government. Public administration
(7)	Directories. Registers see 1.A11-19 in this table
(8)	History see 10.A4-Z in this table
9.5.A-Z	Special topics, A-Z
9.5.A8	Automatic data processing. Electronic data processing
(9.5.B8)	Business and politics. Pressure groups see 14.P7 in this table
9.5.C54	Communication systems
	Confidential information, see 9.5.S4
9.5.C55	Consultants
9.5.C57	Correspondence
9.5.C6	Corruption. Political corruption
9.5.C75	Crisis management
9.5.D42	Decentralization
9.5.D45	Decision making
	Electronic data processing, see 9.5.A8
9.5.E8	Ethics. Political ethics
9.5.I6	Intelligence service. Espionage
9.5.I63	Investigations
9.5.M37	Marketing
9.5.O35	Office practice
9.5.O4	Ombudsman
9.5.O73	Organizational change
9.5.P37	Paperwork
9.5.P64	Political planning. Public policy
9.5.P75	Productivity
9.5.R4	Records. Public records
9.5.S4	Secret and confidential information. Government information
9.5.T4	Telecommunication systems
9.5.T7	Transportation

Tables

	Government. Public administration
	Special topics, A-Z -- Continued
9.5.W55	Whistle blowing
(10.A3)	Administration law see class K
10.A4-Z	General works
	Executive branch
11	General works
	Civil service
12.A-Z1	General works
12.Z13A-Z	Special topics, A-Z
12.Z13A25	Accidents
12.Z13A4	Alcoholism
12.Z13A6	Appointments and removals
12.Z13C53	Charitable contributions
12.Z13C55	Classification
12.Z13D4	Details. Transfers
12.Z13D5	Discipline
12.Z13D77	Drug abuse. Drug testing
12.Z13E48	Employee assistance programs. Problem employees
12.Z13E87	Examinations
12.Z13E9	Executives. Government executives
12.Z13F55	Financial disclosure
12.Z13H35	Handicapped
12.Z13H4	Health insurance
12.Z13H6	Homosexuals. Gays. Lesbians
12.Z13H65	Hours of labor
12.Z13H68	Housing
12.Z13I52	Incentive awards
12.Z13I6	In-service training. Interns
12.Z13J66	Job satisfaction
12.Z13L53	Life insurance
12.Z13M35	Mentally handicapped
12.Z13M54	Minorities
12.Z13O4	Older employees. Age and employment
12.Z13P35	Part-time employment
(12.Z13P4)	Pensioners see 12.Z2 in this table
12.Z13P44	Personnel management
12.Z13P64	Political activity
	Problem employees, see 12.Z13E48
12.Z13P7	Promotions
	Propaganda, see 12.Z13P85
	Public relations, see 12.Z13P85
12.Z13P85	Publicity and propaganda. Public relations. Government publicity
12.Z13R3	Rating of employees
12.Z13R47	Relocation of employees
	Removals, see 12.Z13A6
	Selection and appointment, see 12.Z13A6
12.Z13S56	Shift systems
12.Z13T57	Titles of officials

	Government. Public administration
	Executive branch
	Civil service
	Special topics, A-Z -- Continued
12.Z13T7	Travel
12.Z13T85	Turnover of employees
12.Z13V35	Vacations. Annual leave. Sick leave
12.Z13V64	Volunteer workers
12.Z13W6	Women in the civil service
12.Z13W68	Work sharing
12.Z2	Salaries. Pensions. Retirement
	Individual departments or ministries
12.Z3	Department of the Interior
	Other departments or ministries limited to a particular subject see the subject
	Legislative branch
13	General works
13.5	Legislative reference bureaus
13.7	Upper house
13.8	Lower house
14.A-Z	Special topics, A-Z
14.B74	Broadcasting of proceedings
14.E45	Employees
14.E85	Ethics
14.F34	Filibusters
(14.L39)	Legislative power see class K
(14.L4)	Legislative process see class K
	Lobbying, see 14.P7
14.O6	Opposition
14.P53	Political planning. Public policy
14.P7	Pressure groups. Lobbying
14.P8	Publication of proceedings
(14.R4)	Reporters and reporting see J9 14.P8
14.S65	Speaker. Presiding officer
(15.A-Z2)	Judiciary see class K
15.Z3-Z7	Government property. Public buildings
	Political rights. Political participation. Practical politics
16	General works
17.A2	Citizenship
(17.A3)	Naturalization see class K
	Elections. Voting. Suffrage. Right to vote
18	General works
18.5.A-Z	Local results of national elections. By place, A-Z
19.A15	Election statistics. Election returns

Tables

	Government. Public administration
	Political rights. Political participation. Practical politics
	Elections. Voting. Suffrage. Right to vote -- Continued
(19.A2)	Election law see class K
19.A4	Election fraud. Corrupt practices
	Political parties
19.A45	General works
19.A5A-A59Z	Special parties, A-Z Assign one Cutter to each party
	State, provincial, prefecture government (General and comparative)
19.A598	General works
19.A9-Z8	By state, province, prefecture, A-Z For local government, see JS

0	History
1.A1	Periodicals. Societies. Serials
1.A11-A19	Directories. Registers
1.A25	Dictionaries
(1.A3-3)	Constitutional history. Constitutional law. Constitutions
	see class K
3.2	Separation of powers
3.5.A-Z	Special topics, A-Z
3.5.C58	Civil-military relations
	Federal and state relations, see 3.5.S8
	Language question
	see P119.32
3.5.M5	Minorities
3.5.R43	Regionalism
3.5.S8	State rights. Federal-state relations. Central-local relations
	Government. Public administration
(4)	Directories. Registers
	see 1.A1 in this table
(5.A1)	History
	see 5.A7-5.Z in this table
5.A55A-Z	Special topics, A-Z
5.A55A8	Automatic data processing. Electronic data processing
(5.A55B8)	Business and politics. Pressure groups
	see 7.9.P7 in this table
5.A55C54	Communication systems
	Confidential information, see 5.A55S4
5.A55C55	Consultants
5.A55C57	Correspondence
5.A55C6	Corruption. Political corruption
5.A55C75	Crisis management
5.A55D42	Decentralization
5.A55D45	Decision making
	Electronic data processing, see 5.A55A8
5.A55E8	Ethics. Political ethics
5.A55I6	Intelligence service. Espionage
5.A55I63	Investigations
5.A55M37	Marketing
5.A55O35	Office practice
5.A55O4	Ombudsman
5.A55O73	Organizational change
5.A55P37	Paperwork
5.A55P64	Political planning. Public policy
5.A55P75	Productivity
5.A55R4	Records. Public records
5.A55S4	Secret and confidential information. Government information
5.A55T4	Telecommunication systems
5.A55T7	Transportation
5.A55W55	Whistle blowing

Government. Public administration -- Continued

(5.A6) Administration law
see class K

5.A7-Z General works

Executive branch

6 General works

Departments. Ministries

Civil service

6.Z1 General works

6.Z13A-Z Special topics, A-Z

6.Z13A25 Accidents

6.Z13A4 Alcoholism

6.Z13A6 Appointments and removals

6.Z13C53 Charitable contributions

6.Z13C55 Classification

6.Z13D4 Details. Transfers

6.Z13D5 Discipline

6.Z13D77 Drug abuse. Drug testing

6.Z13E48 Employee assistance programs. Problem employees

6.Z13E87 Examinations

6.Z13E9 Executives. Government executives

6.Z13F55 Financial disclosure

6.Z13H35 Handicapped

6.Z13H4 Health insurance

6.Z13H6 Homosexuals. Gays. Lesbians

6.Z13H65 Hours of labor

6.Z13H68 Housing

6.Z13I52 Incentive awards

6.Z13I6 In-service training. Interns

6.Z13J66 Job satisfaction

6.Z13L53 Life insurance

6.Z13M35 Mentally handicapped

6.Z13M54 Minorities

6.Z13O4 Older employees. Age and employment

6.Z13P35 Part-time employment

(6.Z13P4) Pensioners
see 6.Z2 in this table

6.Z13P44 Personnel management

6.Z13P64 Political activity

Problem employees, see 6.Z13E48

6.Z13P7 Promotions

Propaganda, see 6.Z13P85

Public relations, see 6.Z13P85

6.Z13P85 Publicity and propaganda. Public relations. Government publicity

6.Z13R3 Rating of employees

6.Z13R47 Relocation of employees

Removals, see 6.Z13A6

Selection and appointment, see 6.Z13A6

6.Z13S56 Shift systems

6.Z13T57 Titles of officials

	Government. Public administration
	Executive branch
	Departments. Ministries
	Civil service
	Special topics, A-Z -- Continued
6.Z13T7	Travel
6.Z13T85	Turnover of employees
6.Z13V35	Vacations. Annual leave. Sick leave
6.Z13V64	Volunteer workers
6.Z13W6	Women in the civil service
6.Z13W68	Work sharing
6.Z2	Salaries. Pensions. Retirement
	Individual departments or ministries
6.Z3	Department of the Interior
	Other departments or ministries limited to a particular subject see the subject
	Legislative branch
7	General works
7.5	Legislative reference bureaus
7.7	Upper house
7.8	Lower house
7.9.A-Z	Special topics, A-Z
7.9.B74	Broadcasting of proceedings
7.9.E45	Employees
7.9.E85	Ethics
7.9.F34	Filibusters
(7.9.L39)	Legislative power see class K
(7.9.L4)	Legislative process see class K
	Lobbying, see 7.9.P7
7.9.O6	Opposition
7.9.P53	Political planning. Public policy
7.9.P7	Pressure groups. Lobbying
7.9.P8	Publication of proceedings
(7.9.R4)	Reporters and reporting see J10 7.9.P8
7.9.S65	Speaker. Presiding officer
(8)	Judiciary see class K
9.A13	Government property. Public buildings
	Political rights. Political participation. Practical politics
9.A15	General works
9.A2	Citizenship
(9.A3)	Naturalization see class K
	Elections. Voting. Suffrage. Right to vote
9.A5	General works
9.A53A-Z	Local results of national elections. By place, A-Z
9.A55	Election statistics. Election returns

Government. Public administration
Political rights. Political participation. Practical politics
Elections. Voting. Suffrage. Right to vote -- Continued
(9.A6) Election law
see class K
9.A79 Election fraud. Corrupt practices
Political parties
9.A795 General works
9.A8A-Z Special parties, A-Z
State, provincial, prefecture government (General and comparative)
9.A88 General works
99.A9-Z8 By state, province, prefecture, A-Z
For local government, see JS

.A1	Periodicals. Societies. Serials
.A12	Directories. Registers
.A127	Dictionaries
(.A13-.A32)	Constitutional history. Constitutional law. Constitutions see class K
(.A34)	Treatises see .A58 in this table
.A36	Separation of powers
.A38A-Z	Special topics, A-Z
.A38C58	Civil-military relations
	Federal and state relations, see .A38S8
	Language question see P119.32
.A38M5	Minorities
.A38R43	Regionalism
.A38S8	State rights. Federal-state relations. Central-local relations
	Government. Public administration
(.A4)	Directories. Registers see .A1-.A12 in this table
(.A5)	History see .A58 in this table
.A56A-Z	Special topics, A-Z
.A56A8	Automatic data processing. Electronic data processing
(.A56B8)	Business and politics. Pressure groups see .A792P7 in this table
.A56C54	Communication systems
	Confidential information, see .A56S4
.A56C55	Consultants
.A56C57	Correspondence
.A56C6	Corruption. Political corruption
.A56C75	Crisis management
.A56D42	Decentralization
.A56D45	Decision making
	Electronic data processing, see .A56A8
.A56E8	Ethics. Political ethics
.A56I6	Intelligence service. Espionage
.A56I63	Investigations
.A56M37	Marketing
.A56O35	Office practice
.A56O4	Ombudsman
.A56O73	Organizational change
.A56P37	Paperwork
.A56P64	Political planning. Public policy
.A56P75	Productivity
.A56R4	Records. Public records
.A56S4	Secret and confidential information. Government information
.A56T4	Telecommunication systems
.A56T7	Transportation
.A56W55	Whistle blowing

Tables

	Government. Public administration -- Continued
(.A57)	Administration law see class K
.A58	General works
	Executive branch
.A61	General works
	Departments. Ministries
.A63	General works
	Civil service
.A67	General works
.A69A-Z	Special topics, A-Z
.A69A25	Accidents
.A69A4	Alcoholism
.A69A6	Appointments and removals
.A69C53	Charitable contributions
.A69C55	Classification
.A69D4	Details. Transfers
.A69D5	Discipline
.A69D77	Drug abuse. Drug testing
.A69E48	Employee assistance programs. Problem employees
.A69E87	Examinations
.A69E9	Executives. Government executives
.A69F55	Financial disclosure
.A69H35	Handicapped
.A69H4	Health insurance
.A69H6	Homosexuals. Gays. Lesbians
.A69H65	Hours of labor
.A69H68	Housing
.A69I52	Incentive awards
.A69I6	In-service training. Interns
.A69J66	Job satisfaction
.A69L53	Life insurance
.A69M35	Mentally handicapped
.A69M54	Minorities
.A69O4	Older employees. Age and employment
.A69P35	Part-time employment
(.A69P4)	Pensioners see 49.Z2 in this table
.A69P44	Personnel management
.A69P64	Political activity
	Problem employees, see .A69E48
.A69P7	Promotions
	Propaganda, see .A69P85
	Public relations, see .A69P85
.A69P85	Publicity and propaganda. Public relations. Government publicity
.A69R3	Rating of employees
.A69R47	Relocation of employees
	Removals, see .A69A6
	Selection and appointment, see .A69A6
.A69S56	Shift systems

Government. Public administration
Executive branch
Departments. Ministries
Civil service
Special topics, A-Z -- Continued
.A69T57 Titles of officials
.A69T7 Travel
.A69T85 Turnover of employees
.A69V35 Vacations. Annual leave. Sick leave
.A69V64 Volunteer workers
.A69W6 Women in the civil service
.A69W68 Work sharing
.A691 Salaries. Pensions. Retirement
Individual departments or ministries
.A693 Department of the Interior
Other departments or ministries limited to a particular subject
see the subject
Legislative branch
.A7 Directories. Registers
.A71 General works
(.A72) Constitution. Prerogatives. Powers
see class K
(.A75) Procedure
see class K
.A76 Legislative reference bureaus
.A77 Upper house
.A78 Lower house
.A792A-Z Special topics, A-Z
.A792B74 Broadcasting of proceedings
.A792E45 Employees
.A792E85 Ethics
.A792F34 Filibusters
(.A792L39) Legislative power
see class K
(.A792L4) Legislative process
see class K
Lobbying, see .A792P7
.A792O6 Opposition
.A792P53 Political planning. Public policy
.A792P7 Pressure groups. Lobbying
.A792P8 Publication of proceedings
(.A792R4) Reporters and reporting
see J11 .A792P8
.A792S65 Speaker. Presiding officer
(.A8-.A87) Judiciary
see class K
.A9 Government property. Public buildings
Political rights. Political participation. Practical politics
.A91 General works
.A92 Citizenship

Tables

	Government. Public administration
	Political rights. Political participation. Practical politics -- Continued
(.A93)	Naturalization see class K
	Elections. Voting. Suffrage. Right to vote
.A95	General works
.A953A-Z	Local results of national elections. By place, A-Z
.A956	Election statistics. Election returns
(.A96)	Election law see class K
.A975	Election fraud. Corrupt practices
	Political parties
.A979	General works
.A98A-Z	Special parties, A-Z
	State, provincial, prefecture government (General and comparative)
.A988	General works
.A99A-.A99Z8	By state, province, prefecture, A-Z For local government, see JS

	Replace .x in the table by the Cutter number for the country, province, etc., e. g. .G6 for Goa, .G6A1-3, .G6A4-49, .G6A5-Z, .G62A-Z, .G63A-Z, etc.
.xA1-.xA3	Periodicals. Societies. Serials
.xA4-.xA49	History
(.xA5-.xZ)	General works see .x2 in this table
	Public administration
.x2	General works
.x25A-Z	Special topics, A-Z
.x25A8	Automatic data processing. Electronic data processing
.x25C54	Communication
	Confidential information, see .x25S43
.x25C58	Consultants
.x25C6	Corruption. Political corruption
.x25D42	Decentralization
	Electronic data processing, see .x25A8
.x25I6	Intelligence service. Espionage
.x25M37	Marketing
.x25O4	Ombudsman
.x25P37	Paperwork
.x25P64	Political planning. Public policy
.x25P75	Productivity
	Public relations, see .x25P95
.x25P95	Publicity and propaganda. Public relations
.x25R43	Records. Public records
.x25S43	Secret and confidential information. Government information
.x25W55	Whistle blowing
	Executive branch
.x3	General works
.x4	Civil service
.x5	Legislative branch
.x58	Government property. Public buildings
	Political rights. Political participation. Practical politics
.x59	General works
.x6	Civics. Citizenship
.x65	Elections. Voting. Suffrage. Right to vote
	Political parties
.x7	General works
.x73A-Z	Special parties, A-Z
.x8A-Z	Other topics, A-Z
.x8C58	Civil-military relations
.x8D4	Decentralization
	Federal and State relations, see .x8S8
	Military power, see .x8C58
.x8S8	State rights. Federal and State relations. Central-local relations. Regionalism
.x9A-Z	By state, province, prefecture, A-Z For local government, see subclass JS

Tables

1	Periodicals. Societies. Serials
12	Directories. Registers
(18)	Laws, ordinances, codes
	see class K
	History
20	General works
	By period
23	To 1800
25	19th century
27	20th century
33	General works
35	Local government and the state. Home rule. Central-local government relations
	Local finance
	see HJ9011-HJ9695
37.A-Z	Other special, A-Z
37.A56	Annexation
37.C7	Commission government. Municipal government by commission
	Correspondence, see 37.R42
37.E4	Electronic data processing
(37.F4)	Federal and city relations
	see 35, etc. in this table
(37.I3)	Incorporation. Charters
	see class K
(37.L2)	Land use. Public land
	see HD166-HD1130.5
37.L7	Limits, Territorial. Administrative and political divisions
37.P7	Publicity and propaganda. Public relations. Government publicity
37.P8	Punched card systems
37.R42	Records and correspondence. Public records
38	Local government other than municipal. County government. Township government. Village government
	Executive branch. Mayor. Administration
40	General works
41.A-Z	Individual departments and agencies, A-Z
	For other departments or agencies limited to a particular subject, see the subject
	Civil service
47	General works
(48)	Rules
	see class K
49	Salaries. Pensions. Retirement
50	Legislative branch. Aldermen. City councils
(60)	Judiciary. Municipal courts
	see class K
69	Government property. Government purchasing
70	Political participation
	Elections. Local elections. Municipal elections
(83-85)	Election law
	see class K

Elections. Local elections.
Municipal elections -- Continued
86 General works
87 Statistics. Election returns
90 Political corruption
99.A-Z Local. By city, borough, parish, district, ward, etc., A-Z

1	Periodicals. Societies. Serials
2	Directories. Registers
(4)	Laws, ordinances, codes see class K
	History
5.A5-Z	General works
	By period
6	To 1800
7	19th century
8	20th century
10	General works
11	Local government and the state. Home rule. Central-local government relations
	Local finance see HJ9011-HJ9695
12.A-Z	Other special, A-Z
12.A56	Annexation
12.C7	Commission government. Municipal government by commission
	Correspondence, see 12.R42
12.E4	Electronic data processing
(12.F4)	Federal and city relations see 11, etc. in this table
(12.I3)	Incorporation. Charters see class K
(12.L2)	Land use. Public land see HD166-HD1130.5
12.L7	Limits, Territorial. Administrative and political divisions
12.P7	Publicity and propaganda. Public relations. Government publicity
12.P8	Punched card systems
12.R42	Records and correspondence. Public records
13	Local government other than municipal. County government. Township government. Village government
	Executive branch. Mayor. Administration
14.A1	General works
14.A13A-Z	Individual departments and agencies, A-Z For other departments or agencies limited to a particular subject, see the subject
	Civil service
14.A2	General works
(14.A3)	Rules see class K
14.A4	Salaries. Pensions. Retirement
15	Legislative branch. Aldermen. City councils
(16)	Judiciary. Municipal courts see class K
16.A9	Government property. Government purchasing
17.A2	Political participation
	Elections. Local elections. Municipal elections
(18.A2-A5)	Election law see class K

	Elections. Local elections.
	Municipal elections -- Continued
18.3	General works
18.5	Statistics. Election returns
19	Political corruption
20.A-Z	Local. By city, borough, parish, district, ward, etc., A-Z

1.A1	Periodicals. Societies. Serials
1.A3	Directories. Registers
(1.A9)	Laws, ordinances, codes see class K
	History
2.A2	General works
	By period
2.A3	To 1800
2.A5	19th century
2.A8-Z	20th century
3.A2	General works
3.A3	Local government and the state. Home rule. Central-local government relations
	Local finance see HJ9011-HJ9695
3.A6A-Z	Other special, A-Z
3.A6A56	Annexation
3.A6C7	Commission government. Municipal government by commission
	Correspondence, see 3.A6R42
3.A6E4	Electronic data processing
(3.A6F4)	Federal and city relations see 3.A3, etc. in this table
(3.A6I3)	Incorporation. Charters see class K
(3.A6L2)	Land use. Public land see HD166-HD1130.5
3.A6L7	Limits, Territorial. Administrative and political divisions
3.A6P7	Publicity and propaganda. Public relations. Government publicity
3.A6P8	Punched card systems
3.A6R42	Records and correspondence. Public records
3.A8	Local government other than municipal. County government. Township government. Village government
	Executive branch. Mayor. Administration
4.A1	General works
4.A13A-Z	Individual departments and agencies, A-Z For other departments or agencies limited to a particular subject, see the subject
	Civil service
4.A2	General works
(4.A3)	Rules see class K
4.A4	Salaries. Pensions. Retirement
5	Legislative branch. Aldermen. City councils
(6)	Judiciary. Municipal courts see class K
6.A9	Government property. Government purchasing
7.A15	Political participation
	Elections. Local elections. Municipal elections
(7.A7-A8)	Election law see class K

	Elections. Local elections.
	Municipal elections -- Continued
7.3	General works
7.5	Statistics. Election returns
8	Political corruption
9.A-Z	Local. By city, borough, parish, district, ward, etc., A-Z

.A1	Periodicals. Societies. Serials
.A12	Directories. Registers
(.A3)	Laws, ordinances, codes see class K
	History
.2.A2	General works
	By period
.2.A3	To 1800
.2.A5	19th century
.2.A8-.Z	20th century
.3.A2	General works
.3.A3	Local government and the state. Home rule. Central-local government relations
	Local finance see HJ9011-HJ9695
.3.A6A-Z	Other special, A-Z
.3.A6A56	Annexation
.3.A6C7	Commission government. Municipal government by commission
	Correspondence, see .3.A6R42
.3.A6E4	Electronic data processing
(.3.A6F4)	Federal and city relations see 3.A3, etc. in this table
(.3.A6I3)	Incorporation. Charters see class K
(.3.A6L2)	Land use. Public land see HD166-HD1130.5
.3.A6L7	Limits, Territorial. Administrative and political divisions
.3.A6P7	Publicity and propaganda. Public relations. Government publicity
.3.A6P8	Punched card systems
.3.A6R42	Records and correspondence. Public records
.3.A8	Local government other than municipal. County government. Township government. Village government
	Executive branch. Mayor. Administration
.4.A1	General works
.4.A13A-Z	Individual departments and agencies, A-Z For other departments or agencies limited to a particular subject, see the subject
	Civil service
.4.A2	General works
(.4.A3)	Rules see class K
.4.A4	Salaries. Pensions. Retirement
.5	Legislative branch. Aldermen. City councils
(.6)	Judiciary. Municipal courts see class K
.6.A9	Government property. Government purchasing
.7.A15	Political participation
	Elections. Local elections. Municipal elections
(.7.A7-.7.A8)	Election law see class K

Elections. Local elections.
Municipal elections -- Continued

.7.73 General works

.7.75 Statistics. Election returns

.8 Political corruption

.9.A-Z Local. By city, borough, parish, district, ward, etc., A-Z

Tables

To be divided as follows, using successive Cutter numbers in place of (1), (2), (3), (4), as, for example, .B5, .B52, .B53, .B54; .C65, .C66, .C67, .C68

.xA1-.xA19	Periodicals. Societies. Serials
.xA2	Directories. Registers
.xA6-.xZ	General works
.x3A3-.x3A39	Executive branch. Mayor
.x3A4-.x3A49	Civil service
.x3A5-.x3A59	Legislative branch. City councils
.x3A7-.x3A79	Political participation
.x3A8-.x3A89	Elections. Local elections. Municipal elections
.x3A9-.x3A99	Political corruption. Corruption
.x4A-Z	Local, A-Z

1 Periodicals. Serials
2 Societies
3 Congresses
3.5 Museums. Exhibitions
7 Dictionaries. Encyclopedias
(8) Atlases
  see G1027-G3102
Study and teaching
  see JV57
Biography
9.A2 Collective
9.A3-Z Individual
History
11 General works
14-18 By period
14 Early to 1600
15 17th century
16 18th century
17 19th century
18 20th century
27 General works
(29) Colonial companies
  see HF481-HF491
35 Relations with indigenous peoples
Relation to central government
41 General works
43 Colonial Office
45 Relation to legislature
(53-59) Law
  see class K
Administration. Colonial administration
60 General works
(63) Economic policy
  see HC94-HC610
Executive
  Including viceroy, governor
71 General works
75 Civil srvice
85 Legislative bodies
(91-95) Judiciary
  see class K
96 Political rights. Politcal participaiton. Citizenship
97 Elections

Tables

1.A2	Societies
1.A3-Z7	General works
3.A-Z	Local, A-Z

2 Periodicals. Societies. Serials
  For immigrant relief societies, see HV4013
(4) Serial documents
  see 2 in this table
(5) Laws
  see class K
Emmigration
10 General works
  History. By period
12 To 1800
14 19th century
15 20th century
(18) Emigration to individual countries, regions, etc.
  see classes D, E, F
19 Aid to emigrants. Information bureaus. Manuals
Immigration
20 General works
  History. By period
22 To 1800
24 19th century
25 20th century
25.5 Statistics
33 Immigration policy. Government policy
(41-45) Regulation and control. Legislation
  see class K
(51-55) Restriction and exclusion
  see class K
(71-75) Services for immigrants. Social work with immigrants
  see HV4013
  Special groups of immigrants
81 Children
82 Refugees
84 Women
(85) By ethnic group
  see classes D, E, F
  Local
90.A-Z By state or province, A-Z
95.A-Z Other local, A-Z

Tables

0.A1	Periodicals. Societies. Serials
	For immigrant relief societies, see HV4013
(0.A2-A5)	Serial documents
	see 0.A1 in this table
(0.A7-A8)	Laws
	see class K
	Emigration
1	General works
(1.Z79)	Emigration to individual countries
	see classes D, E, F
1.Z8	Aid to emigrants. Information bureaus. Manuals
	Immigration
2.A-Z2	General works
2.Z5	Statistics
3	Immigration policy. Government policy
(4)	Regulation and control. Legislation
	see class K
(5)	Restriction and exclusion
	see class K
(7)	Services for immigrants. Social work with immigrants
	see HV4013
8	Special groups of immigrants (children, refugees, women, etc.)
	By ethnic group
	see classes D, E, F
	Local
9.A2A-Z5Z	By state or province, A-Z
9.Z6A-Z	Other local, A-Z

.A1-.A19 General collections
Foreign relations and diplomatic correspondence
Secretary of State, Minister of Foreign Affairs
.A2-.A29 Reports
Including bureau reports and documents
.A3 Diplomatic correspondence
Class here general collections, routine correspondence
For correspondence covering special affairs, negotiations, wars, etc., see classes D, E, F, etc.
.A4-.A48 Legislative documents
Including Senate (Upper house), House (Lower house), and Other
.A5 Other documents
Treaties and Conventions
.A58 Official serials
.A6 Collections, by imprint date of first volume
.A7 Separate treatises. By date
.A75 Indexes
Cases, claims, etc.
(a) Place claims under defendant nation, unless the United States or an American citizen is a party, in which case prefer JX238-JX239;, (b) Prefer JX238, and (.A8) using JX239, and (.A85) only for claims which can not be otherwise disposed of; (c) Group claims under name of plaintiff nation, e. g. .C5 Chilean claims, .C7 Colombian claims, .M5 Mexican claims, etc.; (d) Under each claim subarrange using successive Cutter numbers (for material not dealing with a particular claim, arrange in a single chronological series)
.A8A-Z By name, A-Z
.A85 By date
.A9-.Z States which at some time maintained independent foreign relations, treaty rights, etc.
e. g. Under German Empire: Bavaria, Hanover, Saxony, Wurttemberg, etc.
e. g. Under Italy: Venice, Kingdom of the Two Sicilies, etc.

Tables

1 General collections
Foreign relations and diplomatic correspondence
Secretary of State, Minister of Foreign Affairs
2 Reports
Including bureau reports and documents
Diplomatic correspondence
Class here general collections, routine correspondence
For correspondence covering special affairs, negotiations, wars, etc., see classes D, E, F, etc.
3.A1-A4 Serial
3.A5 Special (not limited to special countries). By date
3.A6-Z Relations with particular countries
4 Legislative documents
Including Senate (Upper house), House (Lower house), and Other
Other documents
5.A1-A5 Adminsitrative
5.A6 Digests of decisions, opinions, etc.
Treatises and Conventions
5.8 Official serials
6 Collections, by imprint date of first volume
7 Separate treaties. By date
7.5 Indexes
Cases, claims, etc.
(a) Place claims under defendant nation, unless the United States or an American citizen is a party, in which case prefer JX238-JX239, (b) Prefer JX238, and (8) using JX239, and (9) only for claims which can not be otherwise disposed of; (c) Group claims under name of plaintiff nation, e. g. .C5 Chilean claims, .C7 Colombian claims, .M5 Mexican claims, etc.; (d) Under each claim subarrange using successive Cutter numbers (for material not dealing with a particular claim, arrange in a single chronological series)
8.A-Z By name, A-Z
8.A2 General collections
9 By date
10 States which at some time maintained independent foreign relations, treaty rights, etc.
e. g. Under German Empire: Bavaria, Hanover, Saxony, Wurttemberg, etc.
e. g. Under Italy: Venice, Kingdom of the Two Sicilies, etc.

.A2	Collections
.A28	History of the science
	History and other general works
.A3	To 1800
.A4-.Z4	1800-
.Z5	Contemporary works. By date
.Z6A-Z	Special topics, A-Z
.Z7	Relations with particular powers

.A2-.A4	Collections
.A5	Organization. Administration
.A6-.Z	General works. By author

1	Collections
2	Organization. Administration
3	General works. By author

	Manuals, yearbooks, diplomatic lists
1.A15-A19	Serials
1.A2	Nonserials. By date
	Periodicals see JX1-JX18
	General works
1.A3	Early, to 1860. By date
1.A5A-Z	1860- . By author, A-Z
	Organization and administration
	Documents
2.A2	Serial Including budget, estimates and appropriations, and other general special For the annual reports of the State Department with or without diplomaic correspondence, and other general serial documents, see JX200, JX1195 subdivisions 1, 2, 3, etc. under each country
2.A3	Special. By date
2.A33	Upper House (Senate). By date
2.A34	Lower House (Representatives, etc.). By date
2.A37	Other. By date
2.A4	Department of foreign affairs, Minister of state, etc. By date
	Legations, etc.
2.A5	General
	Legations, etc. in particular regions
2.A52	North America
2.A53	South America
2.A54	Europe
2.A55	Asia
2.A56	Other
2.A58A-Z	By place, A-Z
2.A585	Foreign legations
2.A59	Ambassadors, ministers, envoys, etc.
	Consular service
	Documents
2.A6	Serial
	Cases
2.A65	Collections
2.A65Z5	Particular cases. By date
2.A7	Organization, duties, regulations, forms, etc.
2.A75	Special. By date (inspection, etc.)
2.A8-Z3	General works. By author, A-Z
(2.Z4)	Consular courts see class K
2.Z5	Civil service For lists, see 1.A2
2.Z55	Messengers, interpreters, etc.
2.Z6	Examinations for diplomatic and consular service
2.Z7A-Z	Other works. By author, A-Z
2.Z8	States
2.Z9	Miscellaneous uncataloged material

1 Collections and selections
3-8 Separate works
Separate works are to have separate numbers, 3-8, arranged by alphabetical order of original titles
Texts in original language: .A1 and date
Translations to be arranged alphabetically by language: .E5, English; .F5, French; .G5, German; .I5, Italian; .S5, Spanish
9 Criticism

1.A1	Collections and selections
1.A3-Z	Separate works
	Arrange using successive Cutter numbers for translations, e. g. JX2542.P3 1915, Lawrence, Principles of international law, 1915; JX2542.P35 1920, a French translation, 1920
2	Criticism

.x Table for individual publicists

Authors are to be arranged: 1 Collections and selections; 2 Separate works; 3 Criticism. The Cutter number for original title follows the author number

0	Preliminaries. By date
	Proceedings
0.2	Indexes and digests
0.3	General. By editor
0.4	Statements by participants. By author Including indictments, speeches by prosecution and defense, proceedings in chambers
0.5	Evidence. By date
0.6	Judgments and minority opinions. By author
0.7	Post-trial. By author
0.8	General works on the trial. By author

.xA15	Preliminaries. By date
	Proceedings
.xA2-.xA29	Indexes and digests
.xA3-.xA39	General. By editor
.xA4-.xA49	Statements by participants. By author Including indictments, speeches by prosecution and defense, proceedings in chambers
.xA5	Evidence. By date
.xA6-.xA69	Judgments and minority opinions. By author
.xA7-.xA79	Post-trial. By author
.xA8-.Z	General works on the trial. By author

INDEX

A

Aargau
  Switzerland
    Government: JN9100+
    Legislative and Executive
  papers (General): J418
Abbreviations
  Political science (General):
    JA65
Abdication
  Monarchy: JC392
Abgeordnetenhaus
  Prussia: JN4597
Absentee voting: JF1033
Absolute monarchy: JC381
Abstention
  United States
    Elections: JK1987
  Voting: JF1047
Abyssinia
  Government: JQ3750+
  Legislative and Executive
  papers (General): J861
  Local government: JS7755
  Municipal government: JS7755
Access to the sea
  International law: JX4449.A25
Accession
  Treaties and treaty making:
    JX4171.A3
Accidents
  United States
    Civil Service: JK850.A3
Achenwall: JX2303+
Adams, John
  Messages and papers: J82.A2+
Adams, John Quincy
  Messages and papers: J82.A6+
Aden (Colony and Protectorate)
  Emigration and immigration:
    JV8750.55
Adjoining territory
  International law: JX4147
Administration
  Diplomatic Service: JX1684+
  United States
    House of Representatives:
    JK1410+
    Senate: JK1220+
    State government
      Legislative branch: JK2495
Administration, Colonial:
  JV412+
Administration, Public
  United States: JK401+
    State government: JK2443+
Administrative divisions
  Great Britian
    Local and municipal
  government: JS3152.L5
Administrative papers (Federal
  and state)
  United States: J83+
Advertising
  Political campaigns: JF2112.A4
  United States
    Government and public
  administration: JK468.A3
    State government: JK2445.A4
Aegean Islands (Greece and
  Turkey)
  International status:
    JX4084.A13
Aerial warfare
  Intractions of neutrality
    International law: JX5397.A4
Aeronautics
  International law: JX5760+
Affirmative action programs
  United States
    Civil Service: JK766.4
    Local and municipal government
      Civil service: JS362.5
Afghanistan
  Emigration and immigration:
    JV8752.3
  Government: JQ1760+
  International status:
    JX4084.A34
  Legislative and Executive
  papers (General): J685
  Local government: JS7441+
  Municipal government: JS7441+
Africa
  Colonies and colonization:
    JV246
  Emigration and immigration:
    JV8790+
  Government: JQ1870+
  Legislative and Executive
  papers (General): J704+
  Local government: JS7525+
  Municipal government: JS7525+

INDEX

American Republican Party:
JK2341
American Samoa
Emigration and immigration:
JV9466
Government: JQ6220+
Local government: JS8481
Municipal government: JS8481
American Samoa (U.S. Territory)
Legislative and Executive
papers (General): J958
Americanization
United States
Citizenship: JK1758
Americanization (U.S.): JK1758
Americas
Legislative and Executive
papers (General): J9.7+
Amnesty
Ancient Greece: JC75.A5
Amos: JX2505+
Ämter
Germany
Local government: JS5421
Ancien Régime
France
Government: JN2320+
Ancient colonies and
colonization: JV71+
Ancient local and municipal
governments: JS58
Ancient state: JC51+
Andaman and Nicobar Islands
Government: JQ620.A66
Legislative and Executive
papers (General): J511
Andhra Pradesh
Government: JQ620.A69+
Legislative and Executive
papers (General): J512
Andorra
Emigration and immigration:
JV8259.5
Government: JN3100+
Legislative and Executive
papers (General): J343
Andra Kammaren
Sweden: JN7928
Angary
International law: JX4449.A6
Angola
Emigration and immigration:
JV9011
Government: JQ3651
Legislative and Executive
papers (General): J841
Local government: JS7723
Municipal government: JS7723
Anguilla
Emigration and immigration:
JV7341.6
Government: JL609.2
Legislative and Executive
papers (General): J139.13
Local government: JS1871
Municipal government: JS1871
Anhalt
Government: JN4020+
Legislative and Executive
papers (General): J355
Anhalt-Bemberg
Legislative and Executive
papers (General): J355.4
Anhalt-Dessau-Kothen
Legislative and Executive
papers (General): J355.6
Annexation
United States
Local and municipal
government: JS344.A5
Annexation of territory
International law: JX4098
Annual leave
United States
Civil Service: JK770
Antarctic regions
Local government: JS8499
Municipal government: JS8499
Antarctica
Emigration and immigration:
JV9475
Antartic regions
International status: JX4084.A5
Antigua and Barbuda
Emigration and immigration:
JV7341.7
Government: JL649.2
Legislative and Executive
papers (General): J135
Local government: JS1871.5
Municipal government: JS1871.5

Antiquity, Political theory
 in: JC51+
Appenzell-Ausser Rhoden
 Switzerland
  Government: JN9120+
Appenzell Ausserrhoden
 Switzerland
  Legislative and Executive
 papers (General): J419
Appenzell Inner Rhoden
 Switzerland
  Government: JN9140+
Appenzell Innerrhoden
 Switzerland
  Legislative and Executive
 papers (General): J420
Appointment
 France
  Civil service: JN2746
 The Diplomatic Service: JX1665+
 United States
  Local and municipal government
   Civil service: JS364
Appointments
 Civil service: JF1651
 Germany
  1945-
   Civil service: JN3971.A69A6
 Heads of state: JF274
 Italy, United
  Civil service: JN5519.A6
 United States
  Civil Service: JK731+
  State government
   Civil service: JK2471
Arab countries
 Emigration and immigration:
  JV8760
 Government: JQ1850
 Local government: JS7510
 Municipal government: JS7510
Arabia
 Emigration and immigration:
  JV8750+
 Government: JQ1840+
 Legislative and Executive
 papers (General): J692
 Local government: JS7504+
 Municipal government: JS7504+
Arabian Peninsula
 Emigration and immigration:
  JV8750+
 Government: JQ1840+
 Local government: JS7504+
 Municipal government: JS7504+
Arabian Peninsula (General)
 Legislative and Executive
 papers (General): J692
Aragon
 Old kingdom
  Government: JN8137
Archipelagoes
 International law: JX4149
Arctic regions
 Emigration and immigration:
  JV9472+
 International status:
  JX4084.A68
 Local government: JS8495+
 Municipal government: JS8495+
Arenal: JX2975+
Argentina
 Emigration and immigration:
  JV7440+
 Government: JL2000+
 Legislative and Executive
 papers (General): J201+
 Local government: JS2301+
 Municipal government: JS2301+
Armed merchant ships
 Maritime war
  International law: JX5244.A7
Armed neutrality
 International law: JX5383
Armenia
 Emigration and immigration:
  JV8739.6
 Government: JQ1759.3
 International status: JX4084.A7
 Legislative and Executive
 papers (General): J690
 Local government: JS7437
 Municipal government: JS7437
Armistices
 International law: JX5173
Arms control
 International arbitration:
  JX1974+
Arms of war
 International law: JX5127+

Arrest
International law: JX4263.A8
Arrondissement
France: JS4912
Art treasures
International law: JX5311
Arthur, Chester A.
Messages and papers: J82.C4 +
Artificial boundaries
International law: JX4145
Artificial islands
International law: JX4427
Aruba
Emigration and immigration: JV7356.2
Government: JL769.3
Legislative and Executive papers (General): J153.15
Local government: JS1913
Municipal government: JS1913
Arunachal Pradesh
Legislative and Executive papers (General): J513
Arunchal Pradesh
Government: JQ620.A782
Ascension
Legislative and Executive papers (General): J753
Asia
Colonies and colonization: JV241
Emigration and immigration: JV8490 +
Legislative and Executive papers (General): J500 +
Local government: JS6950 +
Municipal government: JS6950 +
Political institutions and public administration: JQ1 +
Assam
Government: JQ320 +
Legislative and Executive papers (General): J527 +
Assemblies, Colonial: JV461
Assembly of the Republic
Portuguese: JN8585
Assimilation of immigrants: JV6342
Assyro-Babylonian Empire
Ancient state: JC61
Asturias
Old kingdom
Government: JN8130
Asylum
Neutrality
International law: JX5388
Asylum, Right of
International law: JX4275 +
Atlantic Ocean islands
Emigration and immigration: JV9029 +
Local government: JS7820 +
Municipal government: JS7820 +
Atlantic Union
International law: JX1393.A8
Atomic bomb
International law: JX5133.A7
Australasia
Government: JQ3995
Legislative and Executive papers (General): J903
Australia
Colonizing nation: JV5300 +
Emigration and immigration: JV9100 +
Government: JQ4000 +
Legislative and Executive papers (General): J905 +
Local government: JS8001 +
Municipal government: JS8001 +
Australian ballot: JF1111
Australian ballot system
United States: JK2215
Australian Capital Territory
Government: JQ4400 +
Austria
Emigration and immigration: JV7800 +
International status: JX4084.A8
Legislative and Executive papers (General): J311 +
Local government: JS4501 +
Municipal government: JS4501 +
Austria-Hungary
Government: JN1601 +
Austria, Lower
Legislative and Executive papers (General): J314
Austria, Upper
Legislative and Executive papers (General): J315

Austrian Empire
  Government: JN1601+
Austrian Parliament
  Austrian Empire: JN1815+
Austrian Republic
  Government: JN2011+
Austro-Hungarian Monarchy
  Legislative and Executive
  papers (General): J310
Austro-Hungarian Parliament:
    JN1792
Automatic data processing
  Canada
    Government: JL86.A8
  Netherlands
    Government: JN5810.A8
  Public administration:
    JF1525.A8
  Spain
    Government: JN8237.A87
  United States
    Government and public
  administration: JK468.A8
    State government: JK2445.A8
Automation
  Germany
    1945-
      Government: JN3971.A56A8
  Italy, United
    Government: JN5477.A8
Automotive spare parts
  United States
    Government supplies: JK1677.A8
Autonomous communities
  Spain
    Government: JN8231
Aves Island
  International status:
    JX4084.A86
Awards
  United States
    Local and municipal government
      Civil service: JS362.3
Ayala: JX2072+
Azerbaijan
  Emigration and immigration:
    JV8739.7
  Government: JQ1759.5
  Legislative and Executive
  papers (General): J690.2
  Local government: JS7438
  Municipal government: JS7438
Azores
  Emigration and immigration:
    JV9030
  Government: JN8661, JQ3982
  Local government: JS7820
  Municipal government: JS7820
Azuni: JX2371+

B

Baden
  Government: JN4040+
  Legislative and Executive
  papers (General): J356
Baden-Württemberg
  Government: JN4139.5
  Legislative and Executive
  papers (General): J383.B3
Bahamas
  Emigration and immigration:
    JV7329.3
  Government: JL610+
  Legislative and Executive
  papers (General): J136
  Local government: JS1841
  Municipal government: JS1841
Bahrain
  Emigration and immigration:
    JV8750.75
  Government: JQ1846
  Local government: JS7507
  Municipal government: JS7507
Bahrein
  Legislative and Executive
  papers (General): J694
Baker, Sir George S.: JX3211+
Balance of power
  Foreign relations
    International law: JX1318
Bali (Island)
  International status: JX4084.B3
Balkan Peninsula
  Political institutions: JN97
Balkan question
  Foreign relations
    International law: JX1319
Balkan States
  Emigration and immigration:
    JV8295+
  Government: JN9600+
  Local government: JS6899.5+
  Municipal government: JS6899.5+

Belgium
Colonizing nation: JV2800+
Emigration and immigration: JV8160+
Government: JN6101+
Legislative and Executive papers (General): J393
Local government: JS6001+
Municipal government: JS6001+
Belize
Emigration and immigration: JV7412.5
Government: JL670+
Legislative and Executive papers (General): J176
Local government: JS2151+
Municipal government: JS2151+
Belligerency
International law: JX4571+
Belligerency, Recognition of
International law: JX4574
Belligerent measures
International law: JX5001+
Belligerent occupation
International law: JX5003+
Belligerents
International law: JX4591
Bello: JX2978+
Benelux Countries
Emigration and immigration: JV8149+
Government: JN5700
Local government: JS5928+
Municipal government: JS5928+
Bengal
Government: JQ360+
Legislative and Executive papers (General): J527+
Benin
Emigration and immigration: JV9020.5
Government: JQ3376
Legislative and Executive papers (General): J768
Local government: JS7672
Municipal government: JS7672
Benue State (Nigeria)
Legislative and Executive papers (General): J746.B464
Bergholm: JX2941+
Berlin
International status: JX4084.B38
Berlin Conference, 1878
Foreign relations: JX1383
Bermuda
Emigration and immigration: JV7310+
Government: JL590+
Legislative and Executive papers (General): J131
Local government: JS1830, JS7821
Municipal government: JS1830, JS7821
Bern
Switzerland
Government: JN9200+
Bern (Canton)
Switzerland
Legislative and Executive papers (General): J423
Bessarabia
International status: JX4084.B4
Bevilagua, C.: JX3651.B3
Bhutan
Emigration and immigration: JV8752.8
Government: JQ628.5
Legislative and Executive papers (General): J626
Local government: JS7090.5
Municipal government: JS7090.5
Bicameral systems: JF541+
Bihar
Government: JQ620.B52
Bihar and Orissa
Legislative and Executive papers (General): J530
Biography
United States
Woman suffrage: JK1899.A+
Biography (Collective) of political scientists: JA92
Biological warfare
International law: JX5133.C5
Birkenhead, Frederick Edwin Smith: JX3220+
Black Sea
International status: JX4084.B55

INDEX

Blacks
United States
Civil Service: JK723.A34
Blockade
Martime war
International law: JX5225
Blue collar workers
United States
Civil Service: JK723.B58
Bluntschli: JX2775+
Bobhuthatswana
Legislative and Executive papers (General): J706
Bodin: JX2075+
Bohemia
Government: JN2210+
Legislative and Executive papers (General): J316
Local government: JS4721+
Municipal government: JS4721+
Bolivia
Emigration and immigration: JV7450+
Government: JL2200+
Legislative and Executive papers (General): J204
Local government: JS2351+
Municipal government: JS2351+
Bombardments
International law: JX5117
Bombay (State)
Government: JQ400+
Bombay Presidency
Legislative and Executive papers (General): J531
Bonaire
Emigration and immigration: JV7356.3
Government: JL769.5
Legislative and Executive papers (General): J153.2
Local government: JS1915
Municipal government: JS1915
Bonfils: JX2608+
Borough government
Great Britain: JS3265
Bosnia-Herzegovina
Emigration and immigration: JV8339.5
Government: JN9679.B6
Legislative and Executive
Bosnia-Herzegovina
papers (General): J460.2
Local government: JS6949.2
Municipal government: JS6949.2
Bosses, Party: JF2111
Botswana
Emigration and immigration: JV9007.2
Government: JQ2760
Legislative and Executive papers (General): J723
Local government: JS7638
Municipal government: JS7638
Boule
Ancient Greece: JC75.V6
Boundaries
France
Local and municipal government: JS4965.5.B6
Geopolitics: JC323
Boundary disputes
International arbitration: JX1981.B65
Bowen, H.W.: JX2451.B6
Boycott
International law: JX4489
Brabant, North
Legislative and Executive papers (General): J392.B7
Bradenburg
Legislative and Executive papers (General): J357.5
Brandenburg
Government: JN4239.3
Brandenburg (State, 1990-
Government: JN4239.5
Brazil
Emigration and immigration: JV7460+
Government: JL2400+
Legislative and Executive papers (General): J207+
Local government: JS2401+
Municipal government: JS2401+
Bremen
Government: JN4240+
Legislative and Executive papers (General): J358
Bribery
United States
Civil Service: JK850.B7

British Central African
Protectorate
Government: JQ2780+
Legislative and Executive
papers (General): J725
Local government: JS7641
Municipal government: JS7641
British Columbia
Government: JL420+
British Guiana
Emigration and immigration:
JV7499.3
Government: JL680+
Legislative and Executive
papers (General): J146
British Honduras
Emigration and immigration:
JV7412.5
British Honduras question
International law: JX1393.B74
British New Guinea
Legislative and Executive
papers (General): J981.N4
British Solomon Islands
Legislative and Executive
papers (General): J968.S6
British West Indies
Emigration and immigration:
JV7330+
Government: JL600+
International status:
JX4084.B75
Local government: JS1851+
Municipal government: JS1851+
Broadcasting of proceedings
Germany
1945-
Legislative branch:
JN3971.A78B74
Great Britain
Parliament: JN611
Legislative bodies: JF539
United States
Congress: JK1129
Brunei
Emigration and immigration:
JV8755.7
Government: JQ1064
Legislative and Executive
papers (General): J609.5
Local government: JS7185
Municipal government: JS7185
Brunswick
Government: JN4260+
Legislative and Executive
papers (General): J359
Brunus: JX2081+
Brussels Conference, 1875
Foreign relations: JX1381
Bry, Georges: JX2613.B8
Buchanan, James
Messages and papers: J82.B7+
Buildings, Public
Austrian Empire: JN1941
Belgium: JN6290
Denmark: JN7279
Germany: JN3759
1945-
Great Britain: JN851+
Hungary: JN2163
Italy, United: JN5589
Netherlands: JN5933
Norway: JN7606
Portugal: JN8600
Public administration:
JF1525.P7
Spain: JN8340
Sweden: JN7943
Bukowina
International status: JX4084.B8
Legislative and Executive
papers (General): J317
Bulgaria
Emigration and immigration:
JV8300+
Government: JN9600+
Legislative and Executive
papers (General): J451+
Local government: JS6901+
Municipal government: JS6901+
Bulmerincq: JX2778+
Bundesrat
Austrian Republic: JN2022
Germany: JN3623+
1945-
Switzerland: JN8812
Bundestag
Germany
1945-
Bundestagsprasident
Germany
1945-
Bundesversammlung
Switzerland: JN8845+

Bureaucracy: JF1501
  Italy, United: JN5503+
Burgenland
  Legislative and Executive papers (General): J317.5
Burkina Faso
  Emigration and immigration: JV9021.6
  Government: JQ3398
  Legislative and Executive papers (General): J780
  Local government: JS7679
  Municipal government: JS7679
Burlamaqui: JX2401+
Burma
  Emigration and immigration: JV8752.5
  Government: JQ751
  Legislative and Executive papers (General): J648
  Local government: JS7111+
  Municipal government: JS7111+
Burns, C.D.: JX3225.B8
Burundi
  Emigration and immigration: JV9001.7
  Government: JQ3566
  Legislative and Executive papers (General): J815
  Local government: JS7694
  Municipal government: JS7694
Bush, George
  Messages and papers: J82.E6
Business and politics: JK467
Byzantine Empire
  Ancient state: JC91+

C

Cabinet
  Canada: JL97+
  Confederate States of America: JK9919
  Great Britain: JN401+
  Ireland: JN1444
  United States: JK610+
Cabinet and Congress
  United States: JK616
Cabinet Office
  Great Britain: JN452
Cabinet system of government: JF331+
Cables
  International law: JX5135.C3
Calcaño: JX2980.C3
Calvo: JX2984+
Calvo doctrine and clause
  International law: JX5485
Camara dos Deputados
  Portuguese: JN8585
Camara dos Pares
  Portuguese: JN8581
Cambodia
  Emigration and immigration: JV8754
  Government: JQ930+
  Legislative and Executive papers (General): J642
  Local government: JS7150
  Municipal government: JS7150
Cameroon
  Emigration and immigration: JV9018
  Government: JQ3520+
  International status: JX4084.C33
  Legislative and Executive papers (General): J805
  Local government: JS7692
  Municipal government: JS7692
Campaign contributions
  United States: JK1991+
Campaign debates: JF2112.D43
Campaign funds: JF2112.C28
  Great Britain: JN1039
  United States: JK1991+
Campaign management: JF2112.C3
  United States: JK2281
Campaign methods: JF2085+

Canada
  Emigration and immigration: JV7200+
  Legislative and Executive papers (General): J100+
  Local government: JS1701+
  Municipal government: JS1701+
  Political institutions and public administration: JL1+
Canadian Confederation: JL65
Canary Islands
  Emigration and immigration: JV9032
  Government: JQ3984
  International status: JX4084.C34
  Local government: JS7823
  Municipal government: JS7823
Canton
  France: JS4917
Canton-federal relations
  Switzerland: JN8788
Cantonal government
  Switzerland: JN9015+
Cape of Good Hope
  Legislative and Executive papers (General): J707
Cape Verde
  Emigration and immigration: JV9033
Cape Verde Islands
  Government: JQ3661
  Legislative and Executive papers (General): J844
  Local government: JS7725
  Municipal government: JS7725
Capital
  United States: JK1606
Capitals
  Public administration: JF1900
Capitol
  United States: JK1616
Capitol pages
  United States
    Congress: JK1084
Capitulations
  Foreign relations: JX1568
  International law: JX5177
Capture
  Martime war
    International law: JX5228
Caribbean Area
  Emigration and immigration: JV7320+
  Government: JL599.5
  Legislative and Executive papers (General): J133+
Carinthia
  Legislative and Executive papers (General): J318
Carnazza-Amari: JX2858+
Carolingian period
  France: JN2334
    Crown: JN2365
Cartago, Costa Rica. Corte de justicia centroamericana: JX1990.C2
Cartels
  International law: JX5169
Carter, Jimmy
  Messages and papers: J82.E4+
Carthage
  Ancient colonies and colonization: JV85
Casanova: JX2862+
Castile and Leon
  Old kingdom
    Government: JN8140
Caucasus
  Emigration and immigration: JV8739.5+
  Government: JQ1759+
  Legislative and Executive papers (General): J690+
  Local government: JS7436+
  Municipal government: JS7436+
Cauchy: JX2614+
Caucus
  Political parties: JF2085
  United States
    Elections: JK2071+
Cavalcanti: JX3651.C3
Cavarreta: JX3545.C3
Cayman Islands
  Government: JL629.5
  Legislative and Executive papers (General): J137.5
Celli: JX2865+
Central Africa
  Emigration and immigration: JV9010+
  Government: JQ2720+
  Local government: JS7637+
  Municipal government: JS7637+

Central African Empire
(Ubangi-Shari)
Legislative and Executive
papers (General): J784
Central African Republic
Emigration and immigration:
JV9016.8
Government: JQ3404
Legislative and Executive
papers (General): J784
Local government: JS7682
Municipal government: JS7682
Central America
Emigration and immigration:
JV7412+
Government: JL1400+
Legislative and Executive
papers (General): J175+
Local government: JS2145+
Municipal government: JS2145+
Central Asia
Government: JQ1070+
Local government: JS7261+
Municipal government: JS7261+
Central Australia
Legislative and Executive
papers (General): J907
Central Europe
Political institutions: JN96
Central India
Legislative and Executive
papers (General): J541
Central Intelligence Agency:
JK468.I6
Central-local government
relations
Belgium: JN6175
France: JS4895
Germany: JS5409+
Great Britain: JS3134+
Sweden: JN7835
Central Provinces (India)
Government: JQ480+
Central Provinces and Bera
(India)
Legislative and Executive
papers (General): J543
Centuriate Assembly
Ancient Rome: JC85.C73
Ceremonials
The Diplomatic Service: JX1678+
Cession of territory
International law: JX4098
Ceylon
Emigration and immigration:
JV8752.7
Government: JQ650+
Legislative and Executive
papers (General): J611
Local government: JS7121+
Municipal government: JS7121+
Chad
Emigration and immigration:
JV9017
Government: JQ3405
Legislative and Executive
papers (General): J785
Local government: JS7683
Municipal government: JS7683
Chamber of Deputies
France: JN2858+
Italy, United: JN5564+
Chamber of Representatives
Belgium: JN6271
Chancellor
Austrian Republic: JN2021.3
Germany
1945-
Weimar Republic.
JN3961.3
Chandagarh
Government: JQ620.C48
Chandigarh
Legislative and Executive
papers (General): J543.5
Change of form of the state:
JC489+
Channel Islands
Europe
Legislative and Executive
papers (General): J307.8.A+
Government: JN1573
Charitable contributions
United States
Civil Service: JK850.C53
Checks and balances
Organs and functions of
government: JF229
Chemical warfare
International law: JX5133.C5

Computers
United States
Government supplies: JK1677.C65
Condominium
International law: JX4068.C7
Confederation of states
Forms of the state: JC357
Conference committees, Congressional
United States: JK1111
Conference on Security and Cooperation in Europe
International law: JX1393.C65
Confidential information
Canada
Government: JL86.S43
France
Civil service: JN2738.S43
Germany
1945-
Government: JN3971.A56S4
Great Britain
Government: JN329.S4
Italy, United
Government: JN5477.S33
Netherlands
Government: JN5810.S4
Public administration:
United States
Government and public administration: JK468.S4
Conflict of interest
Great Britain
Civil service: JN450.C6
Congo
Legislative and Executive papers (General): J786
Congo (Brazzaville)
Emigration and immigration: JV9016.5
Government: JQ3406
Local government: JS7684
Municipal government: JS7684
Congo (Democratic Republic)
Emigration and immigration: JV9015
Government: JQ3600+
Local government: JS7715
Municipal government: JS7715
Congo Conference, 1884-1885
Foreign relations: JX1385
Congreso de los Diputados
Spain: JN8319+
Congress
United States: JK1001+
Congress and the Cabinet
United States: JK616
Congress and the Executive
United States: JK585+
Congresses
Political science (General): JA35.5
Congressional committees
United States: JK1029+
Congressional districts
United States: JK1341+
Congressional employees
United States: JK1083+
Congro Free State (Belgian Congo)
Legislative and Executive (General): J831
Consecration
Monarchy: JC391
Conseil d'Etat
France: JN2701
Conseil-Général
France: JS4907
Consejo de estado
Spain: JN8266
Consensus
State: JC328.2
Consent of the governed: JC328.2
Conservatism
State and the individual: JC573+
Consiglio di Stato
Italy, United: JN5497
Constance, Lake of
International status: JX4084.C63
Constantine I
Greece: JN5056
Constitutional monarchy: JC405
Consular personnel
Citizenship
International law: JX4231.D5
Consultants
France
Civil service: JN2738.C58
Germany
1945-

Cuba
  Emigration and immigration: JV7370+
  Government: JL1000+
  Legislative and Executive papers (General): J162+
  Local government: JS2001+
  Municipal government: JS2001+
Culture and political science: JA75.7
Cumberland: JX2084+
Curaçao
  Emigration and immigration: JV7356.4
  Government: JL770+
  Legislative and Executive papers (General): J154
  Local government: JS1918
  Municipal government: JS1918
Cussy: JX2624+
Cybichowski: JX3425.C9
Cyprus
  Emigration and immigration: JV8746
  Government: JQ1811
  International status: JX4084.C86
  Legislative and Executive papers (General): J691.5
  Local government: JS7500
  Municipal government: JS7500
Czech Republic
  Emigration and immigration: JV7899.15
  Government: JN2210+
  Legislative and Executive papers (General): J338.3
  Local government: JS4721+
  Municipal government: JS4721+
Czech Socialist Republic
  Legislative and Executive papers (General): J338.2.C97
Czechoslovak Repbulic
  Legislative and Executive papers (General): J338+
Czechoslovakia
  Emigration and immigration: JV7899.15
  Government: JN2210+
  International status: JX4084.C9
Czechoslovakia
  Legislative and Executive papers (General): J338+
  Local government: JS4721+
  Municipal government: JS4721+

D

Dadar and Nagar Haveli
  Government: JQ620.D2
Dadra and Nagar Haveli
  Legislative and Executive papers (General): J548
Dahomey
  Emigration and immigration: JV9020.5
  Government: JQ3376
  Legislative and Executive papers (General): J768
  Local government: JS7672
  Municipal government: JS7672
Dalmatia
  Legislative and Executive papers (General): J320
Damages
  Property in war
    International law: JX5326
Daman
  Legislative and Executive papers (General): J550
Daman and Diu
  Government: JQ620.D225
Danzig
  Legislative and Executive papers (General): J359.5
Data tapes
  United States
    Government supplies: JK1677.D3
Davis, C.K.: JX2455+
Davis, G.B.: JX2458+
Deaf
  United States
    Civil Service: JK723.D4
Death on the high seas
  International law: JX4449.D4
Debating
  Campaign methods: JF2112.D43
Debrett
  Great Britain: JN671
Deceit
  International law: JX5121

Decentralization
Germany
1945-
Government: JN3971.A56D42
Great Britain
Government: JN329.D43
Italy, United
Government: JN5477.D4
Netherlands
Government: JN5810.D43
Decentralization in government
Denmark: JN7170.D42
Sweden: JN7850.D43
Decision making
Germany
1945-
Government: JN3971.A56D45
Public administration:
JF1525.D4
Sweden
Government: JN7850.D45
Declaration
International law: JX4552+, JX4561
Declaration of Paris
Foreign relations
International law: JX1367
Del Bon: JX2872+
Delegation of powers
France: JN2606
Organs and functions of
government: JF225
Delhi
Government: JQ620.D4
Legislative and Executive
papers (General): J549
Democracy: JC421+
Ancient Greece: JC75.D36
Ancient Rome: JC85.D3
Democratic Party: JK2311+
United States: JK2311+
Democratic party and civil
service reform: JK699
Denmark
Colonizing nation: JV3300+
Emigration and immigration:
JV8200+
Government: JN7101+
Legislative and Executive
papers (General): J403
Local government: JS6151+
Municipal government: JS6151+
Department of foreign affairs
The Diplomatic Service: JX1686+
Department of the Interior
United States: JK864+
Administrative papers: J84+
Department of the Secretary of
State
Canada: JL103
Departmental government: JS251
Dèpartmental government
France: JS4903+
Departments
Austrian Republic: JN2021.4
Canada
Government: JL95+
Germany
1945-
Government: JN3971.A63+
Government: JN3501
Weimar Republic.
JN3961.4
Great Britain
Civil service: JN451+
Greece
Government: JN5075
Italy, United
Government: JN5493+
Prussia
Government: JN4508
Departments, Government
Belgium: JN6205+
Denmark: JN7191
Netherlands: JN5828+
Norway: JN7501
Portugal: JN8536
Spain: JN8258+
Sweden: JN7875
Dependent states
International law: JX4011+
Deportation of aliens
International law: JX4261
Deposition
Monarchy: JC392
Deserters
International law: JX5161
Desks
United States
Government supplies: JK1677.D4
Despagnet: JX2641+
Despotism
Ancient Greece: JC75.D4

Details
  Canada
    Civil service: JL111.D4
Details and transfers
  United States
    Civil Service: JK850.D4
Detente
  International law: JX1393.D46
Devastation
  International law: JX5011
Developing countries
  Emigration and immigration: JV9480
  Local government: JS8500
  Municipal government: JS8500
  Political institutions and public administration: JF60
Díaz de Medina: JX3651.D4
Dictatorships: JC495
Diena, G.: JX3545.D4
Diez de Medina: JX2986.D5
Diplomacy: JX1621+
Diplomatic correspondence: JX232+
Diplomatic language: JX1677
Diplomatic negotiations for pacific settlement
  International law: JX4473
Diplomatic personnel
  Citizenship
    International law: JX4231.D5
Diplomatic protests
  International law: JX4472
Diplomatic questions, History of: JX1407+
Diplomatic relations (Universal collections): JX101+
Diplomatic service: JX1621+, JX1665+
Diplomatic style: JX1677
Direct legislation: JF491+
Directed-energy weapons
  International law: JX5133.D55
Disability
  United States
    President: JK609
Disarmament
  International arbitration: JX1974+
Discipline
  United States
    Civil Service: JK768.7
Dismissal
  Civil service: JF1651
  France
    Civil service: JN2746
  United States
    Civil Service: JK744
    Local and municipal government
      Civil service: JS364
Dissolution
  Legislative bodies: JF513
  Lower House: JF619
  Upper House: JF549
District government
  Great Britain: JS3270
  Portugal: JN8660
Diu
  Legislative and Executive papers (General): J550
Divine right of kings: JC389
Djibouti
  Emigration and immigration: JV8998.5
  Government: JQ3421
  Legislative and Executive papers (General): J788
  Local government: JS7687
  Municipal government: JS7687
Doctrine of continuous voyage
  International law: JX5234
Documentation
  United Nations: JX1977.8.D6
Dodecanese
  International status: JX4084.D64
Domicile
  International law: JX4241
Dominica
  Emigration and immigration: JV7345.3
  Government: JL669.2
  Legislative and Executive papers (General): J141.2
  Local government: JS1875
  Municipal government: JS1875
Dominican Republic
  Emigration and immigration: JV7395
  Government: JL1120+
  Legislative and Executive papers (General): J168
  Local government: JS2055
  Municipal government: JS2055

Dominion of Canada: JL65
Double allegiance
  Citizenship
    International law: JX4231.D7
Dover, Strait of
  International status:
    JX4084.D68
Drago doctrine
  International law: JX1393.D8
Drenthe
  Legislative and Executive
  papers (General): J392.D7
Dress
  The Diplomatic Service: JX1681+
Drug abuse
  United States
    Civil Service: JK850.D77
Drug testing
  United States
    Civil Service: JK850.D77
Drugs
  United States
    Government supplies: JK1677.D7
Dual Empire
  Austria-Hungary: JN1635
Duane: JX2460.D7
Dunbarton Oaks Conversations,
  1944: JX1976.3
Duration
  Treaties and treaty making:
    JX4171.D8
Dutch Guiana
  Emigration and immigration:
    JV7499.5
  Government: JL780+
  Legislative and Executive
  papers (General): J228
  Local government: JS2575
  Municipal government: JS2575
Dutch West Indies
  Emigration and immigration:
    JV7356+
  Government: JL760+
  Legislative and Executive
  papers (General): J153+
  Local government: JS1911+
  Municipal government: JS1911+
Duties
  The Diplomatic Service: JX1674+
Duties of kings and rulers:
  JC393

E

East Africa
  Government: JQ2945+
  Local government: JS7647+
East Africa Protectorate
  (British)
  Legislative and Executive
  papers (General): J730+
East Asia
  Emigration and immigration:
    JV8756.5+
  Government: JQ1499+
  Legislative and Executive
  papers (General): J665+
  Local government: JS7350+
  Municipal government: JS7350+
East Bengal
  Legislative and Executive
  papers (General): J529
East Germany
  Local and municipal
  government: JS5472
Eastern Europe
  Emigration and immigration:
    JV7597
  Local government: JS3000.7
  Municipal government: JS3000.7
  Political institutions: JN96
Eastern hemisphere
  Colonies and colonization:
    JV236+
Eastern policy
  Foreign policy
    United States: JX1421
Eastern Rumelia
  Legislative and Executive
  papers (General): J452
Ecology and political science:
  JA75.8
Economic aspects
  United States
    Immigration: JV6471
Economic aspects of
  immigration: JV6217
Economic causes of emigration:
  JV6098
Economic effects of
  emigration: JV6118

Economic groups, Representation of
  Representative government: JF1057+
Economic policy
  Colonies and colonization: JV420
Economic zones, Maritime
  International law: JX4144.5
Economics
  International law: JX1252
Economics and colonization: JV341
Economics and political science: JA77
Ecuador
  Emigration and immigration: JV7490+
  Government: JL3000+
  Legislative and Executive papers (General): J225
  Local government: JS2551+
  Municipal government: JS2551+
Education and colonization: JV331
Education of princes: JC393
Eerste Kamer
  Netherlands: JN5887+
Eggers: JX2305.E5
Egypt
  Ancient colonies and colonization: JV75
  Ancient state: JC66
  Emigration and immigration: JV8989
  Government: JQ3800+
  Legislative and Executive papers (General): J866
  Local government: JS7761+
  Municipal government: JS7761+
Egyptian Sudan
  Legislative and Executive papers (General): J868
Eichman trial: JX5441.E3
Eighteenth century political theory: JC171+
Eisenhower, Dwight D.
  Messages and papers: J82.D8+
El Salvador
  Emigration and immigration: JV7423
  Government: JL1560+
  Legislative and Executive papers (General): J185
  Local government: JS2191+
  Municipal government: JS2191+
Election
  Heads of state: JF285
  Legislative bodies: JF513
  Lower House: JF619
  United States
    President: JK526+
  Upper House: JF549
Election costs: JF2112.C28
Election districts
  United States: JK1341+
    State government: JK2493
Election finance: JF2112.C28
  Great Britain: JN1039
Election finances
  United States: JK1991+
Election forecasting: JF1048
  United States: JK2007
Election fraud: JF1083
  Germany: JN3901
    1945-
  Great Britain: JN1088
  Greece: JN5181
  United States: JK1994
Election returns
  Austrian Republic: JN2029.5
  Germany
    1945-
  Great Britain: JN1037
  Greece: JN5166
  Italy, United: JN5609
  Norway: JN7653
  Sweden: JN7958.2
  United States: JK1967+
Election statistics
  Germany
    1945-
  Great Britain: JN1037
  Greece: JN5166
  Italy, United: JN5609
  Norway: JN7653
  Sweden: JN7958.2
Election, Indirect: JF1177
Electioneering: JF2112.C3
  United States: JK2281
Elections: JF1001+
  Ancient Rome: JC85.E4
  Asia: JQ38
  Austrian Empire: JN1993+
  Austrian Republic: JN2029+

Elections
Belgium: JN6331+
Canada: JL193
Confederate States of America: JK9993
Denmark: JN7321+
European Community: JN45
France: JN2959+
Local and municipal government: JS4975
Germany: JN3838
1945-
Local and municipal government: JS5457+
Weimar Republic. JN3969+, JN3969.5
Great Britain: JN945+
Local and municipal government: JS3215+
Greece: JN5165+
Hungary: JN2183
Ireland: JN1541
Italy, United: JN5607+
Local government: JS221+
Municipal government: JS221+
Netherlands: JN5951+
Norway: JN7651+
Portugal: JN8623+
Prussia: JN4653+
Scotland: JN1341
Spain: JN8371+
Sweden: JN7958+
Switzerland: JN8931+
United States: JK1961+
Colonial period: JK97.A3+
Local and municipal government: JS395+
Electoral college: JF1177
United States: JK529
Electoral system: JF1001+
Canada: JL193
Confederate States of America: JK9993
France: JN2959+
United States: JK1961+
Electron tubes
United States
Government supplies: JK1677.E4
Electronic data processing
Belgium
Government: JN6184.E4
Canada
Government: JL86.A8
France
Civil service: JN2738.E4
Germany
1945-
Government: JN3971.A56A8
Great Britain
Government: JN329.E4
Local and municipal government: JS3152.E4
Italy, United
Government: JN5477.A8
Local government: JS100
Municipal government: JS100
Netherlands
Government: JN5810.A8
Norway
Government: JN7480.E4
Portugal
Government: JN8520.E43
Public administration: JF1525.A8
Spain
Government: JN8237.A87
Sweden
Government: JN7850.E4
United States
Government and public administration: JK468.A8
Local and municipal government: JS344.E5
State government: JK2445.A8
Ellice Islands
Emigration and immigration: JV9456
Government: JQ6313
Local government: JS8469
Municipal government: JS8469
Ellis Island Immigration Station: JV6484
Ellis Island Museum: JV6484
Embargo
Foreign relations
United States: JX1427.E5
International law: JX4491
Emigration: JV6001+
United States: JV6435

Emilia
  Early government: JN5271
Empire: JC359
Empire of 1871
  Germany
    Government: JN3388+
Empire, The
  Ancient Rome: JC89
Employee assistance programs
  United States
    Civil Service: JK850.E48
Employee suggestions
  Canada
    Civil service: JL111.I5
Employees
  Germany
    1945-
      Legislative branch: JN3971.A78E45
  Legislative bodies: JF514
  United Nations: JX1977.8.O35
  United States
    House of Representatives: JK1431
    Senate: JK1255+
Employees, Rating of
  United States
    Civil Service: JK766.6
Employers' liability
  United States
    Civil Service: JK850.E5
Employment tests
  United States
    Civil service
      State government: JK2480.E4
Enemy aliens
  Law of war
    International law: JX5275+
Enemy property
  International law: JX5295+
Enforcement of treaties
  International law: JX1246
England
  Emigration and immigration: JV7600+
  Legislative and Executive papers (General): J301+
  Local government: JS3001+
  Municipal government: JS3001+
English Maritime League
  Foreign relations
    International law: JX1367
English rule
  Canada: JL48
English-speaking Africa
  Government: JQ1880+
  Legislative and Executive papers (General): J705+
  Local government: JS7528+
  Municipal government: JS7528+
English-speaking Caribbean
  Emigration and immigration: JV7330+
  Government: JL600+
Envoys
  The Diplomatic Service: JX1691+
Epirus (Greece and Albania)
  International status: JX4084.E65
Equality
  Confederate States of America: JK9887
  State and the individual: JC575
Equality before the law: JC578
Equatorial Africa
  Emigration and immigration: JV9010+
Equatorial Guinea
  Emigration and immigration: JV9015.3
  Government: JQ3702
  Local government: JS7736
  Municipal government: JS7736
Eritrea
  Government: JQ3583
  Legislative and Executive papers (General): J823
Esperson: JX2875+
Espionage
  Canada
    Government: JL86.I58
  France
    Civil service: JN2738.I58
  Germany
    1945-
      Government: JN3971.A56I6
  Great Britain
    Government: JN329.I6
  Italy, United
    Government: JN5477.I6
  Public administration: JF1525.I6
  United States
    Government and public administration: JK468.I6

F

Index

German (Democratic Republic, 1949-
International status: JX4084.G4
German (Federal Republic, 1949-
International status: JX4084.G3
German Confederation (1815-1866)
Legislative and Executive papers (General): J351 +
German Democratic Republic (1949-1990)
Local and municipal government: JS5472
German Democratic Republic, 1949-1990
Government: JN3971.5
German East Africa
Government: JQ3500 +
Legislative and Executive papers (General): J800
Local government: JS7690
Municipal government: JS7690
German New Guinea
Legislative and Executive papers (General): J981.N42
German Southwest Africa (to 1967)
Legislative and Executive papers (General): J812
Germany
Colonizing nation: JV2000 +
Emigration and immigration: JV8000 +
Government: JN3201 +
International status: JX4084.G3
Legislative and Executive papers (General): J351 +
Local government: JS5301 +
Municipal government: JS5301 +
Germany (Democratic Republic, 1949-1991)
Legislative and Executive papers (General): J352
Gerrymandering
United States: JK1341 +
Gestoso y Acosto: JX3001 +
Ghana
Emigration and immigration: JV9022.3
Government: JQ3020 +
Legislative and Executive papers (General): J743
Local government: JS7655
Municipal government: JS7655
Ghent, Treaty of
Foreign relations
International law: JX1347
Gibraltar
Emigration and immigration: JV8259.7
Government: JN1576
International status: JX4084.G5
Legislative and Executive papers (General): J308
Gibraltar, Strait of
International status: JX4084.G52
Gifts
The Diplomatic Service: JX1683.G5
Gilbert and Ellice Islands Colony
Legislative and Executive papers (General): J968.G5
Gilbert Islands
Emigration and immigration: JV9455
Government: JQ6312
Local government: JS8468
Municipal government: JS8468
Glafey: JX2306 +
Glarus
Switzerland
Government: JN9260 +
Legislative and Executive papers (General): J426
Glenn: JX2469.G4
Goa
Government: JQ620.G6
Gold Coast
Government: JQ3020 +
Legislative and Executive papers (General): J743
Local government: JS7655
Municipal government: JS7655
Gondon: JX2673.G4
Goods, Passage of
Intractions of neutrality
International law: JX5397.P3
Görz and Gradiska
Legislative and Executive papers (General): J322

Government purchasing
Great Britain
Local and municipal government: JS3200
Hungary: JN2163
Public administration: JF1525.P85
United States: JK1671+
Local and municipal government: JS388
Government report writing
Public administration: JF1525.R46
Government, Local: JS2.2+
Government, Municipal: JS2.2+
Government, Organs and functions of: JF201+
Government, Provincial
Canada: JL198
Government, State
United States: JK2403+
Governments in exile
International law: JX4068.G6
Governor
Colonies: JV431+
United States
Colonial period: JK66
State government: JK2447+
Governor general
Canada: JL88
Grant, Ulysses S.
Messages and papers: J82.C1+
Grasso: JX2887+
Graubunden
Switzerland
Government: JN9280+
Great Britain
Colonizing nation: JV1000+
Emigration and immigration: JV7600+
Government: JN101+
Legislative and Executive papers (General): J301+
Local government: JS3001+
Municipal government: JS3001+
Great Lakes
Foreign policy
United States: JX1423
Greece
Ancient colonies and colonization: JV93
Ancient state: JC71+
Emigration and immigration: JV8110+
Government: JN5001+
Legislative and Executive papers (General): J385
Local government: JS5601+
Municipal government: JS5601+
Green movement: JA75.8
Greenland
Emigration and immigration: JV9473
Government: JL599.2, JN7370+
Legislative and Executive papers (General): J126
Local government: JS6187, JS8496
Municipal government: JS6187, JS8496
Grenada
Emigration and immigration: JV7345.4
Government: JL629.6
Legislative and Executive papers (General): J141.4
Local government: JS1876
Municipal government: JS1876
Grievance procedures
United States
Civil Service: JK768.8
Griffith, W.: JX2523.G6
Grisons (Graubünden)
Switzerland
Legislative and Executive papers (General): J427
Groningen
Legislative and Executive papers (General): J392.G7
Grotius: JX2091+
Guadeloupe
Emigration and immigration: JV7360
Government: JL820+
Legislative and Executive papers (General): J159
Local government: JS1942
Municipal government: JS1942

Guam
  Emigration and immigration:
    JV9452
  Government: JQ6000+
  Legislative and Executive
  papers (General): J951
  Local government: JS8466
  Municipal government: JS8466
Guaranty treaties
  Treaties and treaty making:
    JX4171.G8
Guatemala
  Emigration and immigration:
    JV7416
  Government: JL1480+
  Legislative and Executive
  papers (General): J179
  Local government: JS2171+
  Municipal government: JS2171+
Guerrilla warfare
  International law: JX5123
Guiana
  Legislative and Executive
  papers (General): J227.52+
Guianas
  Emigration and immigration:
    JV7499.2+
  Local government: JS2573+
  Municipal government: JS2573+
Guinea
  Emigration and immigration:
    JV9021.2
  Government: JQ3381
  Legislative and Executive
  papers (General): J771
  Local government: JS7673
  Municipal government: JS7673
Guinea-Bissau
  Emigration and immigration:
    JV9024
  Government: JQ3681
  Legislative and Executive
  papers (General): J850
  Local government: JS7727
  Municipal government: JS7727
Gujarat
  Government: JQ620.G8
  Legislative and Executive
  papers (General): J551
Gulfs
  International law: JX4138
Günther: JX2311+
Guyana
  Emigration and immigration:
    JV7499.3
  Government: JL680+
  Legislative and Executive
  papers (General): J146
  Local government: JS2573
  Municipal government: JS2573

H

Hague Conferences: JX1912+
Hague conventions
  Law of war
    International law: JX5136
Haiti
  Emigration and immigration:
    JV7393
  Government: JL1080+
  Legislative and Executive
  papers (General): J167
  Local government: JS2051
  Municipal government: JS2051
Hall, A.B.: JX3110.H3
Hall, W.E.: JX2524+
Halleck: JX2475+
Hamburg
  Government: JN4280+
  Legislative and Executive
  papers (General): J360
Handicapped
  France
    Civil service: JN2738.H35
  United States
    Civil Service: JK723.H3
Hanover
  Government: JN4299.5
  Great Britain
    Crown: JN341
  Legislative and Executive
  papers (General): J361
Harbors
  International law: JX4138
Harding, Warren G.
  Messages and papers: J82.D3+
Harrison, Benjamin
  Messages and papers: J82.C6+
Harrison, William Henry
  Messages and papers: J82.B1+
Hartmann: JX2786.H3

Incentive programs
  Canada
    Civil service: JL111.I5
Indemnity
  Property in war
    International law: JX5326
Independence, Means of
  protecting
  International law: JX4071+
India
  Emigration and immigration:
    JV8500+
  Government: JQ200+
  Legislative and Executive
  papers (General): J500+
  Local government: JS7001+
  Municipal government: JS7001+
Indian Ocean islands
  Emigration and immigration:
    JV9040+
  Local government: JS7900+
  Municipal government: JS7900+
Indian Ocean region
  International law: JX1393.I53
Indigenous peoples, Relations
  with
  Colonies and colonization:
    JV305+
Indirect election: JF1177
Individual and the state:
    JC571+
Individual as subject of
  international law: JX4000
Individual rights
  Political theory: JC585+
Indochina
  Emigration and immigration:
    JV8753.7+
  Government: JQ750+
  Local government: JS7139+
  Municipal government: JS7139+
Indochina (Federation)
  Legislative and Executive
  papers (General): J641
Indonesia
  Emigration and immigration:
    JV8756
  Government: JQ760+
  Legislative and Executive
  papers (General): J631
  Local government: JS7191+
  Municipal government: JS7191+
Information services
  Legislative bodies: JF527
Information services,
  Congressional
  United States: JK1108
Information, Freedom of: JC598
Information, Government
  Germany
    1945-
Information, Secret and
  confidential
  France
    Civil service: JN2738.S43
Infractions of neutrality
  International law: JX5391+
Innocent passage
  International law: JX5237
Installation
  Heads of state: JF289
Instruments of war
  International law: JX5127+
Insurance, Health
  United States
    Civil Service: JK794.H4
    Civil service
      State government: JK2480.H4
Insurance, Life
  United States
    Civil Service: JK794.L5
Insurgency: JC328.5
  Great Britain: JN297.I53
Intelligence service
  Canada
    Government: JL86.I58
  France
    Civil service: JN2738.I58
  Germany
    1945-
      Government: JN3971.A56I6
  Great Britain
    Government: JN329.I6
  Italy, United
    Government: JN5477.I6
  Public administration:
    JF1525.I6
  United States
    Government and public
  administration: JK468.I6
Intercourse of belligerents:
    JX5145+

Ireland
Emigration and immigration: JV7710+
Government: JN1400+
Legislative and Executive papers (General): J307.3
Local government: JS4301+
Irian Barat (Indonesia)
International status: JX4084.I7
Irish Republic
Emigration and immigration: JV7710+
Legislative and Executive papers (General): J307.3
Municipal government: JS4301+
Islamic countries
Emigration and immigration: JV8762
Government: JQ1852
Local government: JS7520
Municipal government: JS7520
Islamic Empire
Government: JQ1758+
Local government: JS7435+
Municipal government: JS7435+
Islamic state: JC49
Islands
International law: JX4148
Isle of Man
Government: JN1170+
Legislative and Executive papers (General): J305.5
Israel
Emigration and immigration: JV8749
Government: JQ1830
International status: JX4084.I8
Legislative and Executive papers (General): J698
Local government: JS7502
Municipal government: JS7502
Isthmian canals
Foreign relations: JX1398+
Istria
Legislative and Executive papers (General): J323
Italian East Africa
Government: JQ3580
Legislative and Executive papers (General): J821
Local government: JS7703
Municipal government: JS7703
Italian Republic
Government: JN5441+
Italian Somalia
Government: JQ3585
Italian Somaliland
Legislative and Executive papers (General): J825
Local government: JS7707
Municipal government: JS7707
Italo-Ethiopian War, 1935-1936
International law: JX1393.I8
Italy
Colonizing nation: JV2200+
Emigration and immigration: JV8130+
Government: JN5201+
Legislative and Executive papers (General): J388+
Local government: JS5701+
Municipal government: JS5701+
Italy, United
Government: JN5441+
Ivory Coast
Emigration and immigration: JV9021
Government: JQ3386
Legislative and Executive papers (General): J773
Local government: JS7674
Municipal government: JS7674

J

Jackson, Andrew
Messages and papers: J82.A7+
Jaipur
Legislative and Executive papers (General): J601.J26
Jamaica
Emigration and immigration: JV7329.5
Government: JL630+
Legislative and Executive papers (General): J138
Local government: JS1861+
Municipal government: JS1861+
Jammu
Legislative and Executive papers (General): J559
Jammu and Kashmir
Government: JQ620.K3

K

Index

Lesbians
United States
Civil Service: JK723.H6
Leseur: JX2701.L3
Lesotho
Emigration and immigration: JV9006.7
Government: JQ2740
Legislative and Executive papers (General): J722
Local government: JS7639
Municipal government: JS7639
Letters of marque
International law: JX5241
Levi: JX2545+
Liability, Employers'
United States
Civil Service: JK850.E5
Liberalism
State and the individual: JC574+
Liberia
Emigration and immigration: JV9023.6
Government: JQ3920+
Legislative and Executive papers (General): J875
Local government: JS7799
Municipal government: JS7799
Libertarianism: JC585+
Liberty
Ancient Rome: JC85.L53
Rights of the individual: JC585+
Libraries
International law: JX5311
Libya
Emigration and immigration: JV8983
Government: JQ3340+
Legislative and Executive papers (General): J826
Local government: JS7670.5
Municipal government: JS7670.5
Licenses
Law of war
International law: JX5271.L4
Licensing
Aeronautics
International law: JX5775.L5
Lie detectors
United States
Government and public administration: JK468.L5
Lieber: JX2483.L6
Liechtenstein
Emigration and immigration: JV7899.5
Government: JN2270+
Legislative and Executive papers (General): J340
Local government: JS4770
Municipal government: JS4770
Lieutenant-governor
United States
State government: JK2459
Life insurance
United States
Civil Service: JK794.L5
Liguria
Early government: JN5256
Limburg
Legislative and Executive papers (General): J392.L5
Limitation of speeches
Legislative bodies: JF538
Limited monarchy: JC405
Limits, Territorial
Great Britain
Local and municipal government: JS3152.L5
Lippe
Legislative and Executive papers (General): J363, J364
Lippe-Detmold
Government: JN4320+
Liszt, Franz von: JX3445+
Lithuania
Emigration and immigration: JV8194
Government: JN6745
Legislative and Executive papers (General): J401.3
Local government: JS6130.5
Municipal government: JS6130.5
Loans
Intractions of neutrality
International law: JX5397.L6
Lobbying
Belgium
Legislative branch: JN6249
Canada
France

Lucerne (Canton)
  Switzerland
    Legislative and Executive papers (General): J428
Luxembourg
  Emigration and immigration: JV8175
  Government: JN6380+
  Legislative and Executive papers (General): J395
  Local government: JS6049
  Municipal government: JS6049

M

Macao
  Emigration and immigration: JV8757.7
  Government: JQ1519.5
  Legislative and Executive papers (General): J651
  Local government: JS7365.5
  Municipal government: JS7365.5
Macedonia
  Government: JN9679.M3
Macedonia (Republic)
  Legislative and Executive papers (General): J460.4
  Local government: JS6949.7
  Municipal government: JS6949.7
Machiavelli: JX2115+
Mackintosh: JX2552+
Macri: JX2894+
Madagascar
  Emigration and immigration: JV9004
  Government: JQ3450+
  Legislative and Executive papers (General): J791
  Local government: JS7688
  Municipal government: JS7688
Maddalena Archipelago (Italy)
  International status: JX4084.M24
Maddalena Island (Italy)
  International status: JX4084.M24
Madeira Islands
  Emigration and immigration: JV9031
  Government: JQ3983
  Local government: JS7822
  Municipal government: JS7822
Madhya Pradesh
  Government: JQ480+
  Legislative and Executive papers (General): J564
Madiedo, Manuel M.: JX3021+
Madison, James
  Messages and papers: J82.A4+
Madras
  Government: JQ520+
Madras Presidency
  Legislative and Executive papers (General): J563
Magellan, Strait of
  International status: JX4084.M28
Maghrib, The
  Legislative and Executive papers (General): J762+
Magna Charta
  Great Britain: JN147
Maharashtra
  Government: JQ620.M26
  Legislative and Executive papers (General): J565
Maine, Sir Henry: JX2555+
Mainz
  Government: JN4359.5
Majorca
  Old kingdom
    Government: JN8128
Majority leader
  United States
    Senate: JK1227
Malacca, Strait of
  International status: JX4084.M3
Malagasy Republic
  Emigration and immigration: JV9004
  Government: JQ3450+
  Legislative and Executive papers (General): J791
  Local government: JS7688
  Municipal government: JS7688
Malawi
  Emigration and immigration: JV9007.3
  Government: JQ2941
  Legislative and Executive papers (General): J728
  Local government: JS7644
  Municipal government: JS7644

Malaya
  Emigration and immigration: JV8755
  Government: JQ1062
  Legislative and Executive papers (General): J615+
  Local government: JS7161+
  Municipal government: JS7161+
Malayan Union
  Legislative and Executive papers (General): J615+
Malaysia
  Emigration and immigration: JV8755
  Government: JQ1062
  Legislative and Executive papers (General): J615+
  Local government: JS7161+
  Municipal government: JS7161+
Maldive Islands
  Government: JQ3159
Maldives
  Emigration and immigration: JV9041
  Local government: JS7900
  Municipal government: JS7900
Mali
  Emigration and immigration: JV9021.4
  Government: JQ3389
  Legislative and Executive papers (General): J774
  Local government: JS7675
  Municipal government: JS7675
Malloy: JX2118+
Malpur
  Legislative and Executive papers (General): J601.M28
Malta
  Emigration and immigration: JV8141
  Government: JN1580+
  Legislative and Executive papers (General): J309
  Local government: JS5927
  Municipal government: JS5927
Mamiani: JX2897+
Mandates
  International law: JX4021+
Manila war crime trial, 1946: JX5441.M3
Manipur
  Government: JQ620.M29
  Legislative and Executive papers (General): J566
Manitoba
  Government: JL280+
Manning: JX2558+
Manpower planning
  Great Britain
    Civil service: JN450.M36
Manuals for foreign-born citizens
  United States
    Citizenship: JK1758
Marches
  Early government: JN5281
Marianas
  Emigration and immigration: JV9449
  Government: JQ6242
  Local government: JS8464
  Municipal government: JS8464
Marino: JX3545.M3
Maritime law
  International law: JX4408+
Maritime war
  International law: JX5203+
Marketing
  Germany
    1945-
      Government: JN3971.A56M37
  Public administration: JF1525.M37
Marriage
  and
    nationality
      Citizenship
        International law: JX4231.M3
Marshall Islands
  Emigration and immigration: JV9448
  Government: JQ6241
  Local government: JS8463
  Municipal government: JS8463
Martens, F.F.: JX2951+
Martens, G.F. von: JX2324+, JX2814
Martial law
  Belligerency
    International law: JX4595
Martime law
  International law: JX4426

Index

N

National emblems: JC345+
National holidays
  United States: JK1761
National Republican Party
  United States: JK2320
National socialism: JC481
National state: JC311+
Nationalism: JC311+
Nationality
  International law: JX4203+, JX4215+
Nationality of ships
  International law: JX4449.N3
Nationalization
  International law: JX4263.P6
Nationalrat
  Austrian Republic: JN2023
  Switzerland: JN8862
Nationals abroad, Protection of by their home states
  International law: JX4263.P7+
Nations, Colonizing: JV500+
Native American Party: JK2341
NATO
  International law: JX1393.N58+
Natural boundaries
  International law: JX4115+
Naturalization
  International law: JX4216
Nauru
  Legislative and Executive papers (General): J981.N3
Navarre
  Old kingdom
    Government: JN8133
Navigation laws
  International law: JX4431
Near East
  Emigration and immigration: JV8739+
  Government: JQ1758+
  International status: JX4084.N4
  Local government: JS7435+
  Municipal government: JS7435+
Necessity for declaration
  International law: JX4564
Necessity, Doctrine
  International law: JX4079.N4
Neighborhood government: JS211
  United States
    Local and municipal government: JS391
Nepal
  Emigration and immigration: JV8510
  Government: JQ628
  Legislative and Executive papers (General): J625
  Local government: JS7180
  Municipal government: JS7180
Netherlands
  Colonizing nation: JV2500+
  Emigration and immigration: JV8150+
  Government: JN5701+
  Legislative and Executive papers (General): J391+
  Local government: JS5931+
  Municipal government: JS5931+
Netherlands Antilles
  Emigration and immigration: JV7356+
  Government: JL760+
  International status: JX4084.N45
  Legislative and Executive papers (General): J153+
  Local government: JS1911+
  Municipal government: JS1911+
Neuchâtel
  Switzerland
    Government: JN9320+
    Legislative and Executive papers (General): J429
Neumann: JX2817+
Neutral property
  International law: JX5316
Neutral trade
  International law: JX5316
Neutral trade with belligerents
  Intractions of neutrality
    International law: JX5397.N5
Neutrality
  Law of war
    International law: JX5355+
Neutralization
  International law: JX4031+
Neutralized states
  International law: JX4031+
New Brunswick
  Government: JL230+

Norfolk Island (Australia)
  Legislative and Executive papers (General): J912
Norman Conquest
  Great Britain
    Political institutions: JN141
Norman period
  Great Britain
    Crown: JN336
North Africa
  Emigration and immigration: JV8977+
  Government: JQ3198+
  Local government: JS7660.5+
  Municipal government: JS7660.5+
North America
  Colonies and colonization: JV226
  Emigration and immigration: JV6351+
North Atlantic Assembly
  International law: JX1393.N58+
North Atlantic region
  International law: JX1393.N57
North Atlantic Treaty Organization
  International law: JX1393.N58+
North Australia
  Legislative and Executive papers (General): J913
North Borneo
  Legislative and Executive papers (General): J618.S3
North Brabant
  Legislative and Executive papers (General): J392.B7
North German Confederation
  Government: JN3357+
North German Confederation (1866-1870)
  Legislative and Executive papers (General): J351+
North Holland (Province)
  Legislative and Executive papers (General): J392.H6
North Korea
  Emigration and immigration: JV8757.5
  Government: JQ1729.5
  Legislative and Executive papers (General): J677.5
  Local government: JS7400
  Municipal government: JS7400
North Rhine-Westphalia
  Government: JN4399.7
  Legislative and Executive papers (General): J383.N6
North Sea
  International status: JX4084.N65
North West Provinces and Oudh (India)
  Legislative and Executive papers (General): J598
Northeast Africa
  Emigration and immigration: JV8996+
Northeastern fisheries: JX238.N6+
Northern Europe
  Political institutions: JN7009.2+
Northern Ireland
  Emigration and immigration: JV7709.5
  Government: JN1572
  Legislative and Executive papers (General): J307.5
  Local government: JS4295
  Municipal government: JS4295
Northern Marianas
  Government: JQ6242
  Local government: JS8464
  Municipal government: JS8464
Northern Rhodesia
  Emigration and immigration: JV9006.3
  Government: JQ2800+
  Legislative and Executive papers (General): J725.3
  Local government: JS7642
  Municipal government: JS7642
Northern Territory (Australia)
  Government: JQ4640+
  Legislative and Executive papers (General): J913
Northwest Territories
  Government: JL460+
Norway
  Emigration and immigration: JV8210+
  Government: JN7401+
  Legislative and Executive papers (General): J405
  Local government: JS6201+
  Municipal government: JS6201+

Index

Notation
  Political science (General):
    JA65
Nova Scotia
  Government: JL220+
Nuclear crisis control:
    JX1974.8
Nuclear damages
  International law: JX5405
Nuclear hazards
  International law: JX5405
Nuclear nonproliferation
  Disarmament: JX1974.73
Nuclear weapon-free-zones
  Disarmament: JX1974.735+
Nuclear weapons
  Disarmament: JX1974.7+
Nuisances
  International law: JX4147
Nullity
  International arbitration:
    JX1981.N8
Nyasaland
  Emigration and immigration:
    JV9007.3
  Legislative and Executive
  papers (General): J728
Nys: JX2702+

O

Obligation
  Treaties and treaty making:
    JX4171.O3
Obligation, Political: JC329.5
Obsolescence
  Treaties and treaty making:
    JX4171.O32
Obstruction
  Legislative bodies: JF519
Obwalden
  Switzerland
    Government: JN9480+
    Legislative and Executive
  papers (General): J437
Occupation currency
  International law: JX5003.5
Occupations
  International law: JX4263.L2
Ocean bottom
  International law: JX4426
Odelsting
  Norway: JN7581
Office equipment and supplies
  United States
    Government supplies: JK1677.O4
Office of Personnel Management
  United States: JK631+
Office practice
  Germany
    1945-
      Government: JN3971.A56O35
  Public administration:
    JF1525.O35
  United States
    Government and public
  administration: JK468.O4
Officers
  Legislative bodies: JF514
  United States
    House of Representatives:
    JK1411
    Senate: JK1224+
Official Register
  United States: JK5
Officials
  Legislative bodies: JF514
  United Nations: JX1977.8.O35
Offshore structures
  International law: JX4427
Oldenburg
  Government: JN4400+
  Legislative and Executive
  papers (General): J367
Older employees
  United States
    Civil Service: JK723.O4
Oligarchy: JC419
Olivart: JX3034+
Olivi, Luigi: JX2910.O7
Olmeda y Leon: JX2388.05
Oman
  Emigration and immigration:
    JV8750.6
  Government: JQ1843
  Local government: JS7506.5
  Municipal government: JS7506.5
Ombudsman
  Canada
    Government: JL86.O43
  France
    Civil service: JN2738.O47

Ombudsman
  Germany
    1945-
      Government: JN3971.A56O4
  Great Britain
    Government: JN329.O43
  Norway
    Legislative branch: JN7548
  Public administration:
    JF1525.O45
  United States
    Government and public
  administration: JK468.O6
Ompteda: JX2335+
Ontario
  Government: JL260+
Open sea
  International law: JX4423+
Operations research
  Public administration:
    JF1525.O6
Oppenheim, H.B.: JX2821+
Oppenheim, Lassa F.L.: JX3264+
Opposiiton
  State: JC328.3
Opposition
  Germany
    1945-
      Legislative branch:
    JN3971.A78O6
  Legislative bodies: JF518
Option of nationality
  Citizenship
    International law: JX4231.O7
Orange Free State
  Legislative and Executive
  papers (General): J715
Oranje Wystaat
  Legislative and Executive
  papers (General): J715
Organization
  Diplomatic Service: JX1684+
  Legislative bodies: JF514
  Political parties: JF2085+
  United States
    House of Representatives:
    JK1410+
    Senate: JK1220+
    State government
      Legislative branch: JK2495
Organizational change
  Public administration:
    JF1525.O73
Organs and functions of
  government: JF201+
Oriental state: JC47
Orissa
  Government: JQ620.O7
  Legislative and Executive
  papers (General): J575
Országgyülés
  Hungary: JN2115+
Ortega y Cotes: JX2388.07
Otto of Bavaria, King of
  Greece: JN5041+
Oudh
  Legislative and Executive
  papers (General): J597
Outbreak
  International law: JX4552+
Outer Mongolia
  Government: JQ1730
  Local government: JS7400.5
  Municipal government: JS7400.5
Overijssel
  Legislative and Executive
  papers (General): J392.O8
Oyo State
  Legislative and Executive
  papers (General): J746.O956

P

Pacific Area
  Colonies and colonization:
    JV241
  Emigration and immigration:
    JV9290+
Pacific area
  Legislative and Executive
  papers (General): J903+
Pacific Area
  Local government: JS8401+
  Municipal government: JS8401+
Pacific blockade
  International law: JX4494
Pacific islands
  International law: JX1393.P3
Pacific Islands (Ter.)
  International status:
    JX4084.P27

Pacific Ocean islands
Emigration and immigration: JV9290+
Local government: JS8401+
Municipal government: JS8401+
Pacta sunt servanda
Treaties and treaty making: JX4171.P3
Pages, Capitol
United States
Congress: JK1084
Pahang
Legislative and Executive papers (General): J618.P3
Paine, Thomas: JC177+
Pakistan
Emigration and immigration: JV8753
Government: JQ629
Legislative and Executive papers (General): J610
Local government: JS7091+
Municipal government: JS7091+
Palatinate
Legislative and Executive papers (General): J367.5
Palau
Emigration and immigration: JV9450
Government: JQ6591
Local government: JS8465
Municipal government: JS8465
Palestine
Emigration and immigration: JV8749
Government: JQ1830
International status: JX4084.I8
Legislative and Executive papers (General): J698
Local government: JS7502
Municipal government: JS7502
Panama
Emigration and immigration: JV7429
Government: JL1640+
Legislative and Executive papers (General): J184
Local government: JS2211+
Municipal government: JS2211+
Panama Canal
Foreign relations: JX1398+
Panama Canal Treaties, 1977: JX1398.72+
Panama Canal Zone
Emigration and immigration: JV7432
Government: JL1670+
Legislative and Executive papers (General): J184.5
Pando: JX3038+
Papacy
International arbitration: JX1981.P3
Papal States
Nineteenth century
Government: JN5431
Paper
United States
Government supplies: JK1677.P3
Paperwork
France
Civil service: JN2738.P36
Germany
1945-
Government: JN3971.A56P37
Sweden
Government: JN7850.P38
United States
Government and public administration: JK468.P34
Papua New Guinea
Emigration and immigration: JV9453
Government: JQ6311
Local government: JS8467
Municipal government: JS8467
Paracel Islands
International status: JX4084.P28
Paraguay
Emigration and immigration: JV7500+
Government: JL3200+
Legislative and Executive papers (General): J235
Local government: JS2601+
Municipal government: JS2601+
Paris, Treaty of (1856)
Foreign relations
International law: JX1367
Parish government
Great Britain: JS3275

Philippine annexation
Foreign policy
United States: JX1426
Philippines
Emigration and immigration: JV8685
Government: JQ1250+
Legialstive and Executive papers (General): J661+
Local government: JS7301+
Municipal government: JS7301+
Phillimore: JX2565+
Philosophy
Colonies: JV51
Phoenicia
Ancient colonies and colonization: JV81
Piédelièvre: JX2714+
Piedmont
Early government: JN5251
Pierantoni: JX2917+
Pierce, Franklin
Messages and papers: J82.B6+
Pinang
Legislative and Executive papers (General): J618.P5
Pinheiro-Ferreira: JX3041+
Pious Fund cases: JX238.P5+
Piracy
International law: JX4444+
Planning, Political
Germany
1945-
Legislative branch: JN3971.A78P53
Planos Suárez: JX3651.P7
Plantagenet period
Great Britain
Crown: JN337
Plantagenet to 1399
Great Britain
Political institutions: JN158
Plateau State
Legislative and Executive papers (General): J746.P55
Plater, C.D.: JX3275.P5
Platforms, Party
United States: JK2255
Plebiscite
Ancient state: JC55.P7
Plenipotentiaries
The Diplomatic Service: JX1691+
Plural voting: JF1023
Pohl, H.: JX3491.P6
Poland
Emigration and immigration: JV8195
Government: JN6750+
Legislative and Executive papers (General): J399
Local government: JS6131+
Municipal government: JS6131+
Polar regions
International status: JX4084.P65
Police, International
International arbitration: JX1981.P7
Policy, Government
Emigration and immigration: JV6038
Immigration: JV6271
Political action committees
United States: JK1991+
Political activity
Germany
1945-
Civil service: JN3971.A69P64
Great Britain
Civil service: JN450.P6
United States
Civil Service: JK761
Political advertising: JF2112.A4
Political aspects
United States
Immigration: JV6477
Political aspects of immigration: JV6255
Political causes of emigration: JV6104
Political change: JC489+
Political conventions: JF2091
United States: JK2255
Political corruption: JF1081+
Asia: JQ29.5
Belgium: JN6355
Denmark: JN7355
France: JN2988
Local and municipal government: JS4981
Germany
1945-
Government: JN3971.A56C6

Index

Political corruption
Germany
Local and municipal government: JS5463
Weimar Republic. JN3969.9
Great Britain
Local and municipal government: JS3225
Hungary: JN2187
Ireland: JN1561
Italy, United: JN5641
Local government: JS231
Municipal government: JS231
Netherlands: JN5971
Government: JN5810.C67
Norway: JN7480.C67
Portugal: JN8641
Scotland: JN1361
Spain: JN8386
Sweden: JN7985
Switzerland: JN8961
United States: JK2249
Local and municipal government: JS401
Political culture: JA75.7
Political divisions
Great Britain
Local and municipal government: JS3152.L5
Political ecology: JA75.8
Political effects of emigration: JV6124
Political ethics: JA79
Germany
1945-
Government: JN3971.A56E8
Political geography: JC319+
Political institutions: JF5.2+
Political institutions and public administration
Canada, Latin America, etc.: JL1+
Political leadership: JC330.3
Political messianism
Nationalism: JC314
Political obligation: JC329.5
Political offenses
Right of asylum
International law: JX4292.P6
Political participation: JF799+
Asia: JQ36+
Austrian Empire: JN1951+
Austrian Republic: JN2026+
Belgium: JN6301+
Canada: JL186.5
Denmark: JN7296
European Community: JN40
France: JN2916+
Local and municipal government: JS4966
Germany: JN3770+
1945-
Local and municipal government: JS5448
Weimar Republic. JN3966+
Great Britain: JN900+
Local and municipal government: JS3209
Greece: JN5147+
Hungary: JN2165+
Ireland: JN1490+
Italy, United: JN5593
Local government: JS211
Municipal government: JS211
Netherlands: JN5935+
Norway: JN7615+
Portugal: JN8605+
Prussia: JN4623+
Scotland: JN1290+
Spain: JN8341+
Sweden: JN7945+
Switzerland: JN8901+
United States: JK1764
Local and municipal government: JS391
Political parties
Asia: JQ39
Austrian Empire: JN1998.8+
Austrian Republic: JN2030+
Belgium: JN6365+
Canada: JL195+
Denmark: JN7365.A1+
European Community: JN50
France: JN2997+
Germany: JN3931+
1945-
Weimar Republic. JN3970.A1+
Great Britain: JN1111+
Greece: JN5185.A1+

Political parties
Hungary: JN2191.A1+
Ireland: JN1571+
Italy, United: JN5651+
Netherlands: JN5981+
Norway: JN7691.A1+
Portugal: JN8651.A2+
Prussia: JN4681+
Public administration: JF2011+
Scandinavia (General): JN7066
Scotland: JN1370+
Spain: JN8395.A2+
Sweden: JN7995.A1+
Switzerland: JN8971.A1+
United States: JK2255+
Colonial period: JK101+
Political parties and the individual
United States: JK2271
Political patronage: JF2111
Political planning
Canada
Government: JL86.P64
Germany
1945-
Legislative branch: JN3971.A78P53
United States
Government and public administration: JK468.P64
Political psychology: JA74.5
Political rights: JF799+
Asia: JQ36+
Austrian Empire: JN1951+
Austrian Republic: JN2026+
Belgium: JN6301+
Canada: JL186.5
Confederate States of America: JK9981+
Denmark: JN7295+
European Community: JN40
France: JN2916+
Germany: JN3770+
1945-
Weimar Republic. JN3966+
Great Britain: JN900+
Greece: JN5147+
Hungary: JN2165+
Ireland: JN1490+
Italy, United: JN5591+
Political rights
Netherlands: JN5935+
Norway: JN7615+
Portugal: JN8605+
Prussia: JN4623+
Scotland: JN1290+
Spain: JN8341+
Sweden: JN7945+
Switzerland: JN8901+
United States: JK1717+
Political science
International law: JX1250
Political science (General): JA1+
Political science and culture: JA75.7
Political science and ecology: JA75.8
Political science and economics: JA77
Political science and ethics: JA79
Political science and history: JA78
Political science and international law: JA75.5
Political science and law: JA75
Political science and psychology: JA74.5
Political science and science: JA80
Political science and sociology: JA76
Political sociology: JA76
Political theory: JC11+
Political violence
State: JC328.6
Politics and business: JK467
Politics, Practical
Asia: JQ36+
Germany
1945-
Great Britain: JN900+
Ireland: JN1490+
Scotland: JN1290+
United States: JK1717+
Pölitz: JX2824.P7
Polk, James K.
Messages and papers: J82.B3+

Poll tax
  United States
    Immigration: JV6487
Polson: JX2572+
Polygraphs
  United States
    Government and public administration: JK468.L5
Polynesia, French
  Government: JQ6431
Pomerania
  Government: JN4420
Pomeranian Bay
  International status: JX4084.P66
Pomeroy: JX2483.P7
Pondicherry
  Government: JQ620.P6
  Legislative and Executive papers (General): J580
Populists
  United States: JK2371+
Portugal
  Colonizing nation: JV4200+
  Emigration and immigration: JV8260+
  Government: JN8423+
  Legislative and Executive papers (General): J411
  Local government: JS6341+
  Municipal government: JS6341+
Portuguese East Africa
  Legislative and Executive papers (General): J849
  Local government: JS7729
  Municipal government: JS7729
Portuguese Guinea
  Emigration and immigration: JV9024
  Government: JQ3681
  Legislative and Executive papers (General): J850
  Local government: JS7727
  Municipal government: JS7727
Portuguese West Africa
  Government: JQ3651, JQ3671
  Legislative and Executive (General): J841
  Local government: JS7723
  Municipal government: JS7723
Postal administration
  United Nations: JX1977.8.P8
Postliminium
  International law: JX5187
Power
  State: JC330
Powers
  The Diplomatic Service: JX1671+
Practical politics
  Asia: JQ36+
  Germany
    1945-
  Great Britain: JN900+
  Ireland: JN1490+
  Scotland: JN1290+
  Spain: JN8341+
  United States: JK1717+
Pradie-Fodéré: JX2725+
Pragmatic Sanction
  Austrian Empire: JN1625
Prairie Provinces
  Canada
    Government: JL500
Prefect
  France: JS4905
Prefecture government
  Spain: JN8398
Prefectures
  Greece: JN5190+
Preferential ballot
  United States: JK2217
Premier
  Canada: JL99
Preparatory Commission of the United Nations: JX1976.5
President
  Austrian Republic: JN2021.2
  France: JN2665
  Germany
    1945-
    Weimar Republic. JN3961.2
  Organs and functions of government: JF255
  United States: JK511+
President of the Senate
  United States: JK1224
President pro tem
  United States
    Senate: JK1226
Presidential primaries
  United States: JK522
President's messages
  International law: JX234.A1

Presidents' messages
United States
Civil Service: JK641
Presidents' messages and papers
United States: J80+
Presiding officer
Germany
1945-
Legislative branch:
JN3971.A78S65
Press
Intractions of neutrality
International law: JX5397.P7
Press and peace movements:
JX1964.5
Press conferences
United States
President: JK554
Pressure groups
Belgium
Legislative branch: JN6249
Canada
Parliament: JL148.5
France
Legislative branch: JN2794
Germany
1945-
Legislative branch:
JN3971.A78P7
Great Britain
Government: JN329.P7
Italy, United
Government: JN5477.P7
Legislative bodies: JF529
Netherlands
Legislative branch: JN5883
Norway
Legislative branch: JN7549
Switzerland
Legislative branch: JN8852
United States
Congress: JK1118
State government
Legislative branch: JK2498
Primaries: JF2085
United States: JK2071+
Primaries, Presidential
United States: JK522
Prime ministers
Canada: JL99
Great Britain: JN401+
Prince Edward Island
Government: JL210+
Princes, Education of: JC393
Printing, Public
United States: JK1685.A1+
Prisoners of war
International law: JX5141.A1+
Privacy, Right of: JC596+
Private person, Acts of
International law: JX5410+
Private property
International law: JX5305
Privateers of marque
International law: JX5241
Privieges
The Diplomatic Service: JX1671+
Privy Chamber
Great Britain
Crown: JN371
Privy council
Canada: JL93
Privy Council, The
Great Britain
Crown: JN378
Privy purse
Great Britain
Crown: JN365
Prize courts
Maritime war
International law: JX5263
Prize law
Maritime war
International law: JX5245+
Problem employees
United States
Civil Service: JK850.E48
Procedure
Legislative bodies: JF515
Proceedings, Broadcasting of
Legislative bodies: JF539
Proceedings, Publishing of
Legislative bodies: JF540.5
Product descriptions
United States
Government supplies: JK1679
Productivity
Denmark
Government: JN7170.P75
Public administration:
JF1525.P67

Productivity
  Sweden
    Government: JN7850.P75
  United States
    Government and public administration: JK468.P75
    Local and municipal government
      Civil service: JS363
    State government: JK2445.P76
Productivity, Labor
  United States
    Civil Service: JK768.4
    Civil service
      State government: JK2480.L24
Professions
  International law: JX4263.L2
Progressive Party
  United States: JK2386+
Prohibited acts
  Neutrality
    International law: JX5391+
Prohibited instruments and methods
  International law: JX5131
Prohibition Party
  United States: JK2381+
Promotions
  Germany
    1945-
      Civil service: JN3971.A69P7
  United States
    Civil Service: JK767
Propaganda
  Canada
    Government: JL86.P8
  France
    Civil service: JN2738.P8
  Germany
    1945-
      Civil service: JN3971.A69P85
  International law: JX4079.P7
  Public administration: JF1525.P8
Properties and revenues, Crown
  France
    Ancien Régime: JN2377
Property
  Public administration: JF1525.P7
  Rights of the individual: JC605
Property in war
  International law: JX5278+
Property, Government
  Austrian Empire: JN1941
  Austrian Republic: JN2025.5
  Belgium: JN6290
  France: JN2751+
    Local and municipal government: JS4965
  Germany
    Local and municipal government: JS5445
  Great Britain: JN851+
    Local and municipal government: JS3200
  Hungary: JN2163
  United States
    Local and municipal government: JS388
Proportional representation
  Representative government: JF1071+
Proposed courts
  International criminal courts
    International law: JX5428
Protected states
  International law: JX4021+
Protective signs
  International law: JX5147
Protectorates
  International law: JX4021+
Proudhon: JX2728+
Province of Canada: JL55
Provincial administration
  Ancient Rome: JC85.P9
Provincial-Federal relations
  Canada: JL27
Provincial government: JS251
  Canada: JL198
  Germany: JS5417
  Portugal: JN8660
  Spain: JN8398
Provincial legislative bodies
  Canada: JL179
Provinz
  Germany
    Local government: JS5417
Provisional application
  Treaties and treaty making: JX4171.P77
Provisional arrest
  Right of asylum
    International law: JX4292.P8

Public relations
  France
    Civil service: JN2738.P8
  Germany
    1945-
      Civil service: JN3971.A69P85
  Local government: JS105
  Municipal government: JS105
  Public administration: JF1525.P8
  United States
    Local and municipal government: JS344.P8
Publicity
  Belgium
    Government: JN6184.P82
  Canada
  France
    Civil service: JN2738.P8
  Germany
    1945-
      Civil service: JN3971.A69P85
  Great Britain
    Government: JN329.P8
  Italy, United
    Government: JN5477.P83
  Netherlands
    Government: JN5810.P8
  Norway
    Government: JN7480.P82
  Sweden
    Government: JN7850.P8
  United States
    Civil Service: JK849
Publishing of proceedings
  Legislative bodies: JF540.5
Puerto Rico
  Emigration and immigration: JV7380+
  Government: JL1040+
  International status: JX4084.P9
  Legislative and Executive papers (General): J164+
  Local government: JS2021+
  Municipal government: JS2021+
Pufendorf: JX2131+
Punjab
  Government: JQ560+
  Legislative and Executive papers (General): J581
Purchasing
  Public administration: JF1525.P85
Purchasing, Government
  Austrian Empire: JN1941
  Great Britain: JN865
  United States: JK1671+
Purpose of the state: JC501+

Q

Qatar
  Emigration and immigration: JV8750.7
  Government: JQ1845
  Legislative and Executive papers (General): J699
  Local government: JS7506.8
  Municipal government: JS7506.8
Qualifications
  Prussia
    Suffrage: JN4645
Quality management, Total
  United States
    State government: JK2445.T67
Quantitative methods
  Political science (General): JA71.5+
Quaritsch: JX2824.Q3
Quebec
  Government: JL240+
Queensland
  Legislative and Executive papers (General): J916
Queensland (Australia)
  Government: JQ4700+
Quizzes
  International law: JX1299

R

Raad van State
  Netherlands: JN5837
Rachel: JX2141+
Radio broadcasting and peace: JX1964.7
Radio equipment
  United States
    Government supplies: JK1677.R3
Railroads
  International law: JX5135.R3

Republican Party
United States: JK2351+
Republican party and civil service reform: JK698
Requisitions
International law: JX5321
Resch: JX2824.R3
Research
Political instutions and public administration (General): JF130
Political science (General): JA86+
Public administration: JF1338.A2+
Reservations
Treaties and treaty making: JX4171.R4
Resistance to government: JC328.3
Ancient Greece: JC75.R4
Responsibility for acts of agents of the state
International law: JX5402+
Responsibility for acts of organs of the state
International law: JX5402+
Responsibility of shipments
International law: JX4449.R3
Responsibility of the state
International law: JX5402+
Restitution
International law: JX5483+
Retirement
Civil service: JF1671
Germany
1945-
Civil service: JN3971.A691
Great Britain
Civil service: JN447
Local and municipal government
Civil service: JS3175
Local government
Civil service: JS153
Municipal government
Civil service: JS153
United States
Civil Service: JK791
Local and municipal government
Civil service: JS361
Retorsion
International law: JX4484
Return migration: JV6217.5
Returns, Election
Austrian Republic: JN2029.5
United States: JK1967+
Reunion
Emigration and immigration: JV9046
Government: JQ3480+
Réunion
Legislative and Executive papers (General): J793
Reunion
Local government: JS7905
Municipal government: JS7905
Reuss, Elder Branch
Government: JN4700+
Reuss, Elder Line
Legislative and Executive papers (General): J370
Reuss, Younger Branch
Government: JN4720+
Reuss, Younger Line
Legislative and Executive papers (General): J371
Revision
Treaties and treaty making: JX4171.R45
Revolution, French: JN2468+
Revolutionary and modern periods
France
Government: JN2451+
Revolutions: JC491
Rhine Province
Government: JN4739.3
Rhine River and Valley
International law: JX1393.R4
Rhineland-Palatinate
Government: JN4739.5
Legislative and Executive papers (General): J383.R46
Rhodesia
Emigration and immigration: JV9006.15
Government: JQ2780+
Legislative and Executive papers (General): J725
Local government: JS7641
Municipal government: JS7641
Rhodesia, Southern
International status: JX4084.R5
Rhodian law: JX2014.R5

Rumelia, Eastern
Legislative and Executive papers (General): J452
Rural public administration: JS271
United States: JS425
Russia
Colonizing nation: JV3000+
Emigration and immigration: JV8180+
Government: JN6500+
Legislative and Executive papers (General): J397
Local government: JS6051+
Municipal government: JS6051+
Russia (Federation)
Emigration and immigration: JV8190
Government: JN6690+
Local government: JS6117
Municipal government: JS6117
Russia (Federation, 1992-
Legislative and Executive papers (General): J397.2
Russo-Japanese War, 1904-1905
International law: JX1393.R8
Rutherforth: JX2231+
Rwanda
Emigration and immigration: JV9001.5
Government: JQ3567
Legislative and Executive papers (General): J816
Local government: JS7695
Municipal government: JS7695
Ryukyu Islands
International status: JX4084.R9

S

Saafeld: JX2826+
Saarland
Government: JN4739.8
International status: JX4084.S3
Legislative and Executive papers (General): J383.S2
Saba
Emigration and immigration: JV7356.5
Government: JL779.2
Legislative and Executive papers (General): J154.2
Local government: JS1920
Municipal government: JS1920
Sabah
International status: JX4084.S32
Legislative and Executive papers (General): J618.S3
Safe conduct
International law: JX5151
Sahel
Emigration and immigration: JV9020.15
Saint Eustatius
Emigration and immigration: JV7356.6
Government: JL779.5+
Legislative and Executive papers (General): J154.3
Local government: JS1921
Municipal government: JS1921
Saint Gall
Switzerland
Legislative and Executive papers (General): J430
Saint Helena
Emigration and immigration: JV9034
Government: JQ3986
Legislative and Executive papers (General): J754
Local government: JS7825
Municipal government: JS7825
Saint Kitts and Nevis
Emigration and immigration: JV7341.9
Government: JL649.7
Legislative and Executive papers (General): J139.7
Local government: JS1873
Municipal government: JS1873
Saint Lucia
Emigration and immigration: JV7345.5
Government: JL669.4
Legislative and Executive papers (General): J141.5
Local government: JS1877
Municipal government: JS1877

Saint Martin
  Emigration and immigration:
    JV7356.7
  Government: JL779.7
  Legislative and Executive
  papers (General): J154.4
  Local government: JS1922
  Municipal government: JS1922
Saint Pierre and Miquelon
  Legislative and Executive
  papers (General): J132
Saint Thomas Aquinas: JX2060.T4
Saint Vincent and the
  Grenadines
  Emigration and immigration:
    JV7345.6
  Government: JL669.5
  Legislative and Executive
  papers (General): J141.6
  Local government: JS1877.5
  Municipal government: JS1877.5
Salaries
  Austrian Empire
    Civil service: JN1721
  Belgium
    Civil service: JN6235
  Canada
    Civil service: JL111.S3
    Legislators: JL111.S3
  Civil service: JF1661
  Denmark
    Civil service: JN7223
  France
    Civil service: JN2748
  Germany
    1945-
      Civil service: JN3971.A691
    Civil Service: JN3565
  Great Britain
    Civil service: JN443
    Local and municipal government
      Civil service: JS3175
    Parliament: JN581
  Italy, United
    Civil service: JN5526
  Local government
    Civil service: JS153
  Municipal government
    Civil service: JS153
  Netherlands
    Civil service: JN5861
Salaries
  Norway
    Civil service: JN7528
  Portugal
    Civil service: JN8559
  Prussia
    Civil service: JN4548
  Spain
    Civil service: JN8289
  Sweden
    Civil service: JN7904
  Switzerland
    Civil service: JN8839
  United States
    Civil Service: JK771+
    Local and municipal government
      Civil service: JS361
    State government
      Civil service: JK2474
Salaries of members
  Legislative bodies: JF536
Salaries of members of Congress
  United States: JK781
Salary lists
  United States
    Civil Service: JK771
Salary of the President
  United States: JK779
Salvage
  Aeronautics
    International law: JX5775.S3
  Shipwreck
    International law: JX4436
Salzburg
  Legislative and Executive
  papers (General): J325
Samoa, American (U.S.
  Territory)
  Legislative and Executive
  papers (General): J958
Samoa, Western
  Legislative and Executive
  papers (General): J981.W3
Samoan Islands
  Emigration and immigration:
    JV9465+
  Government: JQ6220+
  Local government: JS8480+
  Municipal government: JS8480+

San Andres y Providencia (Colombia)
International status: JX4084.S36
San Francisco Conference, 1945: JX1976.4
San Marino
Government: JN5695
Sanctions
International law: JX1246
United Nations: JX1977.8.S3
Sandonà: JX2924 +
Santerna: JX2144 +
Sao Tome and Principe
Emigration and immigration: JV9015.5
Government: JQ3685
Legislative and Executive papers (General): J851
Local government: JS7731
Municipal government: JS7731
Sarawak
Legislative and Executive papers (General): J618.S37
Sardinia
Early government: JN5291
Sardinia (Kingdom)
Government: JN5391 +
Saripoulos: JX2845 +
Sarmiento Laspiur: JX3651.S3
Saskatchewan
Government: JL300 +
Satisfaction
International law: JX5483 +
Saudi Arabia
Emigration and immigration: JV8750.3
Government: JQ1841
Legislative and Executive papers (General): J700
Local government: JS7506
Municipal government: JS7506
Savigny: JX2831 +
Savoy
Early government: JN5251
Saxe-Altenburg
Government: JN4740 +
Legislative and Executive papers (General): J372
Saxe-Coburg-Gotha
Legislative and Executive papers (General): J373
Saxe-Meiningen
Government: JN4760 +
Legislative and Executive papers (General): J374
Saxe-Weimar
Legislative and Executive papers (General): J375
Saxony
Government: JN4820 +
Legislative and Executive papers (General): J376
Saxony (State, 1990-
Government: JN4839.5
Saxony-Anhalt (State, 1990-
Government: JN4839.7
Legislative and Executive papers (General): J376.5
Saxony, Lower
Legislative and Executive papers (General): J383.S26
Scandinavia
Emigration and immigration: JV8198 +
General Legislative and Executive papers: J402 +
Local government: JS6141 +
Municipal government: JS6141 +
Scandinavia (General)
Government: JN7009.2 +
Schaffhausen
Switzerland
Government: JN9360 +
Legislative and Executive papers (General): J431
Schaumburg-Lippe
Government: JN4840 +
Legislative and Executive papers (General): J377
Schiattarella: JX2928 +
Schleswig-Holstein
Government: JN4859.5
Schmalz: JX2834 +
Schmelzing: JX2836.S4
Schools, Civil service: JK716 +
Schucking, W.M.A.: JX3491.S5
Schulze: JX2838 +
Schuyler: JX2483.S3
Schwartzburg-Rudolstadt
Legislative and Executive papers (General): J378

Slovak Socialist Republic
  Legislative and Executive
  papers (General):
    J338.2.S577
Slovakia
  Emigration and immigration:
    JV7899.2
  Government: JN2240
  Legislative and Executive
  papers (General): J338.5
  Local government: JS4760
  Municipal government: JS4760
Slovenia
  Emigration and immigration:
    JV8339.2
  Government: JN2201
  Legislative and Executive
  papers (General): J460.3
  Local government: JS6949.8
  Municipal government: JS6949.8
Small states: JC365
Snow: JX2486+
Social aspects
  United States
    Immigration: JV6475
Social aspects of immigration:
    JV6225+
Social causes of emigration:
    JV6101
Social effects of emigration:
    JV6121
Social groups, Representation
  of
  Representative government:
    JF1057+
Social sciences
  International law: JX1249+
Social theories of the state:
    JC336
Societies
  Political science (General):
    JA27+
Sociology
  International law: JX1251
Sociology and political
  science: JA76
Solomon Islands
  Emigration and immigration:
    JV9457
  Government: JQ6341
  Legislative and Executive
  papers (General): J968.S6,
      J981.S6
  Local government: JS8470
  Municipal government: JS8470
Solothurn
  Switzerland
    Government: JN9400+
    Legislative and Executive
  papers (General): J433
Somalia
  Emigration and immigration:
    JV8998
  Government: JQ3585
  Legislative and Executive
  papers (General): J825
  Local government: JS7707
  Municipal government: JS7707
Somaliland, British
  Legislative and Executive
  papers (General): J735
Sorel: JX2751+
Souffrance
  Medieval state: JC116.S7
South Africa
  Emigration and immigration:
    JV8800+
  Government: JQ1900+
  International status:
    JX4084.S62
  Local government: JS7531+
  Municipal government: JS7531+
South Africa, Republic of
  Legislative and Executive
  papers (General): J705+
South African War, 1899-1902
  International law: JX1393.S6
South America
  Colonies and colonization:
    JV231
  Emigration and immigration:
    JV7433+
  Government: JL1850+
  Legislative and Executive
  papers (General): J200+
  Local government: JS2300+
  Municipal government: JS2300+
South Asia
  Emigration and immigration:
    JV8752+
  Legislative and Executive
  papers (General): J500+

South Asia
Local government: JS6970+
Municipal government: JS6970+
Political institutions and administration: JQ98+
South Atlantic region
International law: JX1393.S63
South Australia
Government: JQ4900+
Legislative and Executive papers (General): J921
South China Sea islands
International status: JX4084.S63
South Holland (Province)
Legislative and Executive papers (General): J392.H7
South Korea
Emigration and immigration: JV8757
Government: JQ1720+
Legislative and Executive papers (General): J677
Local government: JS7391+
Municipal government: JS7391+
South Moluccas
International status: JX4084.S65
Southeast Africa
Emigration and immigration: JV8998.7+
Southeast Asia
Emigration and immigration: JV8753.7+
Government: JQ750+
Legislative and Executive papers (General): J500+
Local government: JS7139+
Municipal government: JS7139+
Southern Africa
Emigration and immigration: JV9006+
Government: JQ2720+
Local government: JS7637+
Southern Rhodesia
Government: JQ2920+
Legislative and Executive papers (General): J725.5
Local government: JS7643
Municipal government: JS7643
Southern Yemen
Emigration and immigration: JV8750.55
Southwest Africa
Emigration and immigration: JV9007.5
Government: JQ3540+
Local government: JS7645
Municipal government: JS7645
Southwest Africa (to 1967)
Legislative and Executive papers (General): J812
Southwest Asia
Government: JQ1758+
Legislative and Executive papers (General): J685+
Local government: JS7435+
Municipal government: JS7435+
Sovereign states
International law: JX4004.62+
Sovereignty: JC327
Ancient Rome: JC85.S7
Confederate States of America: JK9887
International law: JX4041+
Soviet Union
Colonizing nation: JV3000+
Emigration and immigration: JV8180+
Government: JN6500+
Legislative and Executive papers (General): J397
Local government: JS6051+
Municipal government: JS6051+
Space law
International law: JX5810
Spain
Colonizing nation: JV4000+
Emigration and immigration: JV8250+
Government: JN8101+
Legislative and Executive papers (General): J409
Local government: JS6301+
Municipal government: JS6301+
Spanish-American War
Foreign policy
United States: JX1426
Spanish Civil War, 1936-1939
International law: JX1393.S65

State government: JS251
  Portugal: JN8660
  Spain: JN8398
  United States: JK2403+
State government (General and comparative
  Germany
    1945-
State-local relations: JS113
  United States: JS348+
State of the Union messages
  United States
    President: JK587
State relations
  Confederate States of America: JK9887
State rights
  Germany
    1945-
  United States: JK311+
State succession
  Treaties and treaty making: JX4171.S72
State, Dissolution of a
  International law: JX4061
Statelessness
  Citizenship
    International law: JX4231.S8
Staten-General
  Netherlands: JN5873+
States
  Germany
    Government: JN4000+
States, New
  Political institutions and public administration: JF59
Statistical methods
  Political science (General): JA71.7
Statistics
  Austrian Republic
    Elections: JN2029.5
  Emigration and immigration: JV6019+
  Germany
    Weimar Republic.
      Elections: JN3969.5
  United States
    Civil Service: JK666
    Elections: JK1967+
    Immigration: JV6461
Statistics, Election
  Germany
    1945-
  Great Britain: JN1037
  Greece: JN5166
  Italy, United: JN5609
  Norway: JN7653
  Sweden: JN7958.2
Statsradet
  Sweden: JN7877
Stockholders abroad, Protection of by their home state
  International law: JX4263.P82
Stockton, C.H.: JX3180.S7
Stoerk: JX2841+
Stortinget
  Norway: JN7541+
Story: JX2489+
Stowell: JX2578+
Straits as boundaries
  International law: JX4141
Straits question
  International law: JX1393.S8
Straits Settlements
  Legislative and Executive papers (General): J615+
Strategic Arms Limitation Talks, I, 1969: JX1974.75
Strategic Arms Limitation Talks, II, 1979: JX1974.75
Strategic Arms Reduction Talks: JX1974.76
Stuart period
  Great Britain
    Crown: JN339
Stuart, 17th century
  Great Britain
    Political institutions: JN191+
Students, College
  United States
    Civil Service: JK723.S8
Study and teaching
  Political institutions and public administration (General): JF130
  Political science (General): JA86+
  Public administration: JF1338.A2+
Styria
  Legislative and Executive papers (General): J327

Township government
  United States: JS418
Trading with the enemy
  International law: JX5270+
Traffic control
  Aeronautics
    International law: JX5775.T7
Trans-Jordan
  Legislative and Executive papers (General): J696
Transfers
  Canada
    Civil service: JL111.D4
  Germany
    1945-
      Civil service: JN3971.A69R45
Transfers and details
  United States
    Civil Service: JK850.D4
Transkei
  International status: JX4084.T67
  Legislative and Executive papers (General): J717
Translating
  United Nations: JX1977.8.L35
Transportation
  International law: JX5701+
  United States
    Government and public administration: JK468.T7
Transvaal
  Legislative and Executive papers (General): J719
Travel
  Germany
    1945-
      Civil service: JN3971.A69T7
  Great Britain
    Civil service: JN450.T7
Travelers in foreign countries
  International law: JX4263.T8
Treaties
  Ancient Greek law: JX2014.T7
  and
    convention
      International law: JX4161+
Treaties, Effect of
  International law: JX4525
Treaty making
  International law: JX4161+
Treaty-making power
  United Nations: JX1977.8.T7
Treaty of Utrecht to the French Revolution (1713-1789)
  Foreign relations
    International law: JX1335+
Tremosa y Nadal: JX3058+
Trentino-Alto Adiege (Italy)
  International status: JX4084.T7
Trial of Major German War Criminals, 1945-1946
  World War II: JX5437
Trials by international military tribunals
  World War II: JX5436+
Trials by national courts other than those of the coutry of the defendant (sitting at home or abroad)
  World War II: JX5439+
Trials by the courts of defendant's own country: JX5443
Tribunes
  Ancient Rome: JC85.T7
Trieste
  Legislative and Executive papers (General): J389.5
Trinidad and Tobago
  Emigration and immigration: JV7352
  Government: JL650+
  Legislative and Executive papers (General): J140
  Local government: JS1878
  Municipal government: JS1878
Tripura
  Government: JQ620.T82
  Legislative and Executive papers (General): J595
Tristan da Cunha
  Emigration and immigration: JV9035
  Government: JQ3986.5
  Legislative and Executive papers (General): J755
  Local government: JS7826
  Municipal government: JS7826
Troops, Passage of
  Intractions of neutrality
    International law: JX5397.P3

Uruguay
Emigration and immigration: JV7520+
Government: JL3600+
Legislative and Executive papers (General): J251
Local government: JS2701+
Municipal government: JS2701+
Utrecht
Legislative and Executive papers (General): J392.U8
Uttar Pradesh
Government: JQ600+
Legislative and Executive papers (General): J599
Uzbekistan
Government: JQ1095
Legialstive and Executive papers (General): J659
Local government: JS7275

V

Valais
Switzerland
Government: JN9520+
Legislative and Executive papers (General): J439
Valencia
Old kingdom
Government: JN8142
Valuation
International law: JX4263.P6
Van Buren, Martin
Messages and papers: J82.A8+
Vandalism
International law: JX5420.5
Vanuatu
Emigration and immigration: JV9459
Government: JQ6400
Legislative and Executive papers (General): J968.N57
Local government: JS8472
Municipal government: JS8472
Vassal states
International law: JX4011+, JX4025
Vassals
Medieval state: JC116.V3
Vatican City
Government: JN5697
Vattel: JX2411+
Vaud
Switzerland
Government: JN9540+
Legislative and Executive papers (General): J440
Venda
Legislative and Executive papers (General): J719.5
Venezuela
Emigration and immigration: JV7530+
Government: JL3800+
Legislative and Executive papers (General): J257+
Local government: JS2751+
Municipal government: JS2751+
Venice
Early government: JN5266
Verona (1822), Congress of
Foreign relations
International law: JX1365
Veterans
United States
Civil Service: JK720
Veterans and the civil service
Great Britain: JN441
Veto
United Nations: JX1977.8.V4
Veto power
United States
President: JK586
State government
Governor: JK2454
Vice President
United States: JK609.5
Viceroy
Colonies: JV431+
Victoria
Legislative and Executive papers (General): J931
Victoria (Australia)
Government: JQ5300+
Vienna (State)
Legislative and Executive papers (General): J329.5
Vienna, Congress of
Foreign relations
International law: JX1351

Vienna, Congress of to the American Civil War (1815-1861)
Foreign relations
International law: JX1358+
Vietnam
Emigration and immigration: JV8754.5
Government: JQ800+
International status: JX4084.V5
Legislative and Executive papers (General): J644
Local government: JS7152
Municipal government: JS7152
Village government: JS271
United States: JS425
Violation
Treaties and treaty making: JX4171.V5
Violence
State: JC328.6
Virgin Islands of the United States
Emigration and immigration: JV7397
Government: JL1160+
Legislative and Executive papers (General): J166
Local government: JS2058
Municipal government: JS2058
Vitoria: JX2158+
Volunteer workers
United States
Civil Service: JK723.V64
Voralberg
Legislative and Executive papers (General): J330
Vote count: JF1161
Vote, Right to: JF831+
United States: JK1846+
Voter registration: JF1113
United States: JK2160+
Voting: JF1001+
Asia: JQ38
Austrian Empire: JN1993+
Austrian Republic: JN2029+
Belgium: JN6331+
Canada: JL193
Confederate States of America: JK9993
Denmark: JN7321+
France: JN2959+
Voting
Germany: JN3838
1945-
Weimar Republic. JN3969+
Great Britain: JN945+
Greece: JN5165+
Hungary: JN2183
Ireland: JN1541
Italy, United: JN5607+
Netherlands: JN5951+
Norway: JN7651+
Portugal: JN8623+
Prussia: JN4653+
Scotland: JN1341
Spain: JN8371+
Sweden: JN7958+
Switzerland: JN8931+
United Nations: JX1977.8.V6
United States: JK1961+
Voting age: JF841
Voting behavior
United States: JK1967+
Voting by members of congress
United States: JK1051
Voting machines: JF1128
Voule
Ancient Greece: JC75.V6
Voulé
Greece: JN5123

W

Waldeck
Government: JN4915
Legislative and Executive papers (General): J380
Wales
Emigration and immigration: JV7720+
Government: JN1150+
Legislative and Executive papers (General): J305
Local government: JS4001+
Municipal government: JS4001+
Walker: JX2584.W3
War
Treaties and treaty making: JX4171.W3
War crime trials
International law: JX5433+

Y

Yukon Territory
  Government: JL495

Z

Zaire
  Emigration and immigration: JV9015
  Government: JQ3600+
Zaïre
  Legislative and Executive papers (General): J831
Zaire
  Local government: JS7715
  Municipal government: JS7715
Zambia
  Emigration and immigration: JV9006.3
  Government: JQ2800+
  Legislative and Executive papers (General): J725.3
  Local government: JS7642
  Municipal government: JS7642
Zanzibar
  Emigration and immigration: JV9002
  Government: JQ3510+
  Local government: JS7697
  Municipal government: JS7697
Zanzibar (to 1964)
  Legislative and Executive papers (General): J733
Zealand
  Legislative and Executive papers (General): J392.Z4
Zechin: JX2349.Z3
Zimbabwe
  Emigration and immigration: JV9006.15
  Government: JQ2920+
  Legislative and Executive papers (General): J725.5
  Local government: JS7643
  Municipal government: JS7643
Zorn: JX3491.Z5
Zouch: JX2181+
Zug
  Switzerland
    Government: JN9560+
    Legislative and Executive papers (General): J441

☆ U.S. GPO: 1995 400-749
5-20181-95CDSGP181/2000